The Essential Guide to

Baby's First Year

by Erika Landau, M.D., and Abigail Brenner, M.D.

ALPHA

A member of Penguin Group (USA) Inc.

ALPHA BOOKS

Published by the Penguin Group

Penguin Group (USA) Inc., 375 Hudson Street, New York, New York 10014, USA

Penguin Group (Canada), 90 Eglinton Avenue East, Suite 700, Toronto, Ontario M4P 2Y3, Canada (a division of Pearson Penguin Canada Inc.)

Penguin Books Ltd., 80 Strand, London WC2R 0RL, England

Penguin Ireland, 25 St. Stephen's Green, Dublin 2, Ireland (a division of Penguin Books Ltd.)

Penguin Group (Australia), 250 Camberwell Road, Camberwell, Victoria 3124, Australia (a division of Pearson Australia Group Pty. Ltd.)

Penguin Books India Pvt. Ltd., 11 Community Centre, Panchsheel Park, New Delhi—110 017, India

Penguin Group (NZ), 67 Apollo Drive, Rosedale, North Shore, Auckland 1311, New Zealand (a division of Pearson New Zealand Ltd.)

Penguin Books (South Africa) (Pty.) Ltd., 24 Sturdee Avenue, Rosebank, Johannesburg 2196, South Africa

Penguin Books Ltd., Registered Offices: 80 Strand, London WC2R 0RL, England

International Standard Book Number: 978-1-61564-086-7
Library of Congress Catalog Card Number: 2010913759

13   12   11   8   7   6   5   4   3   2   1

Interpretation of the printing code: The rightmost number of the first series of numbers is the year of the book's printing; the rightmost number of the second series of numbers is the number of the book's printing. For example, a printing code of 11-1 shows that the first printing occurred in 2011.

Printed in the United States of America

Note: This publication contains the opinions and ideas of its authors. It is intended to provide helpful and informative material on the subject matter covered. It is sold with the understanding that the authors and publisher are not engaged in rendering professional services in the book. If the reader requires personal assistance or advice, a competent professional should be consulted.

The authors and publisher specifically disclaim any responsibility for any liability, loss, or risk, personal or otherwise, which is incurred as a consequence, directly or indirectly, of the use and application of any of the contents of this book.

Most Alpha books are available at special quantity discounts for bulk purchases for sales promotions, premiums, fund-raising, or educational use. Special books, or book excerpts, can also be created to fit specific needs.

For details, write: Special Markets, Alpha Books, 375 Hudson Street, New York, NY 10014.

Publisher: *Marie Butler-Knight*
Associate Publisher: *Mike Sanders*
Senior Managing Editor: *Billy Fields*
Executive Editor: *Randy Ladenheim-Gil*
Development Editor: *Susan Zingraf*
Senior Production Editor: *Janette Lynn*

Copy Editor: *Lisanne V. Jensen*
Cover/Book Designer: *Rebecca Batchelor*
Indexer: *Angie Bess Martin*
Layout: *Rebecca Batchelor*
Proofreader: *John Etchison*

I dedicate this book to parents and children everywhere; to my students; to my husband and family and in memory of my father; to my muse, my love, my best friend ... my daughter.
—Erika Landau

With love and gratitude. In memory of my parents. To my husband, children, grandchildren, and family and friends who give meaning to my life.
—Abigail Brenner

Contents

Introduction

Having a baby is one of life's most exciting and satisfying experiences. So much time, hard work, and energy have gone into preparing you for your baby's birth and for getting all the things in order that it takes to start a new life together.

The first year of a baby's life is thrilling and filled with wonder and amazement—and yes, some confusion and a lot of questioning. If you're a parent for the first time, this is a learning experience. After all, you've never done this before.

What you do know is that you've never loved this much, worked so hard, been so exhausted, so worried, or so frazzled. But you never experienced this much joy.

It seems that every area of expertise in this world requires a license or certificate. But there is no license to become a parent. Neither does the little bundle come with instructions or a guarantee.

Think of parenting as a journey: you know where you want to go, but you may not know how to get there. There are lots of unknowns along the way (and sometimes even ordeals). But eventually, the path becomes clearer and you find your way.

This journey, to know your baby, is also about coming to know yourself. Your child's experiences become yours as well. You are afforded challenges and enormous opportunities to learn more about yourself through your baby.

This book is called "the Essential Guide." Essentials are the basics—everything you need to know about the care and development of your baby during his or her first year of life. A guide is just that: a book providing practical guidance to help you during this first crucial year.

We don't want to tell you what to do; after all, you're the parent. We will guide you through all the stages of your baby's first year, including what to expect, what to look out for, and which concerns need special attention. When we say "must" or "should," we don't mean to imply a rigid standard but rather practical and safe solutions.

We will guide you with the knowledge we have as physicians, but even more, as mothers. We were once there, too. This book is not meant, however, as a substitute for good, solid medical care—the kind your baby's doctor can provide. It's always prudent and makes good sense to consult your pediatrician or other healthcare provider for all concerns.

This Essential Guide will give you enough solid information to become well informed, yet enable you to develop and utilize your own instincts and good judgment. Being well informed allows you to gain confidence and techniques as you help your baby master developmental tasks and milestones.

This journey never ends. Although you will have acquired skills, knowledge, and patience throughout your child's life, you'll be just as worried when he or she starts walking and running, going to school, coming home late at night, marrying, and having his or her own children.

These are amazing times. Try to enjoy every minute, because time goes by so quickly. And somewhere down the line, when your teenager rolls his or her eyes at you, you can tell him or her, "You won't understand until you become a parent yourself."

How to Use This Book

This book is divided into six parts that make it easy to understand the transitional changes that will occur throughout the first year:

Part 1, It's an Entirely New World, begins at birth and takes you through what to expect in the hospital, then going home and feeding your new baby. You'll also get an overview of developmental milestones to expect along the way.

Part 2, The First Three Months, covers the necessary preparations at home for your new baby, how to care for your baby at home, how to get out and about, how to handle sleeping, how your baby is growing during this time, and medical concerns and issues.

Part 3, Months Four, Five, and Six, talks about the growth you'll see, appropriate playtime activities, what to expect with eating and sleeping, medical concerns, and childcare.

Part 4, Months Seven, Eight, and Nine, continues to track the baby's growth and addresses baby-proofing, food allergies, teething, first aid, and developmental concerns to watch for.

Part 5, Months Ten, Eleven, and Twelve, covers the new mobility the baby is experiencing, age-appropriate toys and activities, new foods to try, and common concerns at this stage.

Finally, **Part 6, Twelve Months Later,** addresses special-needs children and medical conditions that require special attention. We'll recap the amazing first year of life, highlighting the essential accomplishments, and we'll give you a glimpse of the next exciting year.

Essential Extras

Throughout the book, you'll see additional pieces of information in sidebars. Here's what to look for:

Definitions and explanations of medical terms and material

 Helpful tips and information about a particular issue or topic

 Warning or cautionary information on a subject

 You'll also see a fourth, name-changing sidebar that presents anecdotes, interesting facts, case histories, or other extended background information you should know

Acknowledgments

From Erika Landau:

This book is written for all parents and caregivers who ever held a newborn and looked at him or her with that mixture of happiness, wonder, gratitude, joy, and sheer fright: Now what? What am I going to do?

I was able to watch the babies grow and their personality unfold. Thank you for giving me the honor and privilege to be part of your lives, to be part of the trials and tribulations of being parents.

Many thanks to my friends, Rita Battat-Silverman and Dr. Abigail Brenner—what a joy it is knowing you and working with you.

Thanks to all my family for letting me disappear while I worked on this book. Many thanks to all my little patients, their parents, and my students, who teach me new things every day.

Special thanks to my daughter, Danielle, who taught me to be a mom and a better pediatrician (and helped me with typing), to my husband, David, for his immense knowledge and energy, to Randy Ladenheim-Gil, and to our editor, Susan Zingraf, for their patience and wonderful work.

Many special thanks to Jen Johnson for illustrating our book.

To Steve Silverman for his deep knowledge of computers and for his commitment to our project.

Many thanks to Dr. Ian Holzman for being such a supportive mentor and a great friend.

From Abigail Brenner:

I love to write about life transitions, and I can't think of any other more exciting than having a baby and watching the hundreds of transitions that happen day by day. There's no other time in life that can compare to the discoveries and achievements made during a baby's first year.

To that end, I want to thank my children, David and Robbie—now parents themselves—who were great kids then and are magnificent adults now. I learned so much from you and still do.

To my four granddaughters—Bronwen, Georgia, Isabella, and India—I'm privileged to be "Mommom" (Mom × 2). It's a terrific thing to watch new life come into the world, but this time from a different yet very special perspective. I appreciate my own efforts as a young parent much more now by watching my children parent their children so well. Sometimes it's hard when you're in the middle of it.

To my husband, Ray, who has always put family in front of everything, I am very grateful for everything. Your support and encouragement mean so much to me.

To Dr. Erika Landau, what a privilege and pleasure it has been to work with you. Your dedication to your patients and your profession is so crystal clear.

To Rita Battat-Silverman, my dear friend and agent, and Leap Over It, Inc., thank you for insisting on my being included in the writing of this book. I'm always grateful for your support, encouragement, enthusiasm, optimism, and amazing generosity.

To Randy Ladenheim-Gil at the Penguin Group and Susan Zingraf, our editor, thank you for your understanding, patience, and expertise.

To Jen Johnson, special thanks for your terrific illustrations.

Trademarks

All terms mentioned in this book that are known to be or are suspected of being trademarks or service marks have been appropriately capitalized. Alpha Books and Penguin Group (USA) Inc. cannot attest to the accuracy of this information. Use of a term in this book should not be regarded as affecting the validity of any trademark or service mark.

Part 1

It's an Entirely New World

From the delivery room to the nursery, you'll get a firsthand view and a general understanding of what happens to your baby during the moments and hours after birth—the first touch, the first cry, what your baby looks like, and the bonding experience.

The hospital setting and procedures are explained, including what the doctors do to ensure your baby's well-being, screening tests that will be performed, and what happens if your baby needs special care. You'll get a glimpse of the special care that premature and multiple-birth babies receive in the NICU, as well as learn about hospital procedures for discharge and essentials needed for baby and you to go home.

We'll talk about everything you'll need to know about breastfeeding or bottle-feeding with breast milk or formula. Last, you'll get an overview of the developmental milestones of your baby's first year.

chapter 1

Your Baby at Birth

Expectations in the delivery room

What the newborn looks like

The immediate medical care given to the newborn

Swaddling technique

For months, you've been taking prenatal vitamins, looking at ultrasounds, and listening to a tiny heart beat. You've talked to doctors and nurses and/or midwives, had countless appointments, taken birth facility tours, shopped for a car seat, decorated a nursery, and planned your maternity leave. The preparation that goes into having a baby is immense, challenging, and unforgettable, and yet it's just the beginning. Once your baby arrives, it's an entirely new world with all new things to learn about your little bundle of joy.

This book is designed to fully prepare you for your first year of being a parent and to help you understand the development that takes place over the course of your baby's first 12 incredible months. We will begin with the day your baby is born and what to anticipate and prepare for on the big day and the days to follow.

In the Delivery Room

Once your contractions begin, it's only a matter of time—specifically, how much time—before you will meet your beautiful new baby. Whether you deliver your baby vaginally or by Caesarean section, in 30 minutes or 20-plus hours, your slippery little baby will emerge and a highly orchestrated process of checks and measurements of him or her will begin. Given the tremendous physical and emotional upheaval you will have just been through, it can be overwhelming to see your new baby handled, prodded, and poked by the hospital staff—so it's helpful to know in advance what they will be doing and why they will do it. Rest assured that it's all to keep your new baby as healthy as possible.

When the baby has completely emerged, the doctor (or midwife, depending on your situation) will call out the time of birth to be recorded, then immediately start cleaning mucus from the baby's nose and mouth by gently suctioning with a bulb syringe to remove any fluid that may have been swallowed. This ensures that the baby is able to breathe on his or her own. Next, the umbilical cord is clamped in two places, and once it is cut, you and your baby are separated (but only physically, of course). Next, the baby is dried quickly and wrapped in a blanket, and if necessary, warmers are used to stabilize the baby's temperature. The baby is also weighed, and the body length is measured as well as the circumference of the head.

Apgar Score

A term to be familiar with in the delivery room is *Apgar score,* a standardized numerical assessment that rates a newborn's heart rate, skin color, muscle tone, reflexes, and breathing. Each of the five categories are rated on a scale from zero to two—two being optimum in a category. Then, all five scores are added to get the Apgar score. This assessment is administered to a newborn twice: at one minute and at five minutes after birth. There is nothing invasive done to the baby for this assessment; it is all measured externally.

SIGN	0	1	2	1 min	5 min
Heart Rate	Absent	Less Than 100	Over 100	2	2
Respiratory Effort	Absent	Slow, Irregular	Good Cry	1	2
Muscle Tone	Limp	Some Flexion	Active Motion	1	2
Reflex Irritability	No Response	Grimace	Cry	1	2
Color	Pale	Body Pink, Extr. Blue	All Pink	1	2
TOTAL SCORE				6	10

Sample Apgar score.

The Apgar score was proposed and implemented by anesthesiologist Virginia Apgar (1909–1974) in the 1950s as a way for medical professionals to monitor the health of newborns via standardized assessment.

Your baby will receive the Apgar score assessment to give the medical staff a gauge of how your baby is doing and whether any action needs to be taken in response to the result.

The First Cry

It's the moment you've been waiting for: hearing your baby's first cry—the signal that your baby is alive and breathing on his or her own.

The first cry is the first really good respiratory effort, because in the womb, the lungs are filled with fluid. As the baby cries, the lungs expand. First, it may be a whimper that very quickly turns into a strong cry.

For the parents it's not a cry; it's the first communication, the first real sign that the baby is here and healthy. It is precious music to your ears.

Also, babies aren't spanked anymore to coax the first cry. Their backs are rubbed or the soles are tapped instead.

The First Touch

After the immediate first necessary procedures—suctioning, cutting the cord, warming the baby, and so on—have been performed to ensure your baby's safety and immediate well-being, you can hold your baby (and be sure to ask to hold your baby if he or she is not handed to you!).

Babies are born with very complicated behaviors that demand and promote attachment. The first cry will create a strong urge in you to hold your baby, and if you choose to do so, to nurse. Some newborns will even start breastfeeding immediately. As much as you may have already read about it, and as much as you may have heard other mothers talk about their incredibly strong attachment to their babies, nothing can really prepare you for the intensity of feelings that will occur when you hold your own baby for the first time.

Should a medical complication with your baby prevent you from being with him or her immediately after delivery, ask the nurses whether a quick look or brief physical contact is possible. If you experience some complications yourself such as exhaustion, feeling overwhelmed, or a medical condition/emergency such that you cannot hold your baby right away, don't worry—bonding will occur nevertheless.

Mother and child are a lifetime connection. It may take time, and it will surely evolve over time, but there is nothing stronger or more complex than this bond. It's also not always love at first sight, so don't panic if this is your experience. But the more time you spend with your baby, the faster the bond will solidify. You and your baby will help each other in the process.

Being present from the very beginning for fathers and life partners is essential. Holding the baby in the delivery room and in the nursery establishes their own bonding with a new son or daughter. The same is true for adoptive parents.

The Miracle Organ

The placenta exits the mother approximately five to ten minutes after birth. You may not even know it when it's happening. Dark red, iridescent, and about nine inches in diameter, this elegant and efficient structure has enabled the fetus to receive oxygen and nourishment for nine months. Amazingly, this organ did not exist prior to pregnancy. Its growth is solely for the purpose of sustaining your baby, ensuring the delivery of essential nutrients for healthy development. After birth, the placenta is "delivered" as well.

The First Vaccine

In the hospital, the first vaccine given to a baby is for protection against Hepatitis B. Hepatitis B is a highly contagious disease caused by a virus that affects the liver, making it unable to function. If this condition goes unrecognized, it can lead to a severe liver disease called cirrhosis. Therefore, newborns are given a Hepatitis B vaccine shortly after birth.

Parents can opt not to have their babies given this first, or any other, vaccine. They must sign a refusal to vaccinate form, and be fully advised of the consequences of not vaccinating.

A newborn can acquire Hepatitis B as a fetus (in utero) from an infected mother. The mother could have been exposed to infected blood or contracted it through unprotected sexual contact. The vaccine is given immediately after birth because the disease has no symptoms in early childhood and because it takes 45–160 days to incubate after exposure. Missing this window of opportunity for protection can cause serious problems later in life.

Besides this vaccine, an immunoglobulin is only given that already has antibodies against Hepatitis B in it. Immunoglobulin aids in building immunity against the disease. A baby will receive another Hepatitis B vaccine at one month and then again at three to four months, along with the other necessary vaccines.

Vaccines will be discussed in greater detail in Chapter 10.

Vitamin K

Newborns receive an injection of vitamin K shortly after birth to aid in blood clotting and prevent bleeding. They have a deficiency of vitamin K because their systems are immature and incapable of manufacturing the vitamin. The vitamin is produced in the bowel by bacteria that newborns lack. Pregnant women should increase their intake of food that contains vitamin K: collard greens, broccoli, asparagus, and Brussels sprouts.

MISC.

The 411 on Vitamin K

Vitamin K as an injection was introduced in 1960. Before 1960, spontaneous bleeding was a cause of infant mortality. The more premature the baby, the higher the risk for bleeding. Breastfed babies are at a higher risk, too, because there is not enough vitamin K in breast milk to protect the baby. Once the injection is given, however, the risk decreases to almost zero. There are no known side effects from receiving vitamin K.

Ointment in the Eyes

Another treatment newborns receive shortly after birth is drops of ointment in their eyes. The ointment is an antibiotic to prevent serious eye infections.

It's necessary because babies have low immunity and no tears, and they can contract a disease by passing through the birth canal

If possible, hold your baby for the first time before he or she is given the eye antibiotic so that his or her vision is not blurry when seeing you for the first time.

Your Newborn Head to Toe

Don't be surprised or even shocked if your newborn doesn't look like what you hoped or expected. Remember, your baby has just been through a long, hard journey and hours of upheaval—and he or she has emerged from a world surrounded by fluid. Your baby will appear wet and discolored from a coating of a slippery lubricant provided by nature to help babies withstand the birthing process, and swelling and bruising are to be expected. But it won't be long before your baby begins to look less swollen and more like the beautiful, perfect baby you always dreamed of..

To understand what you will observe about your baby's body after he or she is born, let's get up close and personal with a newborn's body parts from head to toe.

The Head

Your baby's skull is formed to accommodate a huge amount of wear and tear during birth. It is comprised of several bone plates that come together at the *sutures,* fibrous material that allow the skull to move during birth and expand as the brain grows. These plates are not solidified for a long time to enable the movement, flexibility, and molding that is required by the impact of birth.

The shape of a baby's head may be asymmetric or even flat on one side; this happens if your baby had been favoring one particular resting position in the womb. Your baby's head could have a cone shape, resulting from passage through the birth canal. In most cases, these conditions correct themselves after birth.

Two conditions to note concerning a baby's head are:

> *Caput*: this is fluid that has accumulated under the scalp. It is soft, puffy swelling on the skull caused by pressure during delivery. It's often seen on a large area of the skull and tends to diminish in size over days after birth.

> *Cephalhematoma*: a condition over part of the scalp produced when very tiny blood vessels have broken. The swelling can persist for months.

> *Anterior fontanel*: the soft spot on top of your baby's head. Sometimes you may see the pulsation of an artery underneath this spot. It occurs because the bones in this area are separated by half an inch to an inch. The spot will close in approximately 12 to 18 months.

Posterior fontanel: the soft-spot opening at the back of the head. It will close earlier than the anterior one, at about one to three months.

Because newborns' necks are short and flexible, they are unable to hold their heads up on their own at this age. It's very important to keep their heads well supported during the first three months.

The Hair

Some babies are born with little or no hair while others are born with full heads of hair. Often, a baby's first hair will fall out by the second or third month as it is being replaced with new hair, and this new hair growth can look completely different than the birth hair.

A newborn may also have very fine, dark hair on his or her back and shoulders, called *lanugo*. This hair will usually disappear within a month.

The Face

After the trauma of passing through the birth canal, a baby may have a swollen face—often reddish in coloration. Newborns have what are referred to as "doll's eyes" because they haven't learned to focus yet. There may also be a small, red spot on the whites of the eyes that will disappear in about 14–28 days. The nose may appear to be asymmetric and full of mucus, which usually clears within 24–48 hours. The ears are soft and sometimes wrinkled and folded over. The ears can remodel themselves quickly because they are made of cartilage that is softer than bone.

Your baby's mouth may have a blister on the upper lip because of the fetus's sucking movements in the uterus. This will resolve itself in time, and there is no need for treatment. When a newborn opens his or her mouth, two or three small, white, round cysts may be seen on the palate. These too will disappear over time.

Some babies are born with a short *frenulum*, a soft cord under the tongue, which gives rise to the word "tongue-tied." It will grow with the baby and should not be cut unless it interferes with feeding or later with speech.

The Skin

Newborns sometimes have a yellow skin tone that signifies jaundice, which can be easily corrected if treated quickly. Jaundice is the sign of an immature liver that cannot metabolize the high amount of red blood cells. It is marked by yellowing of the skin and of the whites of the eyes. It occurs as the immature liver of the baby takes over the cycling of red blood cells, which in utero was completed by the placenta in combination with the mother's liver. A pigment called bilirubin, also associated with bruising, is responsible for the yellow coloration. Newborns are tested and monitored closely for jaundice, because if it goes untreated, this condition can be associated with brain damage and hearing loss.

Also, yellow-white colored areas on the skin, called *vernix,* can be present on a baby at birth. They function to protect the skin in the uterus and in the first few days after birth. They will soon diminish as the skin adjusts to life on the outside.

While there is commonly a pinkish cast to a newborn's skin, the hands and feet can have a bluish color and feel cold. This is because a newborn's body does not yet know how to regulate its body temperature, which it will do on its own in time.

More on skin conditions is discussed later in this chapter.

The Chest

As you heard from the very beginning through all those ultrasounds, babies have a much more rapid heartbeat than we do. So, once they are born, they breathe much faster than we do to keep that little heart pumping—taking about 40 breaths a minute. This rate can elevate to 60 times a minute when they are upset, agitated, or crying. During sleep, having 20–30 breaths per minute is normal for babies.

Baby watch

It is normal for newborns to demonstrate erratic breathing—sometimes very fast, and sometimes very slow and shallow. When babies stop breathing for one to two seconds, it's called *periodic breathing.* This can occur because the part of the brain that controls breathing is not mature yet. As long as a baby resumes breathing normally, that's fine. But if not, and the baby turns blue, that's an emergency and requires urgent attention.

The Belly

A newborn's belly has a rounded shape and has what's left of the umbilical cord, called the umbilical stump. There may be drops of blood on the stump, and it may appear moist. The stump will eventually dry out and fall off on its own. After the stump has fallen off, what's left is the baby's belly button. If a baby's belly button is an "outie," called an umbilical hernia, it will be pronounced and stick out when the baby cries. This will typically disappear by two to three years old. If not, corrective surgery is necessary.

Baby steps

The breast tissue in both boys and girls may be swollen after birth, and drops of milk may even be produced. This is the result of maternal hormones passing from the mother to the baby. No action is required; the swelling will diminish in a few weeks.

The Genitals

After birth, the genital areas are swollen in both sexes. For girls, there may also be a white discharge or drops of blood due to the mother's hormones causing a "mini period."

For boys, swelling of the testicles will diminish unless it is a hernia, which needs to be repaired immediately, or hydrocele (fluid around the testicles), which is indicated by a small bump in the groin, especially in premature boys. This should go away in six to eight months.

The normal genital swelling in both sexes will go down in two to four weeks.

The Arms and Legs

Newborns continue to hold their arms and legs tucked in close to their bodies, and possibly their palms in fists, as they did in the uterus. After all, there wasn't a whole lot of room in there toward the end. In a few short weeks after birth, their legs and arms will start to stretch out and their hands will open up.

Height and Weight

Average full-term newborns weigh anywhere from 6.5 to 7.5 pounds (around 3.5 kg). In the first week, however, they'll lose 10 percent of their weight because they're adjusting to the feeding, digestion, and higher volume of fluids in their bodies. Don't worry, though; by the second week, the weight will be regained. Then, newborns will start gaining around one half to one ounce (20–30g) a day the first one and a half to two months, then around half an ounce per month after that.

Hospital nurses will weigh your baby at birth and on a daily basis while you're in the hospital because these measurements are important in the beginning. It indicates how much the baby is eating and how his or her body is processing it.

You won't have to weigh your baby once you go home because it will be done at the baby's regular doctor visits. If you want to weigh your baby at home, make sure the scale is accurate and weigh the baby on the same scale without clothes or with a diaper on. You can also weigh yourself first, then while holding the baby, weigh yourself again—then subtract your weight alone from the weight of the two of you.

Newborns have head circumferences of approximately 14 inches (35cm). Head circumference grows from one quarter to one half inch (0.6–1.3cm) per month. Newborn lengths are, on average, 20 inches (50 cm). The doctor or nurse will mention percentiles—where your baby measures on average growth charts. The percentiles at any given age are the percentages of babies who have that weight at the same age.

Birthmarks and Skin Conditions

Because newborn skin is so sensitive and immature, it will easily react to the environment (which is normal). Rashes, for example, will bloom and disappear quickly, and many birthmarks will also lighten over time—so don't despair if these arise on your baby.

Many parents are concerned at the appearance of birthmarks. Parents may not know what they are, whether or not they are normal, and whether anything needs to be done. Your pediatrician will be able to answer your questions about them. In the meantime, here is a list of some of the more common birthmarks and their characteristics:

> **Mongolian spot:** A flat, bluish-black mark that can be large in size. It will fade over the next three years and disappear at puberty (or it will become very light). It's mostly seen on the buttocks and shoulders and more rarely in other areas. It occurs from the cells that give the skin its coloration and are supposed to migrate deeper, yet for unknown reasons they stop at a superficial level of the skin, giving it the dark appearance. The name comes from the first-known babies, from Mongolia, to have the condition (although it is identifiable in all races). Mongolian spot should not be confused with bruises.

> **Nevi:** May appear as small pinpoints to large birthmarks. They can be light brown, dark brown, or even black and are sometimes covered with hair.

Port-wine stain: A large, flat birthmark that's red to purple in color. Capillary malformations in port-wine stains may indicate medical complications, but only if they are seen on the face.

Salmon patch or stork bite: A flat, red mark mostly on the back of the neck—but it may also be see on the forehead and eyelids. These are normal, and in time will fade.

Hypopigmentation: Areas with no color. These need to be evaluated by the doctor.

Hemangiomas: Small groups of enlarged blood vessels, not necessarily birthmarks. They may be flat, raised (strawberry hemangiomas), or light bluish (cavernous hemangiomas).

Café au lait spots: The birthmark color is of coffee with milk. If there is only one it is not a problem. If there are more, the doctor needs to evaluate.

Rashes can be seen immediately after birth or later and may cause unnecessary alarm. They arise due to newborn skin's high level of sensitivity to what it comes in contact with (such as fabrics and/or lotions). If a rash occurs and persists, contact your baby's doctor within a reasonable time. Some common types of rashes are:

Milia: A tiny white rash mostly on and around the nose

Milaria: A small, round, pink rash sometimes filled with fluid. This results from the fact that newborns do not sweat because their sweat glands are still immature.

Erythema toxicum: A small, white point surrounded by a red flat area. This is a normal condition that will come and go for a few weeks.

Pustular melanosis: Many small vesicles around the chin, neck, extremities, palms, and soles. The name sounds nasty, but it's a completely normal condition.

We'll talk more about these and the best ways to treat rashes in Chapter 6.

Reflexes

Babies have reflexes that are seen only in infancy, and most of these vanish within the first few months of life. These reflexes are very important in the neurological assessment:

Moro reflex, or startle reflex: A pediatrician will elicit these responses by placing the baby in a semi-seated position, holding the arms, and then letting them go. The baby will reflexively extend the arms and immediately bring them back together. (This reflex was first described by Dr. Ernst Moro, hence the name.)

Grasping reflex: Demonstrated when an object, or a finger, is placed in the baby's open palm. The baby will respond by grasping it.

Tonic neck reflex: Observed when a baby, lying on a flat surface with its head turned to one side, reaches the arm out on the same side.

Rooting reflex: When you touch the baby's cheek and the mouth opens.

Stepping reflex: When placed in a standing position, the baby will raise a foot as if to start walking.

Sucking reflex: Demonstrated when you place a nipple, pacifier, or finger into the baby's mouth.

Umbilical Cord Care

Outside the womb, breathing and feeding for your newborn changes completely. What was his or her lifeblood, the umbilical cord, is now a stump on his or her belly. For the first two to three days, there will be some blood around the stump. The stump must be kept dry so it can dry up and fall off, which will happen within one to four weeks. There are no nerve endings in the umbilical cord remnant, so the baby won't feel discomfort or pain during this process. What's left after the stump falls off is yellowish, thick, healing tissue.

In the past, mothers might have been instructed to clean the area of the umbilical stump with rubbing alcohol. However, recent studies show that the stump heals faster if nothing is done.

Should any cleaning be needed, such as if the area appears sticky or dirty, gently wash it with water and a cotton ball and leave the stump uncovered so it can dry.

If the umbilical area continues to bleed or ooze, looks red or swollen, has a bad odor, or has not fallen off after one month, be sure to contact your doctor.

Cord Blood Storage

The blood found in the umbilical cord contains very special cells, called stem cells, that are unique to your baby. When the cord blood is stored it may help the baby, or even the immediate family, in the case of future disease. There are almost 80 diseases that can be helped through the use of stem cells. Cord blood may be used for transplants as well. It's important to evaluate early on before giving birth whether you want to store the baby's cord blood and research the options. If you elect not to store, the umbilical cord blood can be donated to a public cord blood bank, which are regulated by the FDA and the American Association of Blood Banks. Parents should talk to their doctors to understand the different options.

Swaddling

There's nothing more adorable than watching new mothers in the hospital carrying their newborns all wrapped up, with only their faces exposed. This cocoon technique, called swaddling, extends the way babies felt in their tight, warm, environment within the uterus. It's important to swaddle babies because it's just too soon for them to feel secure without it, and it also helps them sleep. If you observe babies who aren't swaddled, you will notice that their uninhibited reflexes and movements will keep waking them up. Also, swaddling does not allow babies to turn onto their stomachs (because some can do this early), so there is a decreased risk of Sudden Infant Death Syndrome (SIDS).

The swaddling technique can be compared to making burritos, stuffed cabbage, or crêpes (depending on your culture). A regular square or rectangular receiving blanket is fine to use (such as the cotton newborn blanket most hospitals use). Swaddling blankets with a more rounded shape and Velcro enclosures are available as well and are easier to use; however, they can be more expensive. Some parents use sleep sacks to swaddle their baby, and these look like zipped bags with no wrapping.

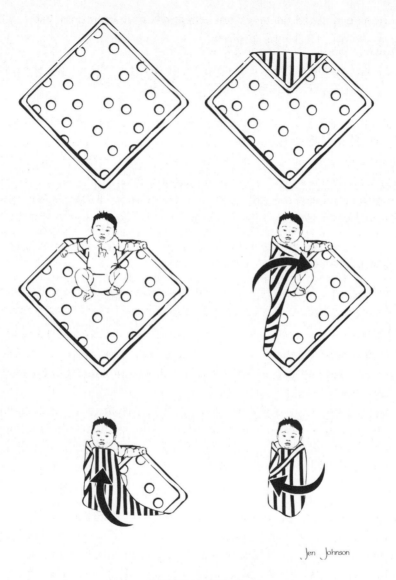

Jen Johnson

Swaddling technique.

Here's how to swaddle your baby with a blanket:

1. Place the blanket on a flat surface, making a triangle with it by folding one side on top of the other; the tip should be facing down.

2. Lay the baby on his or her back so that the neck is at the top line of the blanket.

3. Fold one side of the blanket over one arm and tuck it around the baby.

4. Fold the bottom tip up over the chest.

5. Fold and tuck the other side of the blanket around the baby.

Swaddle the baby for the first few weeks. Sometimes an active baby will be able to kick his or her blanket off. This can be dangerous since the blanket may be pulled over the face. Swaddling should be discontinued if it's being kicked off and before sleep training is started. You'll know when your baby is ready to discontinue swaddling, because he or she will fall asleep quickly after being put to bed swaddled. You may try to stop swaddling "cold turkey" or do it in phases by not wrapping as many parts of the body every night.

Essential Takeaways

- Newborn babies receive several treatments within minutes of being born to keep them healthy, including a Hepatitis B vaccine, a Vitamin K shot, and an antibiotic in their eyes.
- Common characteristics of a newborn baby include fast breathing, a swollen face and genitals, and curled-up legs.
- Bond with your baby right away, from the first moments he or she enters the world (or as close to that time as medically possible).
- Several different types of birthmarks are common on newborns and will usually fade over time.

chapter 2

At the Hospital

Understanding the hospital and nursery settings

The newborn examination and screening

What's needed to take your baby home

Exploring birth alternatives

Today, for most women who have given birth, the hospital, labor and delivery rooms, nursery, and doctors and nurses are the norm for having a baby. We take this scenario for granted, but it wasn't always this way.

Until the late nineteenth century, most women gave birth at home, and the infant and maternal mortality rates were very high.

By 1935, about 37 percent of women gave birth in hospitals. By 1960, this had increased to 97 percent, and now only about 1 percent of births take place outside hospitals—either at home or birthing centers.

A lot goes on in and around the maternity area of a hospital, and it will be helpful to know where your baby will be, what will be happening with your baby, and when you can finally take your bundle of joy home. In this chapter, you will learn about the hospital setting and what to expect during your stay.

definition

Obstetrics, which comes from the Latin *obstare,* meaning "to stand before" or "to stand in front of," was recognized as a specialty around 1828. With the increased use of anesthesia for surgical procedures, the first Caesarean section was performed in Boston in 1894.

Rooming In

If everything goes according to plan at birth with no complications, you and your baby will be transferred from the labor and delivery room to your room on the maternity floor. Keeping your baby with you in your room after birth and during your hospital stay instead of in the nursery, called rooming in, is a major aid to bonding. Of course, if you're too tired, in pain, or experiencing complications, rooming in can be delayed. There may have been complications with the baby at birth, as well, that would keep him or her from being with you right away or as much.

There are advantages to having your baby room in with you. The baby can be soothed and held by you as much as needed, the father or partner can be with the baby as well, you can feed your baby and feed more easily if breastfeeding, and you can change your baby—all of which contribute to bonding and helping you get to know your new baby. Also, with rooming in the parents can notice a problem sooner.

baby watch

Be careful not to fall asleep with the baby next to you in the bed. Place him or her in the bassinet next to your bed before you go to sleep. You'll be exhausted, so this ensures that you won't roll over on the baby inadvertently. This also ensures that you'll be able to sleep as comfortably as you can. After all, you will need to catch rest whenever possible.

Also, in most hospitals, the mothers' rooms have an extra sleeping chair for the father or partner, so the new family can all be together.

The Nursery

Even for healthy newborns, it's necessary for newborns to spend some time in the nursery so the nurses can measure and monitor their well-being. Upon arrival in the nursery, your baby will be placed on a "warming" table to ensure that his or her body temperature is maintained. The nurses will take the baby's vital signs: temperature, heart rate, respiratory rate, blood pressure, weight, height and head circumference. After everything checks out well, the baby will be washed, dried, changed, and taken to his or her mother. You will have the option of having your baby stay in the nursery periodically when you need a break or to rest. Nurses often encourage mothers to utilize the nursery so mothers can recover and get as much rest as possible—because they're going to need it!

When in the nursery, your baby will rest in a bassinet. There are also incubators, or isolettes, which are enclosed bassinets. These are for babies who need phototherapy—the special light treatment used if they become jaundiced (yellow skinned).

The nurses will feed and change the babies in the nursery. The parents can give their preferences for the nurses to follow, such as no pacifier or no formula if breastfeeding.

The NICU

There are times when a newborn needs to be transferred to the Neonatal Intensive Care Unit (NICU). The most obvious reasons are if a newborn (or multiples) is premature (born before 37 weeks), if there are serious infections, if a baby cannot breathe on his or her own, and/or if there are complications of genetic diseases or neurological problems.

Baby steps

The very first NICU was established in 1965 in Connecticut. *Neonatology,* concerned with taking care of a sick newborn, became an official subspecialty in 1975. Advances within the specialty are having a tremendous impact on and making an enormous difference for the lives of newborns.

There are more nurses in the NICU than in the well-baby nursery, and every baby is assigned his or her own nurse. The parents can still visit and hold and feed their baby. There are rooms in the unit where mothers can nurse the baby or pump if breastfeeding is not possible. A baby may only stay for a very short time, just for observation, or a baby may be in the NICU for several days or longer, depending on the situation. Here, babies can also be seen by family practitioners and pediatric or family nurse practitioners.

Seeing their newborn for the first time in the NICU can, understandably, be extremely disconcerting for the parents. The baby will be connected to a monitor—a screen that checks the heart rate, blood pressure, oxygen levels, and respiratory rate at all times. A loud sound will alert the nurse if something is wrong. There may be a feeding tube inserted through the baby's mouth in case he or she is not able to eat normally. There may also be another tube connected to a medication bag that is inserted in the baby's veins.

Some babies in the NICU are not able to breathe on their own. They will be connected to a mechanical ventilator, a machine that will breathe for them. This important machine has saved many lives, and its functioning and capabilities continue to improve.

When a baby is stable enough to leave the NICU, he or she may be transferred to the regular nursery, to the mother's room, or directly home if the mother is home already.

What Are All These Nurses and Doctors Doing?

Regularly, the hospital doctors or nurse practitioners will examine your baby from head to toe. This includes checking the skin, the shape of the skull, the eyes, nose, mouth, ears, neck, collar bone, and chest. They will listen to the lungs and heart and check the abdomen and genital area. They will make sure that your baby is doing well neurologically, checking the reflexes as well as the movement of the arms and legs. They will also ask how the baby is feeding and may want to observe how the baby actually breastfeeds to ensure adequate intake.

The mother will be visited by the doctor and nurses as well, and a by a lactation consultant if breastfeeding.

The Nurses

The nurses, highly specialized in pediatrics, work around the clock in shifts. They will be there at all times to check your baby (and you) and to notify the doctors if anything needs to be attended to immediately. They will regularly take vital signs (pulse, temperature, blood pressure, and weight) and will note the number of wet diapers. This helps them ascertain whether your baby is taking in enough fluids and therefore maintaining normal urinary output. Nurses can also be helpful with issues with breastfeeding.

The Pediatrician

A newborn is examined by a pediatrician within 24 hours of birth. The pediatrician is the doctor specifically for your baby and is one who has either been preselected by you or is on staff at the hospital. In teaching hospitals, the pediatricians do not attend births. However, the neonatalists and residents will be in attendance.

baby steps

Pediatricians do not routinely attend births, except in some cases where a C-section is performed or if complications arise.

If you pre-selected your pediatrician and he or she has admitting privileges at the hospital where you have given birth, he or she will be notified by the hospital when your baby is born. He or she will come to the hospital within 24 hours to do the preliminary examination of your baby. Otherwise, a staff pediatrician and/or resident (doctor in training) will meet you and examine your baby.

Your baby will typically be seen every day in the hospital by the pediatrician, making sure that he or she is growing well and that there are no health problems or complications.

baby steps

Selecting a pediatrician to take care of your newborn is best done in the weeks prior to your due date (or sooner). Leave yourself plenty of time to visit a few practices and interview a few doctors to find the right fit for you and your baby. Many doctors offer a prenatal appointment for this purpose. Ask the hospital or your obstetrician for a referral, and talk to friends who have experience with a particular pediatrician and practice. Remember, this doctor will play a very important role in your family's life, so choose carefully.

More Procedures

Newborns are subject to a battery of tests for the sake of their long-term health. While it may seem like the tests are never ending while you're in the hospital, they are an important part of setting your baby up for the best possible start in life.

The Newborn Screening

All newborns are tested for several inborn diseases at 24 hours after birth; these tests are collectively called a newborn screening. Although the baby may appear to be healthy at birth, diseases could manifest later in life. The purpose of the newborn screening is to detect and help these babies as soon as possible.

Typical newborn screenings test for dozens of diseases that, if left unrecognized and untreated, could lead to serious disease and/or death. For example, if hypothyroidism (a condition where the thyroid gland is incapable of functioning properly) is detected immediately after birth, it can be treated before any symptoms occur and head off a lifetime of health issues for the baby.

The very first newborn screening was done in the 1960s for PKU (phenylketonuria), a condition where babies can't process the amino acid phenylalanine. If untreated, serious developmental problems can occur. With a special diet and good follow-up, these babies will lead a normal life.

The newborn screening is done by a heel stick to draw a few blood drops onto a special paper that is then sent to a laboratory for analysis. The doctors and hospitals are notified of the results, and if the tests reveal an abnormality, the parents will be notified immediately and the baby will be retested.

The newborn screening, the retesting, and the number of diseases screened for are regulated state by state. In New York, for instance, the newborn screening currently tests for 44 diseases. There is an ongoing effort to standardize the screening throughout the United States.

In New York and other states, newborn screening also includes HIV status. Babies born to HIV positive mothers will test positive because they have the mother's immunity, up to the age of 18–24 months. (More on HIV positive babies can be found in Chapter 24.)

Hearing Test

A baby will also undergo a hearing screening test before leaving the hospital. If the screening fails, it will be repeated in a month. If the test is failed again, the baby will be referred to a pediatric ENT (ear, nose, and throat) specialist for further examination and study.

The hearing test is done with non-invasive measures. One way is a small probe is put in the baby's ear that intercepts vibrations in the middle ear. It's called otoacoustic emissions. Another is called auditory brainstem response (ABR) which is done by placing electrodes on the baby's head. It measures the brain's reaction to the sound.

Circumcision

Traditionally, *circumcision* has been done for religious, hygienic, cultural, and social reasons and performed within the first 10 days after birth—but not within the first 24 hours.

Circumcision comes from the Latin *circum* (around) and *caedere* (cut). It means to cut around the foreskin of the penis.

Having your baby boy circumcised is your decision, based on your own research and beliefs—not a medical one. The American Academy of Pediatrics neither endorses nor condones circumcision, because all studies done to support it have been deemed inconclusive. However, recent studies have shown that circumcised men are less likely to have urinary tract infections, have less of a chance of contracting penile cancer (a very rare disease), and may be more protected against HIV transmission.

A doctor performs the procedure with either topical cream or an injection for pain control. The outer layer of skin around the penis is carefully removed, and the penis is bandaged to contain the bleeding. Feeding the baby after the procedure is recommended, or a pacifier dipped in sugar water can be soothing. After circumcision, the penis will look red. As it heals, white, yellowish, small spots will appear (healing granulation tissue).

Keep the general area very clean using water only, not baby wipes, and change the diaper frequently. Put petroleum jelly on the penis to soothe it and keep it from sticking to the diaper. When you need to change the bandage, wet it and apply petroleum jelly.

There is a small risk of continued bleeding and infection. Call the doctor should this occur after three days and if the area is red and swollen or if there has been no urinary output after 12 hours.

Reasons not to circumcise include if the baby is very small or very sick, has a bleeding disorder, or has hypospadias (when the opening is not on the tip of the penis but anywhere else on the shaft).

Premature Babies

Babies who are born before 37 weeks of gestation are called premature, or preemie. The earlier a baby is born, the more complications may arise because the organs did not have time to mature. The good news is that because of advances in the field, premature babies who weigh more than 1.76 pounds (800 g) will survive more than 90 percent of the time.

Premature babies are taken to the NICU for monitoring and treatment. Common problems premature babies have include:

> **Respiratory problems:** These will happen in almost all babies born before 35 weeks. Today, the mother may be given a medication before birth that can help the baby's lung development. A ventilator can aid a preemie's breathing, as well as prongs in their nose called CPAP, or even just

oxygen through a tube. Premature babies tend to stop breathing for a few seconds and drop their heart rate (bradycardia).

Jaundice: The incidence of jaundice increases from 60 percent in full-term babies to more than 80 percent in premature babies.

Intestinal infection: Premature babies are especially prone to developing an intestinal infection called necrotizing enterocolitis (NEC).

Heart problems: These may develop due to the nonclosure of a duct between the lung and heart vessels, referred to as ductus arteriosus. In full-term babies, this closes very soon after birth—but in preemies, it will stay open. The condition can be treated with medication or surgery.

Vision, hearing, and developmental problems: These are all common in premature babies.

Hernias: Premature baby boys frequently have hernias. All premature boys need to be checked for hernia before going home.

Others: Bleeding in the brain or **intraventricular hemorrhage** (could be minimal or more severe), **anemia** which means lower red blood cells, and **retinopathy of prematurity** (new, abnormal vessels which form in the retina). All of these happen because of the organ immaturity and the body's difficulty in handling the adjustment.

For premature babies, breast milk is the best, even if the babies may not be able to breastfeed immediately. The mother can start pumping as soon as possible so the milk can be stored and given through a small tube.

Causes of Premature Birth

MISC.   Malnutrition in the mother, smoking, alcohol consumption, drug use, and poor prenatal care are known reasons for premature births, as are serious or chronic disease, high blood pressure, infection, malformation of the uterus, or hormonal imbalance. And sometimes the reasons cannot be determined.

Twins and Multiple Births

From 1980 to 2000, the number of twins born in the United States increased by 74 percent. Up to three percent of all births are twins or multiples.

Twins and multiples are often born prematurely and therefore require close monitoring and special treatment in the NICU. They can more often be born breech or in transverse positions and via C-section as well. In identical twins, one baby can take more blood from the other; this is called twin to twin transfusion.

To accommodate more than one baby, the mother needs lots of rest. She should strive to get as much rest as possible while the babies are being cared for in the nursery. She is also prone to high blood pressure.

Feeding of twins can be done together or separately; it's actually possible to breastfeed two babies at a time. Mothers need not worry about having enough to feed more than one baby. Given the feedback process, the more the demand, the more the supply. Anyone can lend a helping hand if a combination of breastfeeding and bottle feeding is necessary.

Length of Your Stay

How long you stay in the hospital largely depends on the type of delivery you have, your health, and the baby's health. A mother who has delivered via a normal, spontaneous, vaginal delivery (NSVD) with no complications will typically stay two days. A mother who has delivered via C-section will typically stay four days in the hospital. Check your insurance benefits to confirm what your particular plan offers in terms of your hospital stay. When both mother and baby are healthy, they can go home together at the given time.

What You Need to Go Home

Before going home, your newborn must have a discharge physical examination. The nurses will typically give bathing, dressing, and cleaning demonstrations. You will receive a card on which your baby's birth and discharge weight, length, head circumference, blood type, and any vaccines (if given) were recorded. (It is important to always bring this card to the baby's doctor for all visits.) The newborn screening and hearing test must be done before your baby leaves the hospital. The parents must complete a few forms to receive the baby's birth certificate. Also, request a medical summary for the provider who will see your baby after discharge.

You will want an outfit to take your baby home in and a diaper bag packed with diapers, a change of clothes, burp cloths, a blanket, and a bottle and formula (if using). You will be able to take all of the baby supplies that were brought to you in the hospital room home with you as well.

Baby's Next Doctor Appointment

All babies will see their pediatrician again not long after they leave the hospital. Jaundiced or previously ill babies are usually seen again within 24 hours of leaving the hospital. Parents should call the doctor as soon as possible if they see any problems, such as weight loss or jaundice. Healthy babies will see their doctor in three to five days. This next appointment with the pediatrician is best made prior to you leaving the hospital if possible.

baby watch

Add your baby to your insurance coverage within 30 days of birth or he or she may not be covered.

The Car Seat

One of the most important things you need in order to take your baby home is a car seat. Many hospitals will not allow discharge if the parents do not have a car seat—even if it's only a short distance away or you're going by taxi. You must have a car seat.

The American Academy of Pediatrics (AAP) recommends that all infants up to age 2 ride facing the rear of the car, or at least until they are 1 year old and 20 pounds. Both criteria must be met, such as if a 10 month old is 20 pounds, that doesn't change facing backward. Always read the information provided by the car seat manufacturer for the required minimum weight and height.

You can get an infant-only car seat or a convertible one. The infant-only car seat is small, has carrying handles, and sometimes is a detachable part of a stroller. It can be used typically up to 22–33 pounds. The convertible car seat model is bulkier and does not have handles but accommodates a child up to 80 pounds.

Some basic rules to follow concerning a baby in a car and car seat are:

1. Never leave your baby (or child) alone in a car.

2. The baby's shoulders must be at or below the harness/strap level.

3. Install the seat very securely within your car. If you can wiggle or move it, it is not tight enough.

4. If the baby slouches in the car seat, put blanket rolls on either side of the baby. Do not put anything under or behind the baby.

5. Recheck the harness tightness after changing clothing (for example, from heavier to lighter clothing).

6. Read the manufacturer's manual very carefully. Call them if you have more questions.

Do your research when buying a car seat, as there are quite a variety of styles, models, and prices from which to choose. The National Highway Traffic Safety Administration (NHTSA) is a great resource for information on buying a car seat, car seat safety ratings, recalls, and more. Find this information at www.nhtsa.gov/Safety/CPS.

Many hospitals and fire departments offer free car seat checks to show you how to properly install your car seat in your vehicle. It's a good idea to have this done before you bring your baby home.

Reasons to Remain in the Hospital

A baby may need to remain in the hospital longer than the mother to continue receiving necessary treatments. One condition that often requires a baby to stay longer is jaundice. If a baby's bilirubin levels are high at the time of dismissal from the hospital, the baby will need to stay to receive or continue to receive phototherapy treatment. Other reasons to prolong hospitalization for the baby include administering medication for an infection, observation if the baby is not growing as he or she should, malformations, surgery or prolonged need for nutrition or medication. A nonmedical reason for a newborn to be kept longer in the hospital is instability in a parent's life from drug abuse, a difficult or chaotic home environment, or mental health problems. In these cases, a social worker will determine the time and place of discharge.

In the case of premature babies, they will have to remain in the NICU until they are able to eat, breathe on their own, and show that they are developing well. Preemies have to reach a certain age and weight as well before they can leave. Every situation is different, however.

Many NICUs throughout the country offer support groups for parents with babies in the NICU. Social services and visiting nurses will help families adjust to being apart from their babies. The parents are taught in detail how to take care of their babies, and necessary appointments will be arranged.

Mothers sometimes need to stay longer in the hospital if they have an infection, if there are complications from surgery or anesthesia, if there is abnormal bleeding, or if there is an incapacitating mental illness. If there is a family member available who can take care of the newborn, the baby can go home to be cared for by him or her. If not, the baby will stay until the mother is fully able to take care of her baby.

Alternative Deliveries

Since this is a book about your baby's first year, it's not our goal to discuss how or where to have your baby. That decision is totally yours, after careful consideration of the options and alternatives for delivery. However, it's important to understand the pros and cons of alternative deliveries at home and at birthing centers in light of the potential consequences for your baby.

Homebirths with Midwives

Birth at home is for very healthy women who have had good prenatal care, with no signs of complications.

> **The pros:** Home births provide a relaxed atmosphere in a known environment. A known provider, the same midwife who has seen the mother for prenatal care, is present for the birth. The birth is natural with no medication, and there is a lower risk of infection. There are no restrictions of time for labor or position, and there is no C-section.

> **The cons:** No pain medication is administered, and the mother and baby must be urgently transferred to a hospital if there are any complications. There is no immediate pediatric support, and no Vitamin K given to the baby. Also, there is no insurance coverage for home births.

Before hospitals, midwives delivered babies. The earliest mention of midwives goes back to 1300. Originally, the meaning of the word "wife" was "woman", so midwife literally means "with woman," or "a woman who assists other women in childbirth." These days, many hospitals have midwives on staff.

Birthing Centers

There are birthing centers that are affiliated with a hospital or are independent. Healthy, low-risk pregnancies can consider the birthing center option. The centers are furnished to make the mother feel comfortable and at home.

> **The pros:** The centers provide a pleasant, relaxed environment with known providers and staff, and only natural pain relief is given.

> **The cons:** Some centers are partially covered by insurance while others are not. The mother and baby will need to be transferred to the hospital if complications develop. There is no pediatrician or pediatric support and no newborn screening is done. Discharge is early, usually within 6 to 12 hours of birth. Also, jaundice can become a problem at home.

Adoption or Surrogacy

You don't have to go through pregnancy to become a parent. Adoptive parents, or parents who go the surrogacy route, will have the same feelings and responsibilities as birth parents. Whether you adopt a baby or have a baby through someone else, this is your baby—and all the conditions and concerns for his or her first year apply just the same.

History of Adoption

Adoption did not become legally recognized in the United States until 1850. For a while, adoption took a strange turn. Due to economic conditions, farmers needed help and the orphan trains began. This was less about adoption and more about extra hands. The courts only started to get involved at the beginning of the twentieth century. After the 1960s, adoption practices changed, leading to the present procedures.

The first mother surrogate arrangement was made in 1976. Surrogacy is regulated by state laws and is not legal in certain states.

Many adoptive parents meet their new baby in the hospital right after birth. Parents who use surrogacy will be able to see the baby at birth. Either way, spend as much time as you can with your new baby; hold and carry him or her around. Bonding will happen—sometimes instantly, or sometimes it takes a while. As many adoptive mothers say, "You did not carry them in your belly but in your heart." You can find more on adoption in the Appendix.

Essential Takeaways

- Your time in the hospital will be exciting, tiring, and short. Gather as much information from the doctors and nurses there as you can, and take every opportunity to ask or clarify what you're unsure of.

- Become hands on with your baby as soon as you can. The more familiar you become with what your baby needs and how to provide it, the more comfortable you will feel parenting on your own at home.

- The newborn screening tests your baby for dozens of diseases and is required prior to discharge from the hospital.

- You must have a car seat at the hospital when it's time to bring your baby home.

chapter 3

Feeding Your Baby

Learning to feed your baby

Breastfeeding techniques and positions, pumping, and milk storage

Understanding bottle feeding and the necessities

Feeding schedule and amounts

As a new parent, you will spend a significant amount of time in your day—and night—feeding your baby. It is the most important task you will accomplish each day. It's important to understand the entire spectrum of feeding—breastfeeding, formula, amount, frequency, burping, and more—to be fully prepared for this very special job (one you will grow to love and cherish).

Breastfeeding

A mother's breast milk has always been the best and most important source of feeding for her infant. Not only is it a complex form of nutrition, but breastfeeding also aids in the bonding process between the infant and the mother. Naturally and quite miraculously, the mother's breasts start producing milk at the sound of her newborn crying.

The current recommendation from the American Academy of Pediatrics (AAP) is to breastfeed, if possible, for at least six months. Breastfeeding is such an important topic that a program for teaching breastfeeding was introduced into all pediatric training residency programs in 2010 so that every doctor specializing in pediatrics would gain a deeper knowledge of breastfeeding and understand the many benefits and issues surrounding it.

Baby steps

The American Academy of Pediatrics recommends not introducing solid foods into the baby's diet until about six months of age. Eating solid foods early on diminishes the amount of time breast-feeding; therefore, a baby won't receive as much of the important nutrients from breast milk. Also, large amounts of breast milk or formula on top of solid food can lead to too much weight increase. There is also the danger of food allergies, which increases with the addition of diverse solid foods.

At this very early age, babies don't have the coordination to swallow, which is necessary to accommodate solid foods. Instinctively, babies push with their tongues against any object placed between the lips. This is called the extrusion reflex, and it disappears after four to six months.

Breastfeeding provides many benefits for a baby:

A reduced risk of obesity and autoimmune diseases, such as diabetes

A lower risk of upper respiratory infections as well as ear and lung infections

Easier and better digestion

A lower incidence of SIDS (Sudden Infant Death Syndrome), according to new research

There are many benefits for the nursing mother as well:

The uterus returning to normal pre-pregnancy size much faster

The mother losing her pregnancy weight faster, because there is an increase in the amount of calories burned while breastfeeding

A lower risk of developing breast cancer

Breast milk readily available (no need for preparation in the middle of the night)

Economical, because additional money does not have to be spent on formula, and there is no limit on how long breastfeeding can continue

Learning about breastfeeding and receiving instruction on how to breastfeed is extremely important. Taking a breastfeeding class before birth is helpful, as well as getting help and comfort from others while in the breastfeeding stage..

In the hospital, the doctor, nurses, and lactation specialists are resources for help. Do not get discouraged if satisfactory breastfeeding doesn't happen immediately; it takes time to learn, and you and your baby are learning together and helping each other in the process.

Once you're home, find a breastfeeding support group. It will be helpful to be in the company of other mothers going through the same experience as you. Support groups are usually led by a nurse or lactation consultant and are offered at hospitals for free.

Baby steps — Breast size does not matter in order to effectively breastfeed. Rather, it's the amount of milk ducts, the latching-on technique, and the demand/production response that determine breastfeeding capability.

Friends and even strangers tend to give a lot of advice (mostly unsolicited), make comments, or tell their own stories about breastfeeding, which may or may not be helpful. Take all this information with a grain of salt (and some humor). After doing your own research, make your own decision on what works best for you and your baby.

Reasons Not to Breastfeed

While breast milk is the preferred food for infants, there are situations where breastfeeding is not recommended due to conditions with the mother, including:

- If the mother is HIV positive or has active tuberculosis

- If the mother is undergoing chemotherapy or taking or exposed to radiation

- If the mother has active herpes lesions on both breasts

- If the mother has undergone either the enlargement or reduction of her breasts, which has cut too many of her milk ducts

- If the mother has suffered serious complications after birth

- If the mother is taking medications contraindicated for breastfeeding

- If the baby has certain rare diseases (such as galactosemia or G6PD deficiency)

Talk to your doctor about potential reasons you may have not to breastfeed.

However, in the case of active herpes lesions, the baby can feed from a breast that is clear of the disease. Also, it is possible to breastfeed after breast reduction, augmentation, or lumpectomy. Every surgery is different; it simply depends on the number of milk ducts that have been cut and whether the nipple has been replaced with an artificial one. Retracted nipples are not inhibitors to breastfeeding, either, and lactation specialists can help with this condition.

Mothers who are Hepatitis B antigen carriers can breastfeed. The baby will receive the vaccine and the immunoglobulin immediately after birth. The common cold and bacterial infection are not reasons to stop breastfeeding. Breastfeeding the baby before being exposed to and contracting these infections will actually give him or her immunity through antibodies that have developed in the breast milk. Breast infections such as mastitis or an abscess are also not a cause to stop breastfeeding, although these conditions can be very painful.

Strict hygiene, including washing hands many times a day, is very important during breastfeeding, as always.

The Breastfeeding Mother's Diet

As in pregnancy, a breastfeeding mother's diet should be healthy and balanced. There is simply no need to "eat for two" (or more). The nursing mother needs an extra 500 calories a day, so this is definitely not the time to diet. Good nutrition will result in breast milk that will help the baby grow well. The mother should continue taking prenatal vitamins, because these nutrients will pass to the baby.

While you're breastfeeding, it is advised not to eat raw fish, raw meat, deli meat, or unpasteurized dairy products. Some fish contain high amounts of methyl mercury. Steer clear of swordfish, shark, king mackerel, or tilefish. Tuna is okay (not solid albacore), as is shrimp, salmon (wild, if possible), or catfish once or twice a week.

For daily updates on the safety of fish, visit www.epa.gov/waterscience/fish.

Everything the mother eats or drinks goes through the breast milk. Therefore, if the baby seems physically uncomfortable, it may be caused by something that the mother ate the day before. Eliminating the potentially upsetting food for a week usually takes care of it, then you may restart it after that, watching again for any discomfort. Every newborn is different and will react uniquely to different foods or spices.

Breast milk contains many different substances: lactose, milk fat, proteins, minerals, anti-inflammatory substances, enzymes that aid in the baby's digestion, and immunoglobulins that protect the baby against some infections. However, it is lower in fluoride as well as in vitamins D and K.

Although breastfeeding is considered the best nutrition for an infant, breast milk unfortunately doesn't provide enough vitamin D—a vitamin essential for the development of strong bones and fighting a disease called *rickets*. If you're breastfeeding, you can start giving vitamin D in the first month. In the United States, formulas have enough vitamin D added.

The sun helps the body make vitamin D naturally. But because of the risks of being in the sun (skin cancer), most of us use sunscreen. The sunscreen prevents vitamin D from being made in the body. Moreover, it's not recommended for young infants to be out in direct sun.

All breastfed babies should be given vitamin D, which comes in the form of a solution and is given with a dropper directly into the baby's mouth. Try to give it between feedings, just in case the baby doesn't like it and spits it up. It won't interfere with the rest of the feedings. Make sure you follow the instructions. It's not a prescription vitamin. Your doctor will tell you when to change the vitamin as the baby grows.

definition

Rickets is a disease of the bones when they aren't mineralized and become soft. As a result, bones can easily break, or serious malformations can result. It happens because there is not enough vitamin D, calcium, and phosphate in the body. This is either because of poor diet (for example, breastfed babies who don't get vitamin D, or because of certain diseases such as kidney and liver diseases, and celiac disease, among others). There are still many countries, unfortunately, where rickets is common.

If the mother is on any medication, she may continue taking it, in most cases. Always ask your obstetrician or pediatrician before starting or stopping a new medication. Smoking or drug use should be stopped while breastfeeding. Alcohol in moderation, such as one or two alcoholic drinks per week (with a lower alcohol level) may not be harmful. It takes 30–90 minutes for the alcohol level to peak and up to 13–16 hours to be eliminated completely. The stronger the alcohol level, the more time it takes to clear.

The breastfeeding mother needs to eat well and keep well hydrated with lots of water.

Starting Lactation

Lactation does not start when the baby is born. The process starts at the very beginning of pregnancy. As the breasts enlarge, there may be some pain. This happens because the milk ducts increase in volume and start maturing. There is no need to "prepare" the breasts or "toughen" the nipples. At some point toward the end of pregnancy, a yellowish liquid will be secreted, called *colostrum*. It is the first breast "milk" the baby will consume. Although only available briefly (a few days after birth) and in small quantity, the colostrum is very important because it has a high volume of the substances that help the baby's immature immune system—and it's also very easy to digest. The dark-yellow color of colostrum is due to the presence of beta carotene, an important nutrient for the newborn.

A few days after birth, the milk will come in and be whiter in color, with varying consistency each day. The foremilk is the breast milk that the baby takes in at the beginning of the feeding. The hind milk is the breast milk at the end of the feeding, which contains more fat. This is why it's important for the baby to empty the full breast at each feeding, to get the hind milk.

If the mother is ready, breastfeeding can start at birth—even in the delivery room, if possible. Most babies will breastfeed well; the most important issue is the motion called *latching on*, which is when the baby successfully attaches to the breast for feeding. Latching on is the most important thing for the baby to learn, and sometimes it takes a while for the baby to get it right.

Many mothers will have the *milk ejection reflex*, also known as "let-down." It means that the milk will start flowing at the sound of the baby crying or even before. A mother just seeing her baby may be enough to start the flow of breast milk. It's also totally normal not to have this reflex.

During the first few days of breastfeeding, the mother may feel strong cramps in the uterus, which is normal. The uterus is now contracting and starting to return to its pre-pregnancy size.

Breastfeeding Techniques and Positions

In order to effectively breastfeed, the baby has to take in the nipple and entire areola. The baby's nose should only touch the breast; otherwise, he or she will have difficulty breathing. The mother may feel some pain, but over time this should disappear. Constant pain means inefficient latching on or a possible breast infection.

During breastfeeding, the mother can see the baby's jaw moving, not only the lips. Twenty to thirty minutes on each breast is a sufficient amount of time to feed. The baby will let go of the breast on his or her own when finished. If not, and if you only see the lips moving, it's time to stop. To discontinue breastfeeding, gently put your finger in the side of the baby's mouth or gently on top of the baby's tongue. This will break the latch and allow the mother to pull away.

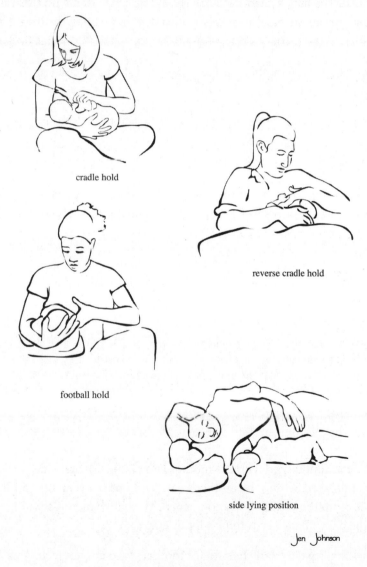

cradle hold

reverse cradle hold

football hold

side lying position

Jen Johnson

Breastfeeding positions.

The Cradle Hold

This is the classic breastfeeding position. The mother should either be sitting in a chair with her feet on a small stool—rocking chairs are great for this—or sitting up in bed with pillows on her lap. The baby's head should rest on the pillows in the mother's lap, almost horizontally and slightly inclined. The baby's head and back should be supported with the mother's opposite arm of the feeding breast. The mother uses her other arm to position the breast into the baby's mouth.

This is a good position for the mother who feels well and strong after an uncomplicated delivery of a full-term baby.

The cross-cradle position is the same as the cradle position but with the opposite arm.

The Football Hold

This position is best accomplished by sitting in a chair with feet on a stool or sitting up on the bed. The baby's head and nose are at the nipple level while the baby's body and legs are to the side under the mother's armpit, with the neck and head supported.

This is a good position for mothers who have had a C-section and/or have flat nipples or for smaller babies or twins—with one at each side. It also works well for babies who only want to feed from one breast.

baby steps

If a baby refuses to feed from the other breast, you can use a small trick. If you hold the baby in a cradle position, don't change the baby's position. Just slide the baby to the other breast, holding him or her in a football position, or do the same thing from football to cradle position.

Reclining

The position is best accomplished with the mother lying in bed on her side with her back very straight. Pillows are placed behind the mother's back and one between her mildly flexed knees. The baby will feed from the breast closest to the bed. The baby's mouth should be at the level of the nipple, and the baby's back needs to be supported.

The reclining position is particularly helpful for mothers who are not feeling well, who have sore backs, or who have had smaller babies.

Make sure that there is somebody checking in with the mother periodically to ensure that she has not fallen asleep with the baby in the bed.

Remember, breastfeeding works when both mother and baby are calm and can enjoy the experience.

Pumping

If the mother is away or the baby is unable to breastfeed yet, breast milk can be pumped. It's necessary to pump as many times as you would normally feed the baby. The action of the pump will give the same signal for milk production as if the baby were at the breast. Most lactation consultants recommend starting as soon as possible after birth if breastfeeding is not possible right away.

There are a few different kinds of breast pumps:

The **manual pump** is small, easy to manage, and less expensive but takes longer to use than an electric one. It can be used for a short time, to relieve pressure, or while traveling.

The **electric pump** is more efficient than the manual pump but can be bulky and noisy. The electric pump can be used to pump both breasts at the same time. Some hospitals rent these pumps. The smaller, personal electric pump has been on the market since the 1990s. If you travel with the electric pump, make sure that it runs on batteries. Take a manual one as well just in case.

Different women are comfortable with different types of pumps. It's a matter of personal preference.

Storage of Breast Milk

If a breastfeeding mother cannot give milk to the baby immediately or if she is working or traveling, the breast milk can be stored. Freshly pumped milk can be stored at room temperature (around 77° Fahrenheit) for four hours, in a refrigerator (39° Fahrenheit) for eight days, and in the freezer (5° Fahrenheit) without a separate door for two weeks, but never longer than that.

If you have a freezer with a separate door and a temperature of 0° Fahrenheit, it can be stored for three to four months. In freezers that are completely separate (deep freezers), where the temperature is at least –4° Fahrenheit, storage of breast milk can last more than six months. There are also insulated coolers specially made to store breast milk.

If the breast milk is stored for a longer period of time, some substances may be lost. Also, your milk changes as your baby grows. The milk expressed when the baby was a newborn may not be as good for the older infant.

Bottles used for breast milk must have a cap and be very clean, either washed in the dishwasher, or washed with hot or boiled water (depending on your water's quality) and dried completely. It is preferable to use smaller bottles made from glass or plastic without BPA (Bisphenol A). Do not use plastic bags if possible. Label every bottle with the time and the day that it was pumped. Put the freshest milk in the back, and use older bottles first.

To thaw breast milk, place the bottle in the refrigerator overnight or place the frozen milk in a bowl with warm water. Very gently, move the bottle to mix the frozen milk that may have separated. Pour a few drops on the inside of your wrist to check the temperature before feeding. The milk is the right temperature if you cannot feel the drops (neither hot nor cold).

Here are some important things to note about the storage of breast milk:

> Never store the milk in the door of the refrigerator or freezer.

> Never refreeze thawed milk. Use it within 24 hours or discard it.

> Never thaw frozen milk at room temperature.

> Never thaw milk in the microwave or on the stove.

How Often the Breastfed Baby Eats

Don't expect the baby to be on a feeding schedule. Feeding is on demand for the first month or two, but the usual number of feedings is 8–12 a day. Babies sleep up to 16–18 hours during the day, so it's important to wake the baby every 2–3 hours during the day, if necessary, to eat. It's not as easy as it sounds; you may need to change or bathe the baby to get him or her up.

baby steps

The more you feed, the more milk you will produce. Resist the urge to feed whenever your baby cries, because it's not always a sign of hunger.

Giving water to the baby before age six months is not recommended. Babies can fill up quickly or even get water toxicity.

It's better to feed the baby before he or she becomes very fussy and cries. There are pre-hunger signs: the baby starts stretching a lot, may make sucking sounds and movements with the mouth, may put the fist to the mouth, or make little noises that sound like the beginning of a cry. As you get to know your baby, you will be able to read these signs early on. A baby who is still calm will latch on much faster and easier.

The baby should feed from both breasts. If that's not possible, start the next feeding with the breast the baby fed from earlier, in order to empty it (getting the hind milk), and then switch to the other breast. Keep in mind that babies have good days and bad days—they will not always eat the same amount. Don't give up. Many new mothers become discouraged very early because it can be a very erratic, unpredictable, and physically challenging stage. Ask for help, and you will succeed.

baby steps

In the first few days, a baby only needs 5–15 ml (or cc) per feeding, so the colostrum is enough. Then the amount the baby eats will increase day by day.

How to Know the Baby Is Eating Enough

You know that the breastfed baby has had enough to eat when he or she is content for at least one and a half to two hours after each feeding, is active and alert, if there are at least four to six wet diapers, and of course if the baby is putting on weight after the first few days. (All babies lose 7 to 10 percent of their weight in the first few days.) If the baby is not getting enough nourishment, he or she will be agitated, will cry after feedings, will want to feed all the time, or will be very sleepy. Also, there will be fewer wet diapers. Instead of clear urine, you may see reddish-looking crystals in the diaper.

If there is a low amount of urine or red crystals in the diaper, call the doctor.

The muscles of the baby's stomach are rigid. If more fluid goes in than the stomach can hold, it will be rejected (spitting up). Call the doctor if the baby spits up more than two teaspoonfuls or if the spit-up is so forceful that it is "projectile."

Understanding Formula

A mother may decide not to breastfeed or may not be able to breastfeed for a variety of reasons: the baby is ill, is adopted, the mother can't stay home and can't pump or store the milk, or the mother is very ill. Sometimes a combination of breast milk and formula is given to the baby.

misc.

Formula Origins

The term *formula* comes from discovering the best mix of substances, as in a mathematical formula. The first use of formula was in Switzerland in the nineteenth century and in the United States in the 1920s. Formulas offer adequate nutrition and hydration for a baby. There are many formulas on the market, and all of them must meet FDA standards.

Formula offers more flexibility to mothers, allows partners and family to help with feeding, can be useful in special diets, and contains vitamin D. Because it is digested more slowly than breast milk, there are fewer feedings than with breastfeeding. However, formula doesn't have immune properties and is more difficult to digest. Formula provides 20 calories per ounce, and premature babies are fed formula that is higher in calories—24 calories per ounce.

Most formulas are based on the properties in cow's milk but are modified to resemble breast milk. All formulas contain iron (4–12 mg per liter). The AAP does not recommend low-iron formulas.

Soy-based formulas are best for vegetarian or vegan families or for babies who may be allergic to the cow's milk protein. However, there is cross-reactivity between soy and cow's milk protein, so babies may be allergic to soy as well.

Protein hydrolysis formulas are partially or extensively hydrolyzed. This means that the protein has been broken down and is much easier to digest. This kind of formula is recommended for allergic infants. There are also amino acid–based formulas for very severe allergies.

Recently, new ingredients—DHA (docosahexonic acid) and ARA (arachidonic acid)—have been added to formulas. They are fatty acids found to be important in the baby's brain and eye development. The research is not yet conclusive about the efficacy of adding these substances to the formula.

Probiotics are another recent addition to formula because they aid in the development of a healthy digestive tract and mimic some immune properties of breast milk. Future research is needed to clarify the long-term effects of the new probiotic-enhanced formula.

Preparing and Storing Formula

There are three ways you can buy formula:

Ready to feed: This type is premixed, so you don't need to add anything. Simply shake the bottle before feeding.

Concentrated: This type needs additional water before feeding. Follow the instructions exactly as they are written on the container. Don't add more or less liquid than what the manufacturer recommends.

Powder: This type needs water added to make the formula. Follow the instructions on the container, and prepare the amount needed for one feeding. When out or traveling, you can bring water separately and prepare the formula right before feeding.

If your tap water is good quality, you can filter it and use it. Well water must be boiled first. Some authorities suggest boiling all water—even bottled water. Be sure that the water is cooled down completely before you start preparing the formula. If the water has high fluoride content, use it only occasionally before age six months, alternating with water from other sources.

Either use warm running water or put the bottle in a bowl of warm water before feeding. Always check the temperature of the formula on your wrist to ensure proper temperature.

You may leave prepared formula at room temperature for one hour. Discard anything that remained in the baby's bottle after feeding. The opened cans, covered, can stay in the refrigerator for 24–48 hours.

Unopened cans of liquid or powder formula should be kept in a dark, cool area. Always check the expiration date. Never freeze the formula, and never warm it up on the stove or in the microwave.

Choosing Bottles and Nipples

There is always talk about "nipple confusion" when it comes to supplementing breastfeeding with formula. This simply means that a baby has been given an artificial nipple and forgets how to breastfeed. To avoid this possibility, it is preferable to start using the bottle only after breastfeeding has been well established. Obviously, if the mother does not produce enough milk and the baby is getting dehydrated, the bottle will be introduced earlier.

Use glass bottles if possible. They are easy to clean and last for a long time. If you use plastic, look for safe materials such as polyethylene/polypropylene, *not* polycarbonate. Recently, a chemical was found in some plastics called bisphenol A (BPA), which can be potentially harmful to the baby. Only use plastic bottles that are BPA free. There are different types of bottles and nipples. You may need to try a few before you choose the one that is most comfortable for your baby. New bottles and nipples should be sterilized before use. Submerge them in hot water for about five minutes. If you have good-quality water, washing the bottles and nipples well after every use is enough. You can also use the dishwasher's full cycle. If you have well water, you may need to sterilize after every use, depending on the quality of the water.

Nipples come in many shapes: shorter, longer, with a round or flat top, and with or without ridges. Allow your baby to try several different kinds to find the one he or she prefers. Be careful to purchase nipples with the right flow for your baby's age. If the flow is too fast, the baby may choke—or if it's too slow, the baby may struggle to suck. As the baby grows, the flow can increase, so change the nipple accordingly and always watch the flow.

Burping

Bottle-fed babies will probably swallow more air than breastfed babies. You can stop the feeding after half an ounce and try to burp (the accumulated air will come up and get eliminated through the mouth). If the baby refuses to let go of the bottle, just move the bottle so the flow stops but the nipple still remains in the mouth.

The most common way to burp the baby is to pick the baby up and hold him or her against your chest, with the baby's chin resting on your shoulder. Pat the baby's back a few times, very gently with one hand. Support the baby with your other hand.

Another way to burp the baby is to lay the baby down on his or her belly on your lap. Make sure you are supporting the baby's head, and gently pat the back. Or put the baby in a sitting position in your lap, support the head and chest, and pat the back gently.

Burping should be done a few times during and at the end of the feeding. Leave the baby in an upright position for about half an hour after feeding is finished.

upright

over the shoulder

lying down

Jen Johnson

Burping positions.

Feeding in the First Three Months

Your baby will eat progressively more each month. The following is a guideline on how much—but remember, every baby is different and these are only approximate numbers.

The first month: One and a half to three ounces at each feeding, every two to three hours

The second month: Four to five ounces at each feeding, every three to four hours

The third month: Four to six ounces at each feeding, every four hours

Newborns' digestive systems are different than in older infants. In the beginning, they will eat small amounts often and have dirty diapers often. As the digestive system matures, feedings will become less frequent, as will the dirty diapers, and the color of the stool will become more brownish. Formula-fed babies may not have a bowel movement every day, whereas breastfed babies will (several). As long as the stool is soft and the baby is comfortable, it's fine.

There will be times when the baby will be eating three to five times during a very short period. These are called "cluster feedings" and occur when there are growth spurts. These usually happen at 7 to 10 days, 3 weeks, 6 weeks, 3 months, 6 months, and 9 months but will depend on the individual baby. Feed the baby as you always do and on demand during these days. Cluster feedings only lasts a few days.

Your Baby's Bowel Movements

The first one to three days, the baby's stool looks black and thick. This is called *meconium*. After three days, the stool becomes dark brown. As the baby begins to digest food better, the bowel movements will start looking yellow-brown. The breastfed baby's stool is yellow-colored with grains that look like mustard seeds. In a formula-fed baby, the stool will be darker or sometimes green. It's not unusual for a baby to have a bowel movement with every feeding. The stool can be very soft and can even change colors depending on the mother's diet.

Call the doctor if all stools are watery and occur between feedings, if there is blood or mucus, if the stool is white or gray, or if the bowel movements resemble little pellets (or conversely, are always very large and very difficult to pass). These are symptoms of problems that may need medical attention.

Using a Pacifier

Some babies take a pacifier, and some don't. Some parents are for them, and some are against. Either way, here are points on both sides to consider regarding the use of pacifiers.

The pros:

> Babies can soothe themselves.

> New research shows they can decrease the incidence of SIDS.

The cons:

> If used too early, pacifiers can interfere with breastfeeding.
>
> It's harder to take away once its use has begun.
>
> During the night, parents will be disturbed if the baby loses the pacifier.
>
> If used for too long, it will interfere with the way the baby's teeth come in.

Ideally, the use of a pacifier begins after two weeks of breastfeeding is well established.

If you choose to use a pacifier, use one that is all one piece. These are more sanitary and easier to clean. Buy a few different ones for the baby to try, and see which one the baby prefers. Discard pacifiers at once if they look worn or have holes or cracks. Take the pacifier away at or before 12 months to prevent problems with incoming teeth. Also, the older the baby gets the more difficult it will be take the pacifier away.

Essential Takeaways

- Deciding to breastfeed or bottle feed is a very personal choice
- Feeding will take up a significant amount of the days and nights during the first three months.
- Proper storage of breast milk and formula is essential.
- Burping is important during and after each feeding.

chapter 4

The Milestones of Baby's First Year

Exploring the developmental milestones of the first year

Understanding developmental delays and when it's time to intervene

Feeding, sleeping, and physical growth through the first year

Your baby is now home and it's time to settle in together. One of the most valuable things you can start to develop once you're home is a routine that will optimally take care of your baby's needs as well as your own. Time frames for feeding, sleeping, bathing, playing, and bonding will be very helpful for both the baby and you to provide structure for your days.

For as much as you may have read about infants by this point and talked to family and friends about what your new life will be like after the baby, nothing can really prepare you for what it's really like. You may look at your baby and think that he or she isn't doing very much, but don't be fooled. So much is subtly happening from day to day.

Take lots of pictures and videos. The way your baby looks and acts today will be very different tomorrow, next week, and next month. During this first year, there are so many things your baby will do. All these new changes are called *milestones*.

definition

The word **milestone** comes from the Latin *miliarium*. In ancient times, stone markers made of local stone were placed alongside roads at regular intervals. That way, travelers could measure distances from one given point to another—and therefore, their progress.

Developmental Milestones

Developmental milestones refer to a complexity of skills and tasks that most children can achieve by a certain age. Milestones do not occur at the same age in all children, however, because every child is different. Try not to be rigid about them, because this will cause you unnecessary anxiety. There is a certain period of time—a "window"—in which each milestone should occur. Of course, if the window has passed by a large margin, such as several months, and the child has not achieved the milestone, it's time to intervene.

Every child is unique and develops the appropriate skills at a different time. Parents who already have other children will readily acknowledge this but will still be amazed by the differences among siblings. Try not to compare one child to another, and allow them to develop at their own pace. Of course, if you have concerns about your baby's development at any time, don't hesitate to express your feelings to your baby's pediatrician.

Four Categories of Developmental Milestones

The developmental milestones are grouped into four categories: motor skills, language skills, cognitive skills, and social skills.

Motor Skills

Motor skills describe the way the baby uses his or her muscles; in other words, the ability to control and move the muscles in the body.

One may think that a newborn doesn't move much or use much muscle, but this is hardly the case. New babies actually have short, repetitive movements of the arms and legs, can slowly push themselves from one side of the crib or bassinet to the other, and can eventually lift their heads.

Examples of motor skills milestones include turning over, sitting, *crawling,* and *cruising.*

definition

Crawling is the movement babies develop to get around on all fours. You may notice different crawling styles: on the knees using full arm motion, or "combat" style, with arms bent at the elbows, using the forearms for leverage, and some other variations.

Cruising develops when a baby is able to stand up and walk around while holding on to furniture.

Motor skills encompass two subcategories:

Gross motor skills refer to the ability of the large muscles to turn, sit, crawl, stand, walk, run, jump, and skip.

Fine motor skills concern other muscles that give the child the ability to perform more refined movements, such as holding a small toy, eating, dressing, and drinking from a bottle or cup.

Language Skills

Language skills encompass the ability to use first sounds, cooing, vowels, consonants, babble, words, and simple and full sentences.

A baby's first language skill is crying. Although the tendency is to want to help whenever the baby cries, it's important to recognize that crying is just the way the baby communicates. He or she may be hungry, sleepy, upset, bored, wet, or just want attention. A quick hug, holding or walking, and changing or feeding may be enough. Inconsolable crying may signify something more serious.

By two months, a baby will make sounds that are described as *cooing,* either on his or her own or as a response to someone's voice. The sounds become louder and more complex. By four to five months, a baby may be able to have a long "conversation," meaning that he or she *babbles* on and on.

Consonants will appear by six to nine months. At age 12 months, a baby will have many understandable words, called jargon or baby talk. They may also say "mama" or "dada," although it may not necessarily be directed at the right person.

Cooing refers to a specific vocalizing sound, as opposed to the baby just making noises. It indicates the ability to use the back of the throat to make sounds.

Babbling refers to a variety of different sounds a baby begins to make at about three to four months. This action indicates progressive speech, because the baby must utilize the tongue and the front of the mouth.

Cognitive Skills

Cognitive skills (from the Latin *cognoscere,* to learn) refer to the complex process involved in understanding and learning.

From birth, a baby is constantly learning from the environment, the parents, and caretakers. A newborn favors his or her mother's face, the four-month-old will laugh and get excited at seeing familiar faces, and the eight-month-old will know who strangers are. These are cognitive skills.

A newborn will respond to visual and auditory stimuli. He or she can see 10–12 inches from the face but can only track objects if they're held right in front, about 30 degrees in either direction. Their vision ranges from 20/200–20/400.

The two- to three-month-old will be able to track objects at 180 degrees. The four- to six-month-old will reach for objects—even a foot away—and will move their head and body, not only their eyes, to see or reach for an object. The eight- to nine-month-old will notice details (can poke at elevator buttons, for example), and the 12-month-old can stack blocks and play with simple puzzles.

Social Skills

Social skills refer to the ability to interact with family, peers, and strangers. It also describes interaction during play, the ability to form relationships, and the response to other people's emotions. Looking at the mother, smiling, and laughing are also social skills.

Milestones: An Overview

The first year of life is full of growth for a baby. While it may seem to be going at a snail's pace to you, to your baby it's quite a busy time of discovering and making sense of the world as well as of himself or herself. The next section provides a general overview of the important milestones in each month of the first year of your baby's life. These major milestones will also be discussed in detail in later chapters. Keep in mind that these are general time frames and the changes are very gradual. Don't be concerned if your baby doesn't hit these milestones exactly at the month indicated. Talk to your doctor if you have concerns about your baby's development. Included at the end of each section are conditions that you should discuss with your pediatrician.

Newborn Through Four Months

In the first four months of life, the changes in your baby are truly amazing. You won't believe the developmental leaps and bounds your baby will make in just this short period of time. Every day brings something brand new, and miraculous.

The Newborn

Gross motor: The baby lies on the back, has curled legs, and lifts the head when lying on the stomach.

Fine motor: The baby grasps when an object is placed in the palm and demonstrates the Moro, rooting, and stepping reflexes. These movements are more reflexive than deliberate, but within the first months, these reflexes disappear.

Language: The baby makes some sounds, mostly during sleep.

Cognitive: The baby may look at light. Newborns' eyes are not as sensitive to light as adults' are, but that will change by months two to three.

Social: The baby prefers his or her mother's voice. The smile everyone gets so excited to see is usually not voluntary.

At Two Months

Gross motor: The baby's legs are straighter and less curled. When placed on its stomach, the baby will lift the head and chest.

Fine motor: The grasp reflex is still evident, but the baby is able to hold a small object for a few seconds.

Language: Cooing begins.

Cognitive: The baby is able to follow objects past the midline (180 degrees).

Social: Now the baby actually smiles in response.

At Three Months

Gross motor: The baby is moving more than before; some babies may even start to turn. When the baby is held in a sitting position, the head lags.

Fine motor: The baby will attempt to reach and grab a toy but misses. The Moro reflex disappears. The baby starts looking at its hands.

Language: A few new sounds emerge, such as "aah" and "gaaah."

Cognitive: The baby responds to different noises and movements.

Social: The baby smiles for a longer period of time.

At Four Months

Gross motor: The baby is now able to lift its head and chest when lying on its back.

Fine motor: The baby reaches and holds objects, looks at his or her hands and brings them to the middle, and pushes with the feet when held up.

Language: The baby laughs and shows emotion.

Cognitive: The baby likes music and starts to show recognition of family members and familiar faces.

Social: The baby shows excitement when seeing a familiar person.

When to Intervene

Talk to your pediatrician if you observe any of the following in your baby:

If the baby doesn't smile or coo by three months of age.

If the body is very stiff or the muscle tone is very low.

If the baby doesn't follow objects past the midline point by three to four months.

Five Through Eight Months

During the period from five to eight months your baby's development will steadily continue. Your baby is quickly building on earlier skills and mastering new ones. During this period your baby will become a more social being, beginning to interact with you in a purposeful way.

At Five to Six Months

Gross motor: The baby can roll over, back to stomach, and is able to sit with support.

Fine motor: The baby is able to hold a bottle or cup.

Language: Babbling begins.

Cognitive: The baby tries to find hidden objects but doesn't yet find them.

Social: The baby continues to respond to different emotions.

At Seven Months

Gross motor: The baby can roll over front to back and is able to put its entire weight on the feet when placed in a standing position.

Fine motor: The baby reaches and grasps larger objects, is able to hold objects with the palm, and can transfer from one hand to the other.

Language: The baby babbles using more vowels.

Cognitive: The baby uses hands to explore everything and puts everything in the mouth.

Social: The baby cries when left alone and prefers the parents and caretakers over others.

At Eight Months

Gross motor: The baby sits well without support, stands holding on to objects (furniture), crawls backward, and starts banging two objects together.

Fine motor: The baby is able to hold objects with the fine pincer grasp (between the thumb and index finger).

Language: The baby may respond to "no" and can imitate sounds.

Cognitive: The baby is able to find a hidden object and can track moving objects.

Social: Stranger anxiety begins. The baby likes the mirror.

When to Intervene

Talk to your pediatrician if you observe any of the following in your baby:

If the baby doesn't hold an object in one hand and place it in the other (transferring) by age nine months

If there is no babbling by eight months

If the baby doesn't follow objects by eight to nine months

If the baby doesn't laugh by six months

If the body is very stiff or the muscle tone is very low

From 9 to 12 Months

From nine months to one year old your baby will become a real little person. The emphasis at this stage is on refinement of skills, especially gross and fine motor and on coordination. In fact, although not the norm, some babies can walk by 10 months old!

At 9 to 10 Months

Gross motor: The baby crawls well and starts walking by holding on to furniture.

Fine motor: A good, fine pincer grasp is present.

Language: The baby speaks louder and uses many syllables in babbling.

Cognitive: The baby points at things with the finger, follows a command with a gesture, and can bang two objects together.

Social: The baby will stop for a short time when told "no" and is able to show emotions.

At 11 Months

Gross motor: The baby cruises well and may start walking with both hands held.

Fine motor: The baby tries to find a dropped object.

Language: The baby starts saying "mama" and "dada."

Cognitive: The baby follows a simple command well, sometimes without a gesture, and can uncover a hidden object.

Social: Peek-a-boo becomes enjoyable.

At 12 Months

Gross motor: Starts walking with one hand held

Fine motor: Can pick up objects when dropped

Language: This is the time when baby talk becomes evident. The child may say "mama" or "dada," but it won't be necessarily directed toward the right person.

Cognitive: Imitates adults and enjoys play

Social: Plays simple games (ball) and can engage in parallel play with other children (they just play but don't interact)

When to Intervene

Talk to your pediatrician if you observe any of the following in your baby:

If your baby doesn't cruise by 12 months

If your baby doesn't show any emotions

If your baby doesn't want to cuddle or play

If your baby can't track a moving object

If your baby's body is stiff or the muscle tone is very low

Please note: Some children may not crawl at all and just go straight to walking, and that's perfectly normal.

Premature Babies and Milestones

Although many premature babies catch up developmentally very quickly after birth, an age correction must be done for them when looking at milestones. This means that if a baby was born one month early, the milestones have to be adjusted to acknowledge and accommodate that. With preemies, you must consider both the chronological age as well as the developmental age.

Making Up the Difference

The **chronological age** refers to the baby's actual birth date, while the **developmental age** refers to the baby's due date. Calculate the baby's developmental age by subtracting the difference in the number of weeks from the actual due date. That's where your preemie is developmentally when he or she comes into the world.

This developmental lag will be made up as the baby gets older. When the premature baby reaches its full-term due date, developmentally he or she is back on track for normal development and growth. Most premature children catch up with their full-term peers. Sometimes, children who are late starters can accomplish developmental tasks faster than those who were not challenged.

When to Intervene

Talk to your pediatrician if you observe any of the following in your premature baby:

If development is delayed by months

If there is a significant delay in more than one category of developmental skills

If the baby fails to show interest in communicating with parents; either having difficulty understanding or responding

Other Milestones

Beyond the normal developmental milestones, there are those special events that should be considered milestones as much as any others. Sleeping through the night or eating solid foods are often considered special events for many parents. In fact, you can consider any "first" for your baby to be a milestone.

The following sections are brief overviews meant to give you an idea of what to expect in the months to come. Later chapters will cover these topics in greater depth.

Feeding Throughout the Year

As previously mentioned, newborns instinctively know how to feed, and it's optimal to feed them immediately after birth. At the beginning of life there will be at least 8–12 feedings a day, but as the baby grows, the interval between feedings will get longer.

After six months, solid foods can be introduced—which is typically rice cereal at first, then baby foods. Breastfeeding mothers can continue breastfeeding in addition to introducing the solid foods. At this point, the baby may have a tooth or two and can sit and be fed from a spoon by an adult.

Giving water to your baby can be started after six months of age. Babies need the fluoride in the water for healthy teeth development, so consult information from your local health department regarding the amount of fluoride in your local water. If there is less than 0.7–1.2 ppm (parts fluoride per million parts of water), children ages 6 months to 16 years should be given a fluoride supplement.

Bottled water typically doesn't contain fluoride, so it's not the best choice for a baby. At stores, however, you will find bottled water that is fluoride supplemented for babies, and it is a suitable choice if you prefer bottled water. Filtered tap water is a good source. If you have well water, call your local health department to have the water tested. It's a good idea to give the water in a small cup, or sippy cup, instead of the bottle, which helps get the baby used to drinking from a cup.

Giving babies fruit juice is not recommended. Juice is very sweet and high in calories, plus the fiber of the fruit has been removed. As a child gets older, juice can be a cause of obesity and dental decay.

Around age 8–10 months, your baby will be able to feed himself or herself (and likely prefer to). A self-feeding baby should always be supervised. If possible, structure your meals as "family time" so the baby is involved and has interaction with others during mealtime.

We'll talk more about how and when to introduce solid foods in Chapter 14.

Changes in Sleeping

The baby's brain takes time to mature. They don't adjust to different environments as adults do; neither can they cope with stimuli in the environment. There is a theory that babies are awake at night because it's a quieter, more peaceful time.

In the first few months, babies sleep around 16–18 hours a day. Up to age three to four months, they need the night feeding in order to achieve optimal growth. Waking them up during the day after three to four hours also helps.

After four months, the night feeding becomes unnecessary. It is the time to allow the baby to soothe himself or herself. Bedtime routines, baths, the same toys, quiet music, and putting the baby in the crib while awake are all helpful.

One can expect a new pattern of unwillingness to sleep by age 6–10 months as separation anxiety emerges. Reassuring the baby, reading, and having a bedtime routine will soon overcome this anxiety.

Weight, Height, and Head Circumference

Percentile refers to the weight, height, and head circumference that the majority of babies achieve at the same age in the same sex. These parameters are always measured at the doctor's office. There are different growth charts for girls, boys, and premature babies.

The baby's weight increases five to seven ounces (140–200g) per week from birth to six months. The weight doubles by five to six months. After six months, it increases more slowly—three to five ounces (85–140g) per week. By 12 months, the baby usually triples the birth weight.

The height increases by one half to one inch (1.5–2.5 cm) per month in the first six months and ⅜ inch (1 cm) per month, from 6–12 months. By 12 months, the baby doubles the birth height.

The head circumference is measured until two years of age and reflects the brain's growth. At birth, the brain is approximately 25 percent of the adult brain size. By 12 months, it is 75 percent of the adult brain size. It grows about 0.39 inches (1 cm) per month.

Developmental Delay

A developmental delay occurs when a baby doesn't meet his or her milestones around the expected time. The delay can be either minor or major and can affect one or more milestone categories.

Genetic abnormalities, severe intrauterine infections, and prematurity are some reasons why developmental delays are thought to occur. But there are times when the reason is completely unknown.

Because the pediatrician is looking for *steady growth* to measure the child's development, an evaluation and further workup is done for any baby who had been developing normally but stops doing so (and even regresses).Autism has become a commonly known, complex neurodevelopmental disorder. There are many forms of autism, but they all have these factors in common: difficulty in expressive language, repetitive movements, inability to play or form a relationship, strange patterns of play, and no interaction with even close family members.

The signs of autism can be subtle, and the diagnosis may not be able to be made before 12–18 months of age. When the developmental signs are caught early, the child can start special programs—and improvement will result earlier.

Essential Takeaways

- Developmental milestones give guidance for normal growth and development within a time frame.
- The four categories of developmental milestones are motor, cognitive, language, and social skills.
- Percentiles are another form of measurement for growth and development.
- Each baby is different and will develop at his or her own pace. Allow your baby to develop naturally, and talk to your pediatrician if you think there is a problem.

Part 2

The First Three Months

So much of what you'll learn about your baby and about parenting will come during the first three months, as you're getting to know and understand your baby's needs and setting schedules and routines for the months to come. We'll take you through establishing a healthy, nontoxic environment at home to setting up the baby's room to getting the essential items you'll need to care for your baby. Then, it's on to bath time and what you'll need and how to carefully evaluate your baby's appearance.

As the world grows bigger for you and your little one, we'll show you how to get out and about and what you'll need when you do. We'll explore ways to relate to your baby and how to begin to stimulate his or her senses.

Creating a sleep routine is one of the big essentials we'll cover, because it will establish what happens in the months to come. You'll also get a good understanding of the early development of your baby's motor skills (gross and fine), cognitive, language, and social skills.

We'll explain the basics about vaccines, their importance, when they're given, and what concerns parents have about them. Finally, we'll discuss your concerns about your baby's health, what to do if your baby gets sick, and what are considered causes of concern from a medical perspective.

chapter 5

Preparations at Home

Making your baby's home environment safe and clean

Getting help at home

Furnishing the baby's room

Stocking up on baby essentials

Bringing home a newborn is an exciting experience, and the environment that you bring your newborn home to live in is an important consideration. In this chapter, we will discuss ways to ensure your home and the items you choose for your baby are safe and in the best interest of his or her health.

A Clean, Nontoxic Space

When it comes to babies, keeping toxins out of the air in your home as much as possible is important. Chemicals used for general household cleaning can do a terrific job removing grease and grime, but they can be particularly dangerous for the young, developing respiratory system of a newborn—and to his or her skin.

Fumes from paints and materials used in carpeting can have an impact on breathing. Of course, smoke, dust, and mold are other known culprits that can cause respiratory problems and allergic reactions.

Window seals, screens, fans, curtains, and upholstery should be freshly cleaned before the newborn comes home, because dust and grime accumulates on them. Make sure that the air conditioner filters are changed and that the heating system is checked and ducts are cleaned if necessary. Smoke and carbon monoxide detectors are absolutely necessary to install and/or check near every room.

Reducing Chemicals

Well before your baby arrives, it's a good idea to get your home improvement projects done and to thoroughly clean your home. You will likely be painting a nursery, which ideally should be done at least a few weeks prior to the baby moving in—using only low- or no-VOC (volatile organic components) paint. Even if the paints you use are organic, some of these fumes can still cause harm. Finishing the painting weeks ahead of time gives the room a chance to dry and the paint fumes to dissipate. It's never a good idea to allow a baby to sleep in a freshly painted room (such as painting it after the baby is home), because the fumes are very dangerous to a baby.

Pregnant women should not be exposed to toxins of any kind including paint, as well as household cleaners, especially aerosol products, insecticides, etc.

Also, if you have other household projects such as removing and/or installing new carpeting, do it two to four weeks before the baby comes home—especially if it is going in the nursery. This allows time for the fumes and odor to subside and the carpet to get worn in a little bit. New carpet has toxic agents sprayed on it at the factory that smell the strongest when it's brand new. It helps to have a window open and a fan on for 24–48 hours after it's installed. If possible, buy carpet made of natural fiber—and of course, one that is non-flammable.

When it comes to household cleaning, choose cleaning products that are environmentally safe and non-toxic. Because you are bringing home your most precious possession, you will want your home to be as clean and safe as possible.

Natural Cleaning Products

In general, the chemical products used for cleaning are harsh; they can cause eye irritation, pulmonary problems, nausea, and allergies. In addition, they can be rather expensive. It's actually very easy to clean an entire home using only natural products that are readily available at the store and often much less expensive. Here are some "staples" of natural cleaning products that are much safer to use, especially when a newborn is living in the house:

> **Vinegar:** Regular white vinegar mixed with equal amounts of water will clean windows, mirrors, floors, and the bathroom.

Baking soda: Mixed with equal amounts of vinegar, this combination will clean sinks, the bathroom, and toilets. On its own with water, it will clean hard surfaces.

Olive oil: Olive oil (extra virgin not necessary!) works great for polishing furniture.

Lemon: Lemons and all citrus fruits cut grease really well.

Tea tree oil: Dilute 8–10 drops in 2 cups water for a good disinfectant.

Borax: This product can be used to combat certain fungi, cockroaches, and fleas.

On a regular basis, try to maintain a clean, safe, and non-toxic environment by dusting regularly, opening windows for fresh air, vacuuming with a filter and changing the filter frequently. Also refrain from using room deodorizers, because they have chemical components.

Plants

Household plants are good to have in your home because they purify the air by absorbing toxins and breaking down chemicals. Don't place them directly in the baby's room, but do place them around your home, away from where your baby will be regularly.

Be very careful of the plants you buy for your home. Some plants can be poisonous to children and pets. Good non-toxic plants include:

- African violets

- Jade plant

- Reed palm

- Boston fern

- Weeping fig

- Spider plant

- Begonia

- Zebra plant

Toxic plants to avoid in the home include:

- Dieffenbachia

- Philodendron

- Bird of paradise

- Elephant ears

- Chrysanthemums

Find a complete list of safe and unsafe plants at the American Academy of Pediatrics (AAP) website, AAP.org.

Family Pets

Like older siblings, family pets will react to a new baby in the house just the same. Your attention will be occupied by someone besides them, and don't think they won't notice, or have an issue with it at first. It is important to consider Fido and Fluffy and work with them before your baby is born to help make the adjustment of the new family dynamic as smooth as possible.

Your pet's health is very important when a newborn is living in the house, so your pet(s) should be up to date on all the appropriate vaccinations before the baby comes home. It's a good idea, too, to cut or file your pet's nails before the baby gets home. Also, have your pet(s) spend time with and get used to being with other family members or friends, because others will need to care for them while you're in the hospital. It can be helpful to have somebody help you take care of your pet(s) for the first weeks after you're home, when you will be very busy with the baby.

Before the baby is even born, you may try carrying a baby doll around the house. Certainly, before you bring the baby into the house, take a piece of clothing the baby has worn in the hospital (such as a hat) and let your pet pick up the baby's scent from the clothing.

Have babies or young children around the pet so they can get used to how they sound. Don't allow your pet to jump on the baby or the furniture, and certainly don't allow your pet to lick the baby. If necessary, have a gate to keep your pet separated from the baby. Especially, as was the case when you were pregnant, a cat's litter box should be far away from the baby. Also, always wash your hands after touching your pet.

The Centers for Disease Control and Prevention (CDC) recommends no interaction for children younger than age five with the following animals: reptiles (snakes, lizards, and turtles), amphibians (frogs, toads, and salamanders), baby chicks, and ducklings. These animals harbor certain bacteria that can be especially harmful to young children.

Getting Help

Every woman who has just given birth needs help. Prior to having your baby, you may think you are capable of managing whatever comes your way. After all, that's the way you've always managed your life and career, right? Why should having a baby be any different? Having and raising a baby is a life changer. It is different than any other experience on the planet. All the planning in the world cannot truly prepare you for all the demands that will be made of you in your role as parent.

The "superwoman syndrome" that has been present for many decades can pressure women into thinking they need to "do it all" or else they may be perceived as weak or a failure of some sort. While a balanced life of work, family, and self is a very good thing, it takes asking for help to be able to achieve it.

There shouldn't be any shame or too much pride to ask for help. Believe us when we say that you'll need it. Family and/or close friends can pitch in around the house, buy groceries, prepare easy meals, and take care of the baby when you need a break. Older children can help, too. Getting them more actively involved and giving them a more "grown-up" role may actually reduce sibling rivalry and give them a sense of increased responsibility.

A nice touch is to buy a present from the baby for the older sibling, and vice versa. And make sure that whenever the baby receives a gift from someone else, older siblings receive something as well.

Household Helpers

There are various types of help for the mother and baby if the family chooses to get outside help and the budget allows. Doulas, baby nurses, nannies, and au pairs are different types of help that can be hired, either short or long term, to lend support around the house in different capacities when a new baby has joined the family.

A doula offers non-medical help. She can help the mother with breastfeeding concerns, take care of the newborn, and sometimes even do light housekeeping. Her role at home is more for the mother.

A baby nurse has more experience to help with the newborn, which is a good helper if the baby had any problems at the hospital.

A nanny typically takes care of the family and other children so the mother can focus on the newborn. Some baby nurses and nannies are willing to sleep in the home during the week. They can be extremely helpful to the family at night.

An au pair is typically someone who lives full time with the family to care for the children in the family.

Postpartum Depression

The mother and those close to her should be aware that at times, instead of feeling happy and contented, the mother may feel tearful, overwhelmed, and unprepared for motherhood. These feelings should be acknowledged without shame or guilt. In fact, the appearance of these feelings is fairly common in women who have just given birth.

Baby blues or postpartum depression is associated with the huge hormonal changes that have occurred in the mother's body during pregnancy through delivery. After the birth of her child, there is a hormonal shift with a gradual return to pre-pregnancy hormone levels. Also in the months following birth, sleep is scarce for a new mother. So the lack of sleep is a contributing factor to the overall feeling of being overwhelmed and unprepared.

With rest and family support, these feelings will gradually improve and the mother will feel like her "old self" again. However, if the mother's distress/depression is not reducing after six months or seems to be getting worse, consult the obstetrician as soon as possible because a more serious depression or other condition may be present.

The Baby's Room Setup

With today's multi-million–dollar baby industry, the sky is the limit as far as how to furnish, decorate, and supply a nursery. However, for the first few months at least, a baby is just fine sleeping in the parent's room in a bassinet, especially if no separate room is available.

But a major part of the tradition—and fun—of having a baby is outfitting and decorating the nursery. Very basically, what you will need is a bassinet or crib, a place to change the baby, a rocking chair (especially for feedings), and drawers for the baby's clothes.

The Bassinet

The AAP does not recommend co-sleeping (having the baby in bed with you) because it is potentially dangerous for the baby to be suffocated or hurt. If you wish to have your newborn near you in the night, the bassinet, also called a cradle or Moses basket, is a great solution for the first baby bed. They are cozy and can be easily moved.

While cribs are federally regulated, bassinets are not. If you buy a bassinet, look for one that has a sturdy bottom and a stable base that barely rocks. Make sure nothing is loose in its construction, that the mattress is firm, and that the mattress cover fits tightly. Do not place any toys, blankets, or pillows in the bassinet. Look for a bassinet that has received the JPMA (Juvenile Products Manufacturers Association) certificate for more peace of mind, which means it has passed a series of tests and inspections.

Baby watch

Don't let your baby sleep on the floor or in improvised sleep areas, such as in the middle of a large bed, because they can easily move and fall.

Look carefully at the manufacturer's manual for the maximum weight and height that the bassinet will safely support. The minute the baby can turn, he or she needs to be moved to a crib.

The Crib

It's perfectly fine to use a crib from the very beginning. Cribs are federally regulated for mandatory safety standards. The vertical slats on the crib must be $2\frac{3}{8}$ inches apart, and none can be loose or missing. If one side drops down, it has to be nine inches above the mattress, and when the side is up, it needs to be 26 inches above the mattress. However, many drop down cribs were recalled, so before using one check the U.S. Consumer Product Safety Commission at www.cpsc.gov.

The crib frame will typically have three height positions for the mattress. The top position is appropriate for a newborn, and the mattress should be lowered as the baby grows and learns to sit and stand up.

Situate the crib away from windows, paintings, drapes (especially with cords), curtain shades or blinds with cords, or anything the baby can eventually touch. Make sure the crib is away from any heat source, heaters, radiators, and/or air ducts.

The mattress should be firm with a tightly fitting crib sheet. If you use bumpers around the sides of the crib, they should be thin and tight to avoid suffocation hazard. Remove them when the baby can stand so he or she can't use them to climb out. There shouldn't be any toys, pillows, or blankets in the crib. It's believed that this precaution can reduce the risk of SIDS (Sudden Infant Death Syndrome).

An overhead mobile attached to the crib can be entertaining and stimulating for a very young baby lying on its back. However, this should be removed as soon as the baby can sit up. If you use a portable crib, make sure to use only the mattress recommended by the manufacturer. Hand-me-downs that may have been recalled or do not meet safety standards should be avoided. Cribs manufactured before 1980 may have lead in the paint.

The Changing Table

A regular place to change the baby's diaper is an essential piece of furniture for the baby's room. The main thing you need is a flat surface for the baby to comfortably lie on and something to hold the diapers and wipes nearby. You can get a very simple table with storage drawers or an elaborate dresser with drawers and a changing surface. A changing pad with a soft fabric covering should be attached to the top of the changing surface to ensure that the baby is comfortable and secure.

A changing table is convenient, but not necessary. The baby can also be changed on a bed or on the floor with a changing pad.

Place diapers, baby wipes, lotions, creams or pastes for rashes, cotton balls, or any other product you prefer or find convenient to use, along with clean cotton cloths, in the designated area next to the changing surface.

As with any other piece of equipment or furniture in your baby's room, make sure that the changing table is away from anything that can fall or be pulled down, from drapery or window blind cords, outlets, or from any other piece of furniture the baby may be able to easily reach.

Other Essential Items

Aside from the old wooden variety, rocking chairs today are comfortable, upholstered, and attractive in design. The rhythmic motion is soothing for the baby, especially while nursing or feeding. It's the perfect place for quiet time and bonding.

The baby monitor allows you to hear the baby without having to go into the room. This way, you can pay attention for sounds, cries, and any kind of distress. A monitor has done much to allow parents to sleep without worrying about what's happening in the baby's room. Monitors are also available with video, allowing you to see your baby in addition to hearing him or her.

A humidifier (runs with cold water) or vaporizer (runs with hot water and therefore must be used with caution) will lend moisture to the air, especially in cold months when the heat is frequently turned on and the air is dry. Moisture helps the baby breathe more easily, preventing stuffiness or hardening of mucous, and is extremely helpful when the baby has a cold. The filters must be cleaned every day.

The diaper pail is essential for obvious reasons. There are many varieties on the market today with various bagging contraptions. They all serve the same basic function, so choose one that will work for you and the space you have.

Equipment for the Baby

A baby swing is very helpful to rock and soothe your baby, especially if you want a break or need your hands for something else at that moment.

There are many models, but certain basics apply to all of them. Choose a swing that is substantially made and has a stable base. Make sure the baby is strapped in securely and sitting appropriately in the seat, not slouched over. Never leave your baby alone while swinging, and limit the amount of time in the swing or until your baby lets you know he or she wants out.

A baby bouncer, or bouncy seat, is a fabric-covered seat where the baby can sit or slightly recline while strapped in. Many are battery powered to be set into motion to bounce, rock, or vibrate, and eventually the baby can bounce on his or her own. It's very soothing and rhythmic for the baby and an opportunity to begin to see the world from a different perspective. The bouncy seat should be placed on the floor, not on a bed, chair, table, or other piece of furniture, because the seat could be bounced over the edge and cause the baby serious injury.

Clothes and Other Necessities

There is nothing more adorable than baby clothes. While difficult to do, try to resist the urge to buy lots of newborn clothes. Babies grow so quickly that they will outgrow them in no time. The basic needs of a newborn really consist of a few essential items—just a few in large quantity. Having a washer and dryer is very helpful because you will be changing the baby's clothes many times a day. Here's a list of clothes and other items and their quantities that should suffice for the first three months:

Short- and long-sleeved onesies or rompers (10)

T-shirts (8)

Sleep sacks or footed sleepers (10)

Baby socks (5–7 pairs)

Hats (1–2)

Warm jacket (1)

Bibs (6–8)

Washcloths (4–6)

Hooded towels or regular towels (2–3)

Receiving blankets (cotton) (6)

Blanket, only for going out (1–2)

Burp cloths (10+)

Diapers and wipes (ongoing; have a supply on hand at all times)

Always wash baby clothes before dressing the baby in them for the first time. Use hypo-allergenic detergent if possible; however, regular detergent can be used if the baby's skin doesn't appear to be overly sensitive.

Diapers

The first disposable diapers appeared about 40 years ago, but the debate is still going on about whether to use cloth or disposable diapers. Cloth diapers were once more difficult to put on and needed safety pins. Now there's Velcro. The newer cloth diapers even have a disposable lining and more layers.

Disposable diapers come in various sizes and thicknesses to accommodate the newborn as well as the older baby. Super-absorbent disposable diapers may be very helpful to get through the night. Cloth or disposable is purely a personal decision. Either type does the job.

Cloth diapers have a lesser impact on the environment and are convenient for home, although not for traveling. They need to be changed more frequently, soaked and washed, and need more energy and water for laundering. The cost is much less if cleaning is done at home as opposed to using a diaper service.

Disposable diapers are easier to use than cloth, are more convenient when traveling, and are simply thrown away after use. However, they create a huge environmental impact, may cause more rashes, and cost as much as using a diaper service.

It's not an easy decision. There are many factors to consider: budget, the environment, and your family's lifestyle. A combination may be a good idea (cloth at home; disposable on the go). There are new biodegradable diapers on the market; however, they are more costly than regular disposable diapers.

Because all babies (and mothers) are different, buy a small amount of different kinds of diapers and decide what works best for both you and baby.

Other Baby Essentials

Have the following items readily available. These are needed for the ongoing, regular care of your baby:

> Baby thermometer
>
> Baby shampoo
>
> Baby nail clippers or baby nail files
>
> Brush and/or comb

Nasal bulb syringe

Diaper rash cream, paste or ointment

Cotton balls

Baby oil/mineral oil

Baby wipes

Baby moisturizer (fragrance free)

Essential Takeaways

- Create an eco-friendly, toxin-free home environment for your baby and your family.
- Ask for help, and don't feel badly about it
- Know the safety standards when buying baby furniture.
- Have all the essential baby items at home and ready for when the baby comes home.

chapter 6

Baby Care

Cleaning and diapering the baby

Essentials for bath time

What to observe in baby's appearance in the first weeks

When to call the doctor

In the beginning, especially if this is your first baby, everything you need to learn and do for your baby may seem quite daunting. While there are a lot of things to learn, in short time you will gain confidence in your ability to take excellent care of your baby—and before you know it, you'll be a total pro at it.

Diaper Changing

When you are learning to change your baby at the beginning, thankfully the baby doesn't move around too much—giving you the opportunity to learn the ropes of wiping and diapering. As your baby gets older and more physical, though, it'll become a real challenge to change him or her. The baby will be squirming and turning while you're trying to fasten the diaper. After a while, you'll get pretty fast at it and the contest is over … until the next change. But here are some basic things to know about diaper changing at the very beginning.

Baby Wipes

For the first two weeks, instead of using commercial baby wipes, trying using a wet cloth (one that has been previously washed) for wiping. Disposable wipes, even the hypoallergenic ones, have some chemicals on them that could cause a rash. You could avoid a potential problem by just using a wet cloth. After the first couple weeks, it's typically fine to use disposable wipes. Try to stick with fragrance-free varieties to reduce the risk of rashes and allergic reactions.

Wiping Procedure

The bottom and genitals of a newborn are delicate, so wipe them very gently. Baby girls always need to be cleaned from front to back to avoid the risk of infection in the vaginal area from waste. Be sure to clean inside the folds of her skin.

Baby boys who were circumcised should be wiped very gently with water until the area heals—making sure that the rectal area is cleaned last. Don't try to pull back the foreskin on uncircumcised boys to clean underneath, this can cause pain and bleeding. The foreskin will separate on its own over time.

Preventing Rashes

No matter how hard you try to prevent it, sooner or later your baby *will* get diaper rash. There's no need to panic, though, because most rashes are not serious. The rash will be red, and it will appear on the buttocks or in the folds. The newborn's skin is very delicate, and the combination of acidity from the urine, the warmth, the lack of air in the diaper area, plus rubbing will contribute to the appearance of a rash. Also, diaper rashes can get supra-infected with fungus or bacteria.

Diaper rash creams and ointments will usually take care of the problem. Changing your baby frequently can help prevent rashes from occurring in the first place. Other things that can help are not putting a diaper on too tight, especially at night, and allowing your baby's skin to air-dry whenever possible. It's also important not to rub when you use wipes. Using a small amount of petroleum jelly on the buttocks can also help because it provides a barrier between the skin and the diaper. Baby powder was once very popular to use, but it's not recommended now because it may cause allergies. Also, the baby can inhale the baby powder particles, which are irritating. If a rash doesn't get better within three to four days of using ointment, gets worse, or if you see pus or areas that look swollen and infected, call the doctor.

A Baby Bath

You can give your baby a gentle sponge bath every day for the first few weeks after you come home from the hospital. Just using a washcloth and warm water is enough. The areas that need a little extra attention are the genitals, to ensure they are clean, and the umbilical cord stump, which may still be swollen and red for a couple of weeks after you arrive home. You can also give your newborn a full bath in a small baby tub if you wish. Bathing your newborn is not an easy task—the baby will be wet, slippery, and somewhat challenging to hold on to. But after a few attempts, you'll know what to do, and the experience will be a terrific one.

The Bathtub

You can use a portable baby bathtub made from plastic, or you can use a large bathroom or kitchen sink as a bathtub as long as you place a nonslippery surface, such as a towel or foam pad, in the tub on which the baby can comfortably semi-recline. Supporting the baby's head with one hand while bathing is a good idea.

infant bath tub

infant bath seat

Jen Johnson

Safe bathing options.

There are many baby tubs on the market, usually made from heavier plastic; some are foldable or inflatable. A good baby bathtub should be sturdy and have smooth edges, a slip-resistant mat, and a plug at the bottom.

Do not bathe the newborn to four to five months old in an adult bathtub if possible, because it's simply too large and deep with a slippery surface that will not allow you to have the same kind of control. A newborn will also feel overwhelmed in such a large space, and many drownings occur accidentally in an adult tub.

Bath-Time Essentials

The essential items to have ready at bath time, in addition to the tub, are:

> One or two washcloths (soft, prewashed ones)
>
> A cup for rinsing
>
> Baby soap
>
> Baby shampoo (optional)
>
> Hooded or regular towels (prewashed)

The bathwater should be warm and never hot, around 90° Fahrenheit. Check the water by testing it on your wrist (because the skin in that area is sensitive). If you gently feel the warmth of the water on your wrist, it's a good temperature. You can also use a baby bath thermometer. Adjust the temperature as needed *before* placing the baby in the water.

Hypoallergenic, fragrance-free soap and/or shampoo can be used. Use a washcloth and gently clean the skin, paying attention to the neck and body folds.

Use a cup to pour water onto your baby's body and head in small amounts to rinse and to keep them warm for the duration of the bath. Be careful not to get soap in the baby's eyes. Shampooing a baby's hair every day is not necessary—a couple times a week is fine. Rinse the baby's head from the forehead back, and make sure that all the soap and shampoo are completely rinsed off.

A bath for a very young baby only needs to last 5 to 10 minutes so the baby doesn't get cold or overwhelmed. When finished, lift the baby from the tub and wrap him or her in a towel immediately. Pat dry, instead of rubbing, with the towel. Gently clean and dry behind the ears.

Never leave a baby alone or with a young sibling in the bathtub.

Soon enough, bath time will evolve into play and fun time. Babies will love to splash and play with rubber ducks, balls, and other soft plastic or rubber toys. Eventually, your baby will try to wash himself or herself—the very beginnings of independence.

Baby's Appearance

During the first year, you'll have ample time to get to know your baby head to toe and on every level. It's important to become aware of everything about your baby. That way, you'll know when something doesn't look or feel right to you. In the very early weeks after birth, it's essential to track changes in your baby—those changes that happen from day to day that mark normal, healthy development as well as those changes that signal a problem.

Your baby's physical appearance is very important to observe. If something seems "off" to you about your baby, it's important to tell your doctor. Many of the things you'll observe are just what's normal, but there are some conditions that may need attention.

Cradle Cap

Sometimes you'll see thick, yellowish, greasy patches of scaly skin on the baby's scalp. This is called "cradle cap," or *seborrheic dermatitis of the scalp.* You may see patches of this behind the ears and on the eyelids and eyebrows as well. This condition doesn't itch and won't bother the baby, thankfully.

The exact cause of cradle cap is unknown. It's thought that hormonal changes from the mother, or maybe a type of fungus, could be the culprit. The bottom line is that it's not a serious problem and gets better with time.

You may put olive oil, mineral oil, or petroleum jelly on the baby's scalp, leave it on for a few hours, and then brush it off gently or shampoo the hair to remove the scales. You may need to do this a few times until you see improvement, but don't pick at the scales. Call the doctor if the area becomes swollen or red or if there is pus.

Molded Head

As discussed in Chapter 1, a baby's skull may look asymmetrical, molded, or flat. It happens either because of a cephalhematoma from birth or because the baby is positioned lying down on one side only, particularly when put to sleep. All babies prefer one side when lying in their cribs. Therefore, your baby's head should be repositioned so it's not always on the same side, and the baby should be put on his or her stomach when awake as much as possible.

baby steps

Always put a baby to sleep on his or her back. The American Academy of Pediatrics (AAP) recommends this position for sleeping because babies who do so are statistically at lower risk for SIDS (Sudden Infant Death Syndrome).

Talk to your doctor if the baby's skull asymmetry, called *positional plagicephaly,* gets progressively worse, making the face asymmetrical as well.

Hair

Your baby may have been born totally bald or with a full head of hair. During the first few weeks, or even months, you may notice hair loss. This doesn't always happen, however. Some babies may keep the hair they were born with. Hair loss is totally natural and no need for concern. Eventually, the hair that was lost will be replaced by hair that may be very different in color, thickness, and texture from the original baby hair.

The Eyes

The newborn's eyes may seem to be cross-eyed. This condition is called *strabismus* (from the Greek, "to squint") and is very common. The muscles of the eyes haven't yet developed the kind of control necessary for both eyes to be coordinated. Most of time it's just a temporary problem, but should it persist (continuing beyond the first few months), consult the doctor.

The eyes may also look swollen and have a discharge. Sometimes a tear duct is closed and gets easily infected. When this happens, wash your hands well and gently massage the outer area of the eye closest to the nasal angle, without touching the eye itself. This will open the clogged tear ducts. You can do this five to six times a day. Clean the eye discharge with a clean cotton ball every morning.

Call the doctor if the discharge gets worse, if the eye looks swollen and red, or if there is a lot of tearing in the first six weeks of life.

Eye Color

The eye color at birth is blue-gray in most babies. Color is determined by the amount of a pigment called *melanin* in the iris of the eye. Light eyes have little pigment, while darker eyes have more. The color of the eyes is largely determined by heredity; it's in your genes. It changes during the first year and sometimes even into the second.

Jaundice

Although we discussed this condition in Chapter 1, it's important to summarize it here again because there are profound implications of this condition if untreated.

Jaundice is a yellow color seen in the baby's skin and eyes. Sixty percent of full-term babies and 80 percent of premature ones will be jaundiced. The substance that accumulates in the body and is responsible for the color is called *bilirubin*.

Bilirubin comes from the breakdown of red blood cells. Usually, old red blood cells travel through the liver, then through the intestines, and are excreted out of the body. When the baby's immature liver is not able to process the cells fast enough, bilirubin increases. The bilirubin level is determined by a blood test.

Because this condition is so frequent in newborns, it's called normal, physiologic jaundice. It starts around the second or third day of life and disappears completely within a few days, and no treatment is necessary.

Any jaundice that is present at birth or in the first day and does not improve after one week needs to be addressed immediately. The blood types in the mother and baby may be different, there may be an infection, the blood cells may be destroyed too quickly, or the liver may not be healthy. Also, babies who do not drink enough fluid may appear to be jaundiced due to extreme dehydration.

The treatment for jaundice is phototherapy. The baby will be put in an incubator under special lights. The eyes will be protected with a mask, and it's important for the baby to drink more fluids while under the lights.

Untreated, very high levels of bilirubin can damage the brain and other nerve tissue, leading to possible hearing loss and problems with vision, as well as other problems.

Kernicterus is the name given to the condition that stems from extreme newborn jaundice and that results in an abnormal buildup of bilirubin in the brain and nerve tissue.

Thrush

Thrush (*Candida albicans*) is naturally occurring yeast that exists in the mouth and the digestive system. This yeast doesn't overgrow when a person has a healthy immune system, and "good" bacteria in the digestive system. Infants' immune systems are not fully developed early on, so they don't have enough of the good bacteria yet, which can enable Candida to overgrow.

Oral candidiasis or thrush causes white patches on the lips, tongue and the inside of the lips and cheeks. You may see similar-looking patches right after the baby has been fed that you can wipe away, but the patches from thrush can't be removed. Thrush isn't usually painful, but sometimes the baby may experience some mild discomfort. The baby's doctor may prescribe an oral solution to get rid of it.

If you are breastfeeding and have painful nipples, you may need medication as well. If the baby is being fed formula, always make sure the nipples and pacifiers are clean. See or talk to your doctor if your baby gets thrush after eight to nine months of age.

Penis

Watch out for inflammation of the penis called balanitis. If your son was circumcised it will take time for the penis to heal. Usually there is some swelling and redness, but there may also be some bleeding from the site and pus.

In either case, carefully clean the area with soap and water (not alcohol) and dry well. The symptoms should clear on their own with no intervention, but if bleeding and/or pus continue and the wound doesn't heal, contact your doctor. A topical antibiotic may be prescribed.

Umbilical Stump

Continue to clean the area around the bellybutton using only soap and water, not alcohol. The stump will turn black, and shrivel up and should fall off in a few weeks. Let your doctor know if this doesn't happen.

Folding the diaper down to keep it away from the stump may help to reduce irritation. If there is redness, bleeding, or pus contact your doctor.

Nail Care

The nails of a full-term baby are sharp and grow fast. Use a baby nail clipper or a nail file to trim them regularly (but never scissors). You may need another person to help make sure the baby is not moving too much so you can safely trim the nails. During the first two months, you can cover the baby's hands so that he or she doesn't scratch the face and eyes.

Common Things Babies Do

Just as it's important to get to know your baby, head to toe, it's very helpful and reassuring to know that there are some common things babies do.

Coughing and sneezing: Don't worry that your baby is sick, unless of course, this is accompanied by fever and congestion. Babies cough and sneeze simply because it's the instinctive way to clear their airways.

Hiccups: This is a frequent occurrence caused by gulping air during feedings or when the baby has been crying. They usually stop on their own and there's not much you can do for them, except to soothe your baby by gently patting him or her on the back.

Spitting up: The infant's immature digestive system allows for regurgitation (when breast milk or formula come back up). This isn't the same as vomiting. Keeping the baby in a semi-sitting position (when bottle feeding), burping during bottle and breastfeedings, and holding the baby upright after feedings may help prevent spitting up.

Essential Takeaways

- Diaper rash is common and can be prevented by changing your baby's diaper regularly and letting his or her bottom air out.
- Sponge baths are fine for newborns, and using a baby bathtub is best for full baths.
- Cradle cap is common and will likely go away on its own after a few weeks.
- Talk to your doctor if cradle cap, molded head, crossed eyes, or jaundice does not improve in a short period of time.

chapter 7

Baby's World Gets Bigger

Helping your baby's development

Taking the baby outdoors

Traveling with your baby

Emergency readiness for you and your baby

Never, ever will a human being learn and develop as much as a newborn will in the first year. You may not think that they're doing very much or understanding anything, but that couldn't be further from the truth. It's a well-known fact that babies are sponges— they take in everything around them, all the time, through all their senses.

Unlike many adults, babies don't yet know about fear and are not afraid to try. Everything they do is a learning experience, and each new experience builds on the last one. Babies are very instinctive creatures. They don't yet know whether something is good or bad or right or wrong, and so they don't stop to think about it. They just do what comes naturally to them.

If little ones had to constantly stop and be consciously aware, they would never be able to accomplish the enormous number of things that are required for life.

What Newborns Know

The newborn baby is able to recognize the mother's face and voice almost from the beginning—and soon also those of close family members. They start learning from the very moment they're born; some would say even in the womb.

Newborns are able to hear and see. They tell us when they're not happy by crying and when they're content by being quiet and calm. They know how to make sucking sounds and put their fingers in their mouth, letting us know they're hungry. They'll rub their eyes and get fussy if they're tired. They will react differently to a stressful or calm environment or caregiver.

Babies actually "know" quite a lot when they're born, but only parents can increase their growth and development by being with them, playing with them, and stimulating their capacity to learn.

Stimulate Your Baby's Senses

People may wonder, "Why bother talking to a baby?" After all, he or she couldn't possibly understand. However, what is not understood today will indeed be understood very soon—maybe even tomorrow or the next day. Long before actual language begins, hearing conversations impacts the baby's language development.

Talk to your baby using a soft voice. Have simple conversations, asking and answering questions. This dialogue, while one-sided for now, will eventually pay off because your baby is taking it all in.

Here are several things you can do to engage and interest your baby and stimulate his or her senses. Beginning these very early on sets the tone for the baby's expectations:

> Read to your baby. It's not what you read that matters as much as your tone of voice.
>
> Put soft music in the background or sing to your baby.
>
> Walk around the house with your baby. Point out things, name them, and tell the baby something about them.
>
> Hold your baby. There are never enough kisses or gentle hugs you can give a baby. He or she will understand your love and care and will feel safe.
>
> Touch your baby's face. In response, your baby will study your face and grasp your finger.

If the baby cries, pick him or her up and address the reason for the crying. Newborns can't soothe themselves. By giving them the assurance that you are there, you are fostering trust. Babies will learn to comfort themselves later.

Massage for Babies

The famous physician Hippocrates wrote about massage in 460 B.C. *Massage* derives from the French word meaning "friction" or "kneading," perhaps from the Arabic word *massa*, which means "to touch, to feel." Massage is used for therapeutic purposes and to relieve pain and stiffness. Massage therapy was introduced in the United States in the nineteenth century. Massage is calming for babies and it helps with sleeping and digestion. It's also a wonderful way to bond. Choose a time when the baby isn't too sleepy and do not massage immediately after feeding. Make sure the room is comfortable and warm, and your hands warm and soft. If the baby gets upset or wants to move, stop and restart the massage later.

Place the baby on a soft blanket, wearing just a diaper.. In order to figure out how much pressure to apply when you massage, close your eyes and press gently on your eyes with eyelids closed. This is the pressure that you'll apply on the baby's body.

Head and face: Start with very light strokes on the baby's forehead, eyebrows, and temples. Massage the top of the head and the ears. Stroke the cheeks. With a circular motion, use one finger to massage the jaw. Touch the nose and make a circular motion around the mouth.

Shoulder and chest: Stroke the shoulders and make circular movements around the chest. Stroke the rib cage up and down.

Arms and hands: Encircle the arm between your thumb and forefinger very lightly and move this "circle" up and down the arms. Do the same with the forearm. Touch and pull every finger gently. Repeat this on the other arm.

Tummy: Wait to massage the tummy until the umbilical cord is healed. Bring the legs up, flexing them towards the abdomen a few times. Stroke downwards from the rib cage, alternating your hands. Make circular movements around the navel.

Legs and feet: Stroke the thighs, then flex and extend the legs. Apply light pressure on the soles. Touch and gently pull each toe. Massage the entire sole with your thumb.

Back: Massage the entire back gently with your palm. Massage the shoulders. With small circular movements, stroke the back, avoiding the spine. Touch the lower back and the hips.

Talk or sing to the baby while you are massaging. Try to do this massage at least once a day toward the evening.

Safe Toys

According to the American Academy of Pediatrics (AAP), toys will enhance your child's physical, social, and cognitive development as early as the newborn stage. At this age, babies like to look at and listen to toys.

All toys you select for your baby should be well made, shatterproof, easily cleaned, and painted with lead-free paint. Small rattles, soft balls, and special baby mirrors that are unbreakable and have rounded edges are suitable toys. Mobiles that hang over the crib and play music are visually stimulating (these should be removed when the baby is able to sit up). Toys should make gentle sounds; nothing too loud, startling, or jarring. Also, toys should not have strings, cords, or any sharp edges. Also, remember not to put any toys in the crib or bassinet.

Be careful not to overstimulate your baby. When you see the signs of fatigue—rubbing the eyes and getting more and more agitated—it's time for quiet, calmer play (and soon, sleep). We will cover sleep in the next chapter.

Television and videos are definitely not recommended for babies at this stage, despite what the videos that claim to "enhance intelligence" try to sell you.

Out of the House

You can take your baby out immediately after birth. You can go for walks, to the park, to visit friends, and so on. You can even take the baby to restaurants, preferably during off hours, or to stores that are not too busy. If at all possible, do not take a baby younger than two months into a subway, crowded bus, or crowded, loud places in general.

baby steps

When your baby is older than six weeks of age, you and caregivers can actually attend movies at theaters. Many cities have special times designated for this, where breastfeeding and crying are not a problem (in fact, they're the norm).

Diaper Bag

The diaper bag becomes as important to you as your purse when you go out with the baby. It won't leave your side, gets totally stuffed with stuff, and is all about style as much as function. Babies have a lot of needs, so when you leave home with your baby, you'll need to carry several essential items in your diaper bag to make the baby comfortable and your time together more peaceful. It can be a lot to lug around, but here are the basics you should have with you at all times:

1–2 changes of clothing

Several disposable diapers

Baby wipes

1–2 burp cloths

2–3 bottles (if using)

Prepared formula (if using)

A breastfeeding cover-up (optional, if breastfeeding)

1–2 pacifiers

Diaper cream/ointment

1 small blanket

Small plastic bags for soiled diapers, clothes, and so on

A few toys and books

Be sure to restock the diaper bag each time before you go out so you don't get caught somewhere without a clean diaper or outfit.

Strollers

You've probably been shopping for a stroller already. It is wise to test drive all different kinds of strollers at the store to find the one that will work best for your needs and feel right to you. You will be using your stroller a lot!

The safest way to transport your baby outside is in a sturdy stroller. Before taking your baby out in the stroller, check all stroller parts and make sure they are tight and the safety belts are adjusted. Check for stroller recalls at www.cpcs.gov.

Be sure the stroller is in a position that allows the newborn to lie flat, because this is the safest position. No toys or any other objects should be in the stroller with the baby. If you need to use a blanket, wrap it snuggly around the baby, only up to his or her chest.

Stroller History
The original stroller was called a *perambulator* and was first used in England at the end of the nineteenth century. People protested because it was very big and took up a lot of space on crowded pedestrian walkways.

There are lots of choices when it comes to strollers—many different styles, colors, and price points. Pick one that will work best for you and your needs. The most important thing is that the stroller is sturdy and safe.

Other Kinds of Carriers

You can carry the baby in the car seat baby carrier if your walk is not too long. Also, there are stroller frames designed for car seat baby carriers to easily snap into. These are very convenient because you don't have to move the baby in and out of the car seat and stroller at each destination.

Slings are becoming more and more popular today, and there are a variety of styles from which to choose. The sling is very practical for newborns or smaller babies—they feel comfortable because of the closeness to the parent. When using a sling, check often to make sure that you can see your baby's face and that there is ample breathing space for the baby.

Sling Time
Slings have been around for centuries. Since ancient times, moms have carried their babies while they worked. Similar to swaddling but without the tight wrap, the sling holds the baby snugly and securely against the mother's body.

Whichever style of sling you choose, be sure that you follow the manufacturer's guidelines and that it fits well and securely on your body. Adjust it whenever necessary, wear comfortable shoes, and watch your step.

When a baby can hold its head up (a baby's neck becomes stronger and more stable at two to three months), other carriers, such as baby backpacks, are suitable. The most important factor in choosing a baby carrier is that both you and your baby feel comfortable.

Playgroups and Activities

When a small group of infants of the same age gather with their mothers or caregivers, called a playgroup, it allows them to see and study each other and to hear others like themselves make sounds or cries similar to their own.

While a playgroup for babies 0–3 months may be more about the mothers getting together, the baby will certainly get some benefit out of it as well. You'll often see your baby staring into space. Actually something is going on—babies learn just by observing. In a playgroup, your baby will see others like him- or herself, maybe for the first time. He or she will hear another cry or coo and the voices of different adults as well. They will also see different colors and objects than they're used to seeing at home.

Going to a music group or class specifically designed for infants is beneficial not only for the companionship your baby will find with other infants (and you will find with other mothers or parents), but participation will allow your baby to hear sounds he or she will enjoy.

For new parents and caretakers, playgroups and activities are a welcome break from the everyday routine. It's also a social venue to help lift your spirits when you're feeling so exhausted. Meeting more experienced parents can be enormously reassuring and helpful as well.

A word of caution, however, is do not expose your baby or yourself to illness at playgroup if at all possible. Stay home if you (or your baby) are sick or if you know someone else in the group is sick. It's far better to wait until everyone is well before returning. Wash your hands and your baby's hands, and change his or her clothing when you get home if someone was sick at the group you attended.

What to Wear

There is always a tendency to overdress your baby when you take him or her outside. A way to gauge the appropriate amount of clothes is to dress your baby as you dress yourself, plus an extra layer. In summertime, buy baby clothes made of natural fabrics (such as cotton) that allow air to circulate. Also, be sure your baby has a hat with a brim to protect his or her head and face from the sun. In warm weather, the baby should stay in the shade until you can apply sunscreen lotion, at about three months. Your baby will need to drink more formula or breast milk when it's very warm outside. No water is needed, though, until age six months.

When the weather is cold in winter months, the baby's head, hands, and feet must be covered when going outside. Dress the baby in layers you can take off so he or she can be comfortable when you go inside.

Take your baby out in all seasons of the year, dressed appropriately for the weather. He or she will benefit from the fresh air (and so will you!).

Traveling with a Newborn

You will want to show off your new bundle of joy just as soon as possible, and that will likely mean traveling to see relatives and friends. You will soon learn that the smallest passenger on your travels will most certainly have the most baggage.

Traveling by Car

First and foremost, the car seat must be the right one for your baby's size and must meet all safety specifications (see Chapter 2). Make sure that there are no air bags in the back where the baby is sitting. Maintain a gentle air flow inside the car or have windows slightly open for fresh air, and don't allow it to get too hot inside the car.

Bring clothing to accommodate temperature changes and toys to soothe and distract the baby. Also, have everything ready for feeding and changing, because you'll be stopping to take care of these situations often. Have a sunshade on the back windows to keep the sun out of the baby's eyes. If possible, try to travel during the day, and stop often.

By Plane

Unless there's an emergency, the recommendation is not to travel on a plane with a newborn younger than six weeks of age. The crowds, air quality, pressure changes, and difficulty of responding to a baby's needs on an airplane are all factors that make air travel stressful for a newborn.

If you must travel by plane, infants younger than two years old fly for free on most airlines if you hold them in your lap. Or you can choose to buy the baby a separate seat—in which case the baby will have to be in a car seat safe for flying.

The key to air travel is to leave yourself enough time. All the logistics at the airport—parking, checking in, security, and boarding—will take you at least twice as long. And don't forget to leave time for that last-minute, emergency diaper change just before boarding.

Take a bag designated just for your baby with everything you will need as carry-on luggage, and have it available at your seat. This way, you'll have easy access for whatever comes up. Make sure the bag has a changing pad, diapers, wipes, bags for soiled diapers, extra clothes, food, and toys. If possible, have the baby sit next to the window so he or she will not be bothered by anyone coming in or out of your row.

There will be a difference in the cabin pressure that may affect your baby's middle ear when the plane takes off and lands. Feeding the baby, either breastfeeding or with a bottle, at these times will help relieve any symptoms from the pressure differences. The pacifier can help as well. If the baby has been ill before the flight, ask your pediatrician for advice on how best to handle the baby's discomfort.

Breastfeeding can be done on a plane, so you'll want to have your cover-up handy. You can give breast milk from a bottle as well. The expressed milk needs to be carried either in a cooler or on ice and discarded if it isn't used within 24 hours.

Airport security does allow liquid baby formula (or stored breast milk) to be taken onto a plane. Formula in powder form works well for travel. Bring the necessary water, and make up as much formula as the baby will have at one feeding. Discard any unused formula that cannot be refrigerated after one hour.

By Bus or Train

Traveling by bus or train with an infant is similar to traveling by plane (except for the pressure changes). Follow the same recommendations, and take the same precautions as for air travel.

At the Hotel

If you stay in a hotel, ask for a nonsmoking room and a crib that meets FDA standards. Having the baby sleep in a stroller or car seat is not recommended. Ask for a room with a refrigerator or for one to be placed in your room so you can store your milk or formula. Never leave your baby alone in a hotel room.

Care for Infants During Disasters

Nobody wants to think about this issue, but life shows us that we must. During emergencies and disasters, infants are at particularly high risk. The facts that contribute are the lack of water or contaminated water, disruption in housing, lack of food, and lack of continuing medical care.

In such an event, breastfeeding mothers should be able to continue to do so, but if breastfeeding is not a possibility, ready-to-feed formula should be used. Water may not be available or may not be clean, so it will be impossible to use either concentrated formula or powered formula. Milk banks may be used as a last resort.

The mother needs to eat and drink but must be very careful of contaminated food and water. Crowded shelters can contribute to disease outbreaks. If there is any way to see a health provider, the vaccines need to continue; otherwise, the baby will be exposed to more potentially serious diseases.

It is advised for everyone to have a plan in case of emergency. Most importantly, the family needs to stay together. Know the locations of shelters, safe havens, and places that will offer food and housing, and have an evacuation plan. Also, consult your local health department and the Centers for Disease Control and Prevention (CDC) for disaster procedures in your area. Buy a radio that functions with batteries, make copies of all important documents, have all emergency numbers at hand, and keep all of these items in a waterproof pouch.

Ideally, have these on hand:

> Water—one gallon of water per person per day. In this case, bottled water is best.
>
> Food—varied canned foods, juices, canned fruit, vegetables, and ready-made formula
>
> Plastic utensils and paper or plastic plates and cups
>
> Can opener
>
> First-aid kit
>
> Personal hygiene items for you and your baby
>
> Baby carrier
>
> Clothing for the baby for different temperatures

Diapers and wipes

Bottles and nipples

We never know when disaster may strike, so take a little time to think about what your plan will be. Preparing can save lives.

Essential Takeaways

- Babies are taking everything in, so provide an environment that is healthy and stimulating.
- The diaper bag is essential anytime you leave the house. Mare sure it's restocked each time.
- Leave plenty of time for packing and traveling with your baby.
- Make a plan in case of emergency or disaster, and prepare in advance.

chapter 8

Through the Night

Differentiating between day and night

Managing fussiness and colic

Creating an atmosphere to help your baby sleep

Establishing a consistent sleep routine

The euphoria, tremendous happiness, and gratitude that you feel when you hold your baby for the first time tends to slowly diminish and fade as exhaustion and sleepless nights set in. While you're in the thick of it—such as it's 4 P.M., you're in the your pajamas, unshowered—you may wonder whether or not you'll get a good night of uninterrupted sleep ever again. Rest assured, however, that in time, you will.

The Day-and-Night Confusion

Why are babies up so often in the night? One of the answers is that feeding for them is more important than sleeping. Having such a small stomach and fast digestion, they will wake up hungry and want to eat every two to three hours.

The other answer has to do with the difference between adult and newborn sleep cycles. For adults, the daily cycle (called *circadian rhythm*) is influenced by external/outside and internal/body factors. During daytime, more *cortisol* is secreted. As the light fades, the level of cortisol decreases and more *melatonin* is secreted. Mel-atonin initiates the sleep process, and drowsiness appears as the body prepares for hours of rest, recovery, and repair.

Cortisol, called the "stress hormone," is a steroid hormone that the body releases in response to physical or psychological stress. Aside from its importance in the wake-sleep cycle, cortisol helps regulate blood pressure and carbohydrate metabolism, and plays an important role in immune functioning.

Melatonin is produced by the pineal gland in the brain. Referred to as "the hormone of darkness," melatonin peaks at night. Its function is to induce sleepiness.

In utero, a baby is totally dependent on the mother and has adapted to her daily rhythm. Newborns, however, haven't developed the day/night cycle as yet.

By three to five months, most babies will sleep through the night, and the first months will be considered a real rite of passage for all new parents. In this chapter, we will provide information to try to make these first months as predictable and bearable as possible.

To help your baby start to develop a sense of day and night, from the beginning it's important to do things that will differentiate the two cycles. During the day, make sure there is a lot of light, and try to take the baby outdoors. But remember not to overstimulate the baby with too many activities and visitors.

At night, dim the lights and have quiet hours with some soft music in the background and very little activity. Keep the television off or volume very low.

Getting Fussy

Babies get fussy for a variety of reasons, and it's important to observe the characteristics of your baby's fussiness to know whether it's just normal or something more.

Evening Fussiness

Up to age two months, even the calmest babies will become fussy—crying, agitated, and wanting to eat all the time yet not looking satisfied even when they do. This lasts a few hours, starting in the early evening. A fussy baby can often be calmed by just holding, changing, singing to, or rocking him or her.

There are a few theories why the early-evening fussiness happens. These hours are referred to as the "witching hours," but it really has to do with the immaturity of the nervous system and the digestive system. The accumulated stress of the day and the inability of the baby to cope results in these hours of discomfort.

Fussiness is your baby's way of handling this overstimulation from the day. As disconcerting as it is to see your baby this uncomfortable and, perhaps, inconsolable, think of fussiness as a normal way for your baby to discharge stress. Tomorrow's another day, and eventually your baby will mature enough to be able to calm him or herself.

Colic

If the fussiness persists beyond the usual and the baby cries and gets red in the face, pulls his or her knees toward the chest, and is gassy, we call this condition *colic*. Colic starts around two to four weeks and may last for around three months.

Definition

The word **colic** comes from the Middle English *colik*, meaning "affecting the colon," which derives from the Latin meaning "suffering of the colon." In describing colic, the "rule of threes" has been used by doctors for a long time: three hours a day, for the last three weeks, for three months. Of course, these "rules" vary from baby to baby.

Colicky babies may be more difficult to calm. The parents or caretakers need to have an immense amount of patience with a colicky baby, with the understanding that eventually, the condition will clear.

There are various factors that can cause colic. One is that the baby's digestive system is very immature. Remember that in the womb, the fetus was fed through the placenta. Now the baby's digestive system has to begin to get used to digesting food for the first time. The muscles of the digestive tract are still rigid; they don't have the mobility of the adult nor do they yet have the good bacteria that aids in digestion. As babies mature, the colic will disappear as mobility increases and the digestive system becomes populated with good bacteria.

Another reason for colic could be traced to certain foods that the breastfeeding mother is eating (see below). This is mainly speculation but it's always worth a try to eliminate the food(s) in question from the diet.

Also, many babies tend to swallow air. This will increase the gas in the abdomen and cause more discomfort and pain. Unfortunately, the baby's crying in response to the discomfort may actually cause the formation of more gas.

Acid reflux, which we'll talk more about next, may also be a cause of colic. Babies may be spitting up a lot or vomiting, but they may also have a very stuffy nose or are wheezing.

Calming Your Baby

There are many things you can try to calm your baby and make him or her more comfortable. Holding the baby in a secure sling or baby carrier can work. Walking around with the baby and talking, dancing gently while holding the baby, or taking the baby outside for a walk in the stroller can help. Some parents even secure the baby in the car seat and drive around in the car to quiet the baby. Try different things to see what will work for your baby.

Lullabies, soft music, white noise, and sounds of nature can effectively quiet and calm most babies. Some babies even like the sound of appliances, such as washers, dryers, vacuum cleaners, and electric toothbrushes.

Some babies like a floor swing. However, do not allow the baby to fall asleep in the swing, car seat, or stroller. You want to produce a sense of calm, quiet, and security rather than sleep. Ideally, the baby should be put to sleep in the crib while still awake but drowsy.

Another thing to try is massaging your baby by placing him or her in your lap on the baby's stomach. Place a warm (not hot) towel or blanket under the tummy, and gently rub the back. This is very soothing and often does the trick. You can also place the baby in a sitting position, propping the back, and bend the legs gently toward the belly, then extend the legs like you're gently exercising them. Swaddling the baby helps him or her feel secure and may calm the baby down. Dim the lights, but don't turn them completely off. You want softly focused, gentle light. Also, a bath often calms a fussy baby.

Always check your baby. For instance, he or she may be bothered by a tag in the sleepwear or a stray thread cutting into a finger or toe; it could be too warm or too cold in the room; he or she may need to be changed, has a stuffy nose, and so on. As you get to know your baby better you will probably be able to zero in on the cause of discomfort.

If the baby's nose is stuffed, clean it by inserting one or two drops of saline into each nostril. Wait for a few minutes, squeeze the nasal pump first, then insert the pump or aspirator into each nostril and release it to remove the mucus. Having a clearer nose could bring the baby some relief.

Giving the baby breast milk, a bottle, or a pacifier can help; however, be careful not to overfeed your baby.

Another consideration is changing your diet if you are breastfeeding. Sometimes certain spices and vegetables, such as broccoli, cabbage, cauliflower, and beans, can make the baby uncomfortable. Try cutting down on dairy products and take calcium tablets instead. Too much soda or sparkling/carbonated drinks may be a culprit. If your baby gets formula, consult your doctor about changing the baby's formula—usually to a hydrolisate one.

You can also consult your doctor about giving traditional or homeopathic medication to the baby. Medication is usually not given unless the doctor is convinced that the baby has *acid reflux*. Many babies tend to arch their back when they have reflux. Other symptoms of this condition include spitting up or vomiting, crying inconsolably, irritability, irritation of the throat, problems maintaining weight, and even respiratory problems. Your doctor will advise you about the appropriate treatment for acid reflux.

Acid reflux or GERD (gastro-esophageal reflux disease) results when a portion of the stomach contents is regurgitated; in other words, it goes back into the esophagus. This condition is similar to heartburn in adults.

Concerning colic, parents often want to know whether there's anything they can do to prevent it. Here are a few things you can try:

> Feed the baby small amounts, and burp him or her often.

> Keep the baby upright for at least half an hour after feeding.

> Change your diet if you are breastfeeding, or change the formula.

> Never feed the baby while he or she is lying flat.

> Don't allow the baby to suck on an almost-empty bottle or too long on a pacifier.

When the baby is crying and being fussy a lot of the time, you'll feel exhausted, frustrated, worried, guilty, and inadequate. This may also make the bonding so much more difficult. But this shall pass. Remember, it's not your fault. It's not that you're doing anything wrong.

For the mother, rest as much as you can. Get help from the rest of the family and other caretakers so you can regroup. Ask the baby's doctor for advice, and talk to other families who have babies with colic. Remember, this situation is temporary!

Also, remember always to never *ever* shake a baby. When a baby is shaken, the small, very fragile blood vessels in the brain can break, depending on the degree and the force of the shaking. Shaken baby syndrome (SBS) is a form of child abuse when a baby is shaken vigorously, causing severe damage, disability, and sometimes death. If you feel overwhelmed by your baby's fussiness, whatever the cause, do not shake your baby. Instead take a deep breath, put the baby down and take a short break, and ask for some help right away.

How to Put the Baby to Sleep

This is an age-old question. There is no exact answer, because babies are ever-changing and no two babies are the same—and a baby's stages are ever-changing. Choose whatever method works for you; the following are some recommendations to try.

Babies up to three months of age will wake up several times to feed. By four months, a baby may sleep five to six hours at night. The older the baby gets and the more the baby grows, the fewer number of times he or she will have to wake up for feedings. After sleeping well for a few months, the seven- to eight-month and older baby may start waking up at night again. So, it's important to know that sleep will be varied for a while.

So let's first go through what *not* to do, because these things will inevitably inhibit healthy sleep for your baby (and therefore you!):

> Don't put the baby to sleep on his or her stomach or side. Sleeping wedges are not recommended.

> Make sure there's nothing in the crib that could be dangerous, such as too much space between the rails, bumpers that are too thick, and loose strings.

> No toys, pillows, or blankets should be in the crib.

> Don't put the baby to sleep in the same clothing he or she has worn all day. Sleep clothes are flame resistant; most day clothes are not.

> Don't overheat the room or have it too cold.

> There is absolutely no smoking permitted in a house with an infant.

> Don't put the baby to sleep in his or her crib with a bottle.

> Don't allow the baby to fall asleep on you or in any place other than the crib or bassinet, if possible. Move the baby to the crib or bassinet if this happens.

Don't overstimulate the baby one to two hours before you intend to put him or her to sleep.

Don't take the baby into your bed to sleep. The American Academy of Pediatrics (AAP) does not recommend co-sleeping because it's very dangerous for the baby.

Co-sleeping

While it's fine for parents to have the bassinet or crib in their room, both the U.S. Consumer Product Safety Commission (CPSC) and the AAP strongly advise against bringing a baby into your bed.

Parents like co-sleeping because it's easier to breastfeed and takes less time, and they feel it makes for better bonding. However, there are several dangers:

You can roll over onto the baby.

The baby can suffocate because of pillows and bed sheets.

The baby can become trapped between the headboard and the mattress or the wall and the mattress.

There have been more than 500 deaths associated with co- sleeping.

Of course, how you put your baby to sleep is your choice. If you decide to put the baby to sleep in your bed, make sure to follow these guidelines:

Have a firm mattress.

Have no pillows or blankets.

Have no space between the head or foot board and no sharp corners anywhere on the bed.

Don't leave the baby unattended in the bed.

Dress the baby in light clothing, making sure that the head is free and not covered with anything.

Don't overheat the room.

Don't drink or take any medication that can make you drowsy.

There are *co-sleepers* that look like a crib or bassinet, without one side, that attach directly to the bed. These are safer to use than co-sleeping.

Creating a Sleep Routine

It's hard to believe, but routines can—and should—start at the newborn stage. A difference between day and night activities can be established, which will make life in the house much smoother.

New research shows that during the day, babies who are carried in closer proximity to an adult are calmer and sleep better. Overdoing activities at this age, however, and later, will make the baby overtired, irritable, and unable to settle down.

Try to do something different when the baby naps during the day versus going to bed for the night. For example, change the bassinet or crib position in the room, use a different swaddle, or change to more light where the baby sleeps. At night, always have the same sequence of events. For example, you can give a warm bath (unless the bath will awaken the baby), feed, read, sing, give the baby a "transitional" object (such as a blanket or a soft toy—you'll remove it from the crib the minute the baby falls asleep), and put some music on. The routine doesn't have to be complicated or very long.

However you do it, consistency is the most important thing. This means that every person who takes care of the baby should adhere to the routine. If the routine changes, the baby will get mixed messages that can result in irritability and not going to sleep!

Amount of Sleep

At first, your newborn will sleep 16–20 hours a day, waking up about every 2 to 3 hours. By the second month, he or she may wake up every three to four hours. There are babies who start sleeping six hours a night at age six to eight weeks, but this doesn't happen too often.

The night feedings should be kept short and boring. Don't turn the lights on or make a lot of noise. Simply feed, burp, and change the baby if necessary.

By the third month, the day and night routine will remain pretty much the same. The only real significant change is an increase in the number of ounces per feeding and a decrease in frequency of feeding due to longer periods of sleep.

Essential Takeaways

- Establish routines for your baby early on—most specifically, for feeding and sleeping.
- Establish the difference between day and night routines from the beginning. Your baby will eventually catch on.
- Be consistent with the way your baby's routines are carried out. Each caretaker must follow the routine to the letter or else the baby will become confused.

chapter 9

This Is the Way We Grow Today

Milestone movements in the first three months

What your baby sees and hears

Your baby becoming a social being with smiling and cooing

When developmental delays require intervention

Babies grow so fast. You won't believe how quickly time passes by. Every day is new and different, although you may not always feel like it is, and you'll be amazed at your baby's accomplishments—big and small.

In the beginning, babies make small, almost unseen movements. Then they kick and sit up and before you know it, your little one is running around the house. In this chapter, we'll explore the growth that happens in the first three months.

Lifting the Head

Immediately after birth, a baby can lift his or her head if placed on the stomach. The neck muscles are weak, so the lift will be very brief. When lying on the back, a newborn is unable to lift the head, but he or she may move it from one side to the other.

If a baby is placed in a sitting position, the head will lag—falling forward or to one side—and the back will be rounded, like being hunched over.

At one to two months, babies are able to lift the head and the chest. They will also keep the head lifted for a longer period of time. It's an important milestone because now the muscles of the neck and the shoulders are stronger.

Pushing and Turning

You may think that newborn babies don't move very much at all, but it's not so. While many of their movements are not very controlled, newborns can slowly push themselves across a surface. For this reason, it's important to never *ever* leave your baby unattended. Do not prop up the baby and think that he or she will stay there or put the baby in a bed or on a sofa, no matter how big a surface. Slowly but surely, the baby will push and push until he or she reaches the end and will fall.

Some three-month-old babies start turning from the back to the stomach. This movement requires increased control of the shoulder and upper-trunk muscles. Rolling from the stomach to the back is more advanced and will happen later.

Discovering the Hands

Newborns are swaddled (arms wrapped close to their bodies) a lot of the time for comfort and a sense of security. Therefore, many newborns don't use their hands much, and the hands still remain in a fist. The exception is babies who suck their fingers. Actually, they put their entire fist in their mouth.

During the second month, hand discovery begins. Babies may look at their own hands with real interest. By about the third month, an infant will start bringing the hands to the midline and will stare at them in wonder. It's something brand new, and some babies may actually be scared. Others find their own hands entertaining and will play with them and smile at them.

Grasping and Holding

Newborns are able to grasp a very small toy for a short period of time. Because of the strong grasp reflex, a newborn baby will grasp everything placed in his or her palms. A baby rattle is perfect because it's small enough and makes sounds. Soon enough, a baby will make the connection that he or she is, in fact, the one shaking the rattle to make the sound. When parents reinforce this concept verbally—"Look, you're shaking the rattle" or, "Listen to the noise the rattle is making"—the baby begins to get the idea.

By two months, the hands are no longer held tightly in a fist. A baby can hold a small ball or a soft toy for a brief period of time, but he or she is not able to reach for objects yet.

At three months, babies start reaching toward an object, but they miss it. If they finally grab it, they will let the object drop. The grabbing and dropping will soon become a game for your baby, and you will pick up the toys just so your baby can drop them again.

Seeing

Vision is the last thing to develop in the womb. It's believed that the womb isn't completely dark and that there are some visual stimuli. Visual development is influenced by genetics, brain development, the nervous system, and outside stimulants. In the beginning, the newborn doesn't coordinate eye movements (called doll's eyes). After one or two months, the eyes start to focus.

If you place your newborn 10 to 12 inches away, face-to-face with you, the baby will look at your face. Although their eyesight is around 20/200 to 20/400 (optimal eyesight is 20/20), they can see a few inches away. By about the end of the first month, the distance your baby can see will have increased to about three feet. Newborns can track a moving object only up to 30 degrees by moving their neck. The object will only be seen in a horizontal line. The baby will not be able to see objects if they are held higher or lower than their eye level.

Research shows that newborns can distinguish black and white and shades of gray. An infant's ability to see color develops later (some believe as early as one week after birth). Bright colors such as red, yellow, orange, and green are seen first; blue and violet come later, and still later, pastel colors.

Baby steps

Decorate your baby's room with bright colors to stimulate his or her vision. Attaching a mobile to the crib provides stimulation of the senses—bright colors, hanging shapes, movement, and accompanying music.

Turning Toward Sound and Light

As opposed to vision, hearing is developed in the fetus by 19–20 weeks. At birth, the newborn hears at nearly adult level. Sound is well transmitted in the womb, and noise can affect a newborn's hearing. Many older children who have hearing problems were exposed to noise in infancy. The preliminary results of a new study from the University of California at Irvine show that babies of mothers who smoked during pregnancy may have hearing-related problems.

Newborns will respond to lights and sounds, even if they don't understand their meaning. A baby enjoys the voices of the parents and other caretakers and will startle at very loud and unpleasant sounds. A baby will calm down with repetitive sounds, soft music, and white noise. As opposed to vision, hearing at birth is close to an adult's level. By three months, babies will react with crying to unpleasant sounds. All babies have a hearing test before they leave the hospital. If the baby was born at home or in a birthing center, the parents should make an appointment as soon as possible to have this test done.

baby steps   Don't worry if the deeply sleeping baby doesn't respond to sounds. Remember the saying, "sleeping like a baby"? Sleeping babies are able to completely block out external sounds.

Babies like light. They like toys with flashing and changing colors because they are visually stimulating. Babies will turn toward flashing and changing lights because they're interesting to them. Be careful of lights that are too bright, however. Similar to adults, babies don't like strong lights (such as a camera flash), so don't use the camera flash in front of the baby's face. Also, don't expose your baby to direct sunlight.

Smiling

You will never forget your baby's first smile. That tiny, toothless smile is one of the most beautiful experiences for a new parent. At about two months of age is when your baby will look at you and smile. The smile will be directed toward you in response to talking, singing, touching him or her, or just being there.

You may sometimes see what looks like a smile before two months. Those smile attempts are mostly involuntary and happen mostly in sleep. By three months, your baby will smile more and more and will start making other sounds that, a month later, will become laughter.

Cooing

Parents can't wait to hear their babies' voices—aside from crying, which is the first way of communicating. The reward will arrive at around two months, when you'll hear a few different sounds (called *cooing*). Those sweet sounds are the baby's first attempt toward language.

Cooing refers to a specific vocalizing sound, as opposed to the baby just making noises. It indicates the ability to use the back of the throat to make sounds.

You'll hear cooing when the baby is content. The sounds become louder and transition into crying if the baby starts to get upset.

"Parentese" is the term given to speech that parents and other adults tend to use with babies. It's an adult's equivalent of cooing. Babies seem to love it; in fact they may even prefer it to adult conversations. Characterized by a high-pitched, sing-song voice, "parentese" actually helps a baby learn language. It also features elongated vowels and consonants pronounced clearly and precisely. These are often accompanied by exaggerated facial expressions that are "up close and personal" with the baby. In contrast to baby talk, "parentese" uses actual words in easy sentences, repetitively.

Reacting to Voices

All infants like the sound of voices. As we know, the parents' or caregivers' voices are recognized by the baby in the first few hours after birth.

A two-month-old baby will coo, giggle to others in response, and locate the voice that comes from *in front* of them, not behind them. They don't turn yet to localize the voice.

By three months, a baby will start responding to voices with their own sounds. They will start turning toward the sounds. They will smile when something amuses or pleases them.

This is the time to talk and respond to your baby. Babies like high-pitched voices. Talking "baby talk" to your baby will not stop their capacity to talk.

Don't assume, though, that speaking baby talk is the only way the baby can understand. Hearing language as spoken by an adult is the way the baby will learn speech and how to put sounds and words together to express himself or herself.

When to Intervene

Consult your doctor if you observe any of the following in your baby:

No lifting of the head by two months

Hands still held in a fist by two months

No social smile by three months

No tracking past the midline by three months

No startling or turning toward a sound by three months

Not liking to be hugged

No interest in toys by two to three months

Activities and Toys

With the plethora of baby toys on the market today, you will have no problem finding a variety of fun things for your baby to play with to help stimulate development. Television and DVDs, even the so-called educational ones, are no replacement for hands-on, direct experience and are not recommended.

Also, remember there is no toy, no activity, and no group that can ever replace the parent's closeness and love. Spend as much time with your baby—holding, kissing, hugging, and cuddling him or her in addition to playing with toys. Don't worry; you won't "spoil" your baby. You'll be teaching your baby how to behave later in life and how to feel safe and have trust.

The First Month

In the first month, your newborn will enjoy a mobile that moves and has music. Music boxes made specifically for the crib have lights and even moving objects (such as a pretend aquarium) and are good at this age, too. A sound machine with gentle sounds, such as nature sounds or music, can help the baby settle down.

Stuffed toys need to be soft and securely in one piece. They should be small enough for the baby to hold but not so small as to present a choking hazard. Wrist and ankle rattles are fun at this age, too.

Activity mats are great during "tummy time," when a baby is on his or her stomach. The activity mat or quilt is simple at this age, with sounds, colors, and different kinds of fabric. The mat is especially helpful to distract babies who don't like to be on their stomachs during the day.

The Second and Third Months

By the second month, your baby will enjoy a floor gym. It's more complex than an activity mat, with lights, hanging and moving objects, and music. The baby can be on the back or stomach to gain different perspectives of the toy. Play with your baby by pretending you are playing with the toy as well.

By the third month if the baby can hold the head well, some babies are ready for bouncy toys, such as a bouncy seat or jumper. They enjoy bouncing up and down (without touching the floor) as well as playing and looking around. If you place your baby in the crib to play with toys, always remove all toys from the crib or bassinet before putting the baby to sleep. Also, remove the mobile once the baby can sit up.

Essential Takeaways

- Lifting the head, turning over, grasping, cooing, and smiling are major milestones for your baby in the first three months.
- Your baby can hear as well as you do, and your voice is very important for your baby to hear. Talk and sing to your baby as much as possible.
- Age-appropriate toys are helpful to stimulate your baby's senses, but nothing is better than just you—your voice, touch, and caring response to your baby's needs.

chapter 10

Understanding Vaccines

Understanding why vaccines are given

The diseases prevented by vaccines

Concerns parents have about vaccinating their children

The vaccine-autism controversy

One of the most important achievements in medicine and public health is the development of vaccines and the prevention of diseases. Your baby will receive several vaccines in the first year (if you don't refuse them by signing a refusal to vaccinate form), so let's explore what they are all about.

How Vaccines Work

Since much earlier than the eighteenth century, when the first vaccine was produced, it was observed that if a person contracted a certain disease and survived it, he or she would never get the illness again. This is possible through the body's natural ability to create its own immunity to certain disease-causing bacteria and viruses, called natural immunity. The way natural immunity works is when disease-causing bacteria or viruses (germs) get into the body, a "defense army" to combat them is produced by different cells of the immune system. These are called *antibodies,* and they develop a "memory" of that specific bacteria or virus.

When that same disease-causing bacteria (or virus) try to come back in the same person, the antibodies recognize it and then clear it out of the body before the disease has a chance to produce. This means that the person is now immune to that disease, because the body successfully fought off the disease-causing bacteria using its natural immunity. Luckily for us, there are millions of antibodies circulating in the blood, and they are what protect us from lots of harmful bacteria.

A vaccine works the same way. The difference is that the vaccine creates the "memory" of the disease *without making a person sick with the disease first*. This is possible through the modification of a small amount of the disease-causing bacteria in a laboratory to remove the cells that cause the sickness but keep the cells that will create the memory of it. These modified cells comprise vaccines, given either by mouth or injection, which offer safe protection from harmful diseases.

Here are the four different ways vaccines are made:

1. **Live, changed viruses** that cannot cause disease (used in MMR, or measles, mumps, rubella, chickenpox, and one flu vaccine)

2. **Inactivated, killed viruses** that are strong enough to give immunity (used in polio, IPV and Hepatitis A vaccines)

3. **Partial virus** made out of a small area of the inactivated virus (used in Hepatitis B vaccine)

4. **Partial bacteria** (used in HIB, Haemophylus Influenzae B, Pneumococcal, and DTaP, Diphtheria, Tetanus, acellular Pertussis vaccines)

The word **vaccine** comes from the Latin word vacca, which means cow. The first vaccine was developed in 1798 for smallpox, from a cow that was infected with a similar disease called cow pox.

Vaccine History

The second vaccine was developed in 1885 for rabies. From 1923 to 1927, vaccines were developed for diphtheria, pertussis, and tetanus and in the early 1960s for measles, mumps, and rubella (MMR).

Smallpox was eradicated in the United States in 1971 and worldwide in 1980. In 1979, the last case of wild polio virus was seen in the United States.

Why We Use Vaccines

Vaccines are an important factor in maintaining public health. It's much safer and easier for someone to get a vaccine instead of a disease. Vaccines protect against some diseases that are life-threatening and others that are not. But even nonlife–threatening diseases can have very serious immediate or long-term effects.

For example, rubella, or German measles, is generally a mild disease for a child who contracts it. But if an unvaccinated woman gives birth, she can pass to her baby the disease, called congenital rubella, which will have devastating consequences for the infant. Also, while an infant or child could get a disease in a milder form, that same disease could be potentially fatal to another person who has a chronic disease, who has a weakened immune system, or who is taking certain medications. Vaccines do save lives. If a child who was vaccinated is actually exposed to the disease, he or she may have a mild form of it for a very short period of time but will not suffer the full consequences.

The first vaccine a baby receives is for the harmful virus Hepatitis B, which causes a disease of the liver. This vaccine is given at birth. Then, regular vaccines start to be administered at two months, which is the earliest age for infants to be protected. There are certain diseases that target young infants, such as whooping cough or **pertussis** (the P in DTaP), which is why it's so important for babies to receive the recommended vaccines.

The vaccines need to be given a few times, in the form of "boosters," because a single dose of the vaccine does not give full protection.

Here is a schedule for vaccines and boosters to be given in the first year and beyond:

DTaP is given at 2, 4, 6, and 15 months, 4 years, and 11 years.

IPV is given at 2, 4, and 6 months and at 4 years.

HIB is given at 2, 4, 6, and 15 months.

Pneumococcal is given at 2, 4, 6, and 15 months and a catch-up at 5 years.

Hepatitis B is given as a series of 3: birth, 1 month, and 5–6 months or 2, 4, and 6 months.

Rotavirus is given in one of two ways: one is in three doses at 2, 4, and 6 months, and the other in two at 2 and 4 months. Both are given by mouth.

MMR is given at 12 months and at 4 years.

Hepatitis A is given at 12 and 18 months.

Varicella (chicken pox) is given at 12 months and at 4 years.

Not everyone can receive all of the vaccines. Some live vaccines cannot be given to people who have a weakened immune system, who are allergic, or who are on certain medications.

Vaccines in the First Two Months

The one-month-old baby receives one vaccine: the second Hepatitis B shot (the first was given at birth). For those babies whose mothers have active hepatitis, they also receive it with immunoglobulin, an antibody that helps build immunity.

Most pediatricians start the vaccine series at about two months. The vaccines will be given during the office visit, even if the baby has a slight cold, as long as there is no fever. Doctors don't want to delay the infant's protection. There are usually no vaccines given in the third month unless the baby needs to catch up.

The vaccines given at two months are:

DTaP (Diphtheria, Tetanus, and acellular Pertussis)

IPV (inactivated polio)

Pneumococcal (for pneumococcal disease)

HIB (haemophilus influenzae B)

Hepatitis B

Rotavirus

Diphtheria is a disease caused by a bacteria called *Corynebacterium diphtheriae*. It can cause respiratory and skin problems. It affects the nose, throat, and vocal cords where a thick membrane is formed on them. When the membrane is in the throat, the individual can stop breathing. The skin can be covered with a thick, gray, scaly membrane that can get infected and is hard to remove.

The disease is spread through close contact with the secretions from an infected person. Symptoms start 2–5 days after the infection. Treatment is with a diphtheria antitoxin and antibiotics, but the disease causes death in 20 percent of infected infants.

Tetanus is also known as lockjaw. Tetanus is a neurological disease caused by a bacteria called *Clostridium tetani*. It gets into the body through a dirty wound (stepping on a rusty nail, for example). The symptoms can start in eight days or even months after the infection and causes muscle spasm (twitching). A very strong substance, or toxin, secreted by the bacteria travels through the blood to the nervous system. The whole body becomes stiff, including the respiratory muscles. Even after having had tetanus, the body will not have immunity due to the toxin's strength.

The dirty wound needs to be thoroughly cleaned and an immunoglobulin administered. Antibiotics should be given. There is no antitoxin for tetanus.

If a newborn is delivered in unsanitary conditions and the mother is unvaccinated, neonatal tetanus can develop if the umbilical stump gets infected. Neonatal tetanus can cause death in 40–70 percent of babies.

Pertussis, also known as whooping cough, is a highly infectious disease caused by the bacteria *Bordetella pertussis*. It starts with a runny nose and fever, then a cough develops that becomes spastic and so strong that one can break a rib. It's called whooping cough because of the "whoop"—a high-pitched sigh at the end of the cough. The cough is often followed by vomiting. Pertussis lasts about six weeks.

The disease is fatal in 1 of 100 infants under 6 months. Infants get the disease from older unvaccinated children and adults. All adults are now advised to get the new Tetanus booster that also contains Pertussis.

Serious complications are encephalitis (disease of the brain) and seizures. Antibiotics only shorten the time of pertussis infection, especially if given in the first few days. All those close in contact with the infant need to take the antibiotic as well.

Polio, Poliomyelitis (infantile paralysis), comes from the Greek polios meaning grey and myelos meaning spinal cord. It's an acute viral infection caused by the Poliovirus, which is spread from one person to another. Polio can cause a mild respiratory disease or paralysis. When it reaches the central nervous system, it destroys the neurons and causes muscle weakness and paralysis, which is permanent.

There is no cure; however, it is important to treat by helping breathing and through physical and pain therapy. Years after the infection, some people may demonstrate the post-polio syndrome with extreme tiredness, pain, and paralysis.

Rotavirus is a virus that causes diarrhea in infants mostly during the winter months. The virus is shed in the stool. Babies get sick by touching something that was infected, mainly through dirty hands. It starts with a fever, runny nose, vomiting, cramps, and diarrhea. The diarrhea can be so severe that the baby becomes dehydrated (dry skin and mouth, dry diapers, and lethargy). Some babies need to be admitted to the hospital for IV treatment, which means replacing fluids and electrolytes into the vein.

Hepatitis A is a highly contagious viral disease caused by the Hepatitis A virus that produces an inflammation affecting the proper functioning of the liver. It's transmitted through contaminated food (raw shellfish) and water, close contact with an infected person, by using illegal drugs, and traveling in areas where Hepatitis A is widespread.

Symptoms don't start immediately; it takes a month or more after being infected with the virus for the following symptoms to appear: tiredness, nausea, vomiting, muscle ache, itching, dark colored urine, and yellowing of the skin and eyes (jaundice). Note that not everyone gets all of these symptoms.

A mild case of the disease may last 1–2 months. In some cases, the symptoms can reappear after a few months. In severe cases, there is acute liver failure, which means that the liver stops functioning suddenly. Many of these patients require a liver transplant.

MISC.

Importance of the Liver

The liver helps digestion and absorbs fat and the fat-soluble vitamins A, D, E, and K. The liver activates important substances called enzymes and produces proteins and substances that are important in the coagulation of the blood. The liver is the body's "filtration system," helping to remove medication, toxins, and alcohol. The whole body is affected when the liver doesn't function properly.

Hepatitis B is a virus that causes inflammation and destruction of the liver. It can be transmitted to the newborn by an infected mother, through transfusions (these days they are checked for the Hep B virus), unprotected sex with an infected person, or infected and shared needles or instruments. It's called acute in the first three to six months after the infection, and chronic after that. In many chronically infected people the virus persists in the body. They are called carriers. The infected patients can have nausea, tiredness, jaundice, and joint pain. Sometimes, even if they are infected, they may not feel anything for more than six months. Mothers, who are not tested for the virus or who aren't showing symptoms, can transmit the disease during delivery. However, it is still okay for them to breastfeed. Babies who are born to Hepatitis B–infected mothers will develop Hepatitis B in 90 percent of cases. The symptoms do not start immediately; it may take years. The symptoms are joint pain, loss of appetite, pain in the right side of the abdomen, and jaundice. Chronic Hepatitis B can lead to liver disease or liver cancer.

Haemophylus Influenzae type B (Hib) is caused by a bacteria and spread through contact with the secretions of a sick patient. Usually symptoms start appearing after 19 days. It causes meningitis (inflammation of the membrane covering the brain and the spine), pneumonia, sinusitis, skin infection (cellulitis), and epiglottitis.

The epiglottis is a tissue at the entrance to the voice box (larynx) and windpipe (trachea) that closes them during swallowing. When it gets infected, it blocks the trachea and the baby can't breathe. A tube must be inserted into the windpipe in order to keep the airway open.

Children less than 5 years old are at risk. They must be treated with antibiotics as soon as possible. Hib is fatal in 5 percent of infants and for those that survive, 20 percent will have brain damage or hearing loss.

Pneumococcal disease is caused by *Streptococcus pneumoniae* pneumococcus). Initially, the bacteria invades the lung and causes pneumonia. Transmitted through the blood, it causes sepsis or blood infection. It can also cause ear infections and sinusitis.

The very young and the very old are at high risk, as well as anyone with immune diseases or chronic diseases. Treatment is with antibiotics, but there's an increase in antibiotic resistance. This makes the treatment more expensive and the hospitalization longer.

For the full schedule of vaccines children receive in their first year and beyond, also see Appendix C.

Vaccine Side Effects

Vaccines can produce side effects including fever, redness, possible swelling and pain at the injection site, and crying or sleeping too much. These side effects can start immediately after receiving the injection and can last up to 48 hours.

To alleviate your baby's discomfort, you can give him or her an infant pain reliever if approved by your doctor and/or place a cold towel on the injection site and massage the area.

Call your doctor immediately if:

Fever is higher than 102° Fahrenheit

The baby does not look well

The area is very red and swollen, more than it was right after the injection

Any of these conditions persist for more than 48 hours

The Controversy Regarding Vaccines

Since the development of vaccines in the eighteenth century, they have been met with questions and fear. Over the years, however, after seeing many diseases disappear, vaccines have become the first strategy against many serious infectious diseases.

Since 1998, after a paper was published in the United Kingdom about the MMR vaccine (more on this topic in a minute), a large controversy began and parents began refusing vaccinations for their children for a variety of reasons. This unfortunately caused the recurrence of many previously eradicated diseases.

Many parents have concerns about the safety of vaccines for their children. Some believe that babies are too young and the vaccines will overwhelm their systems. But in reality, it's desirable to start vaccines as soon as possible because it takes some time for the vaccines to be effective. Vaccines are only a small fraction of the normal germs that exist in your child's environment.

Understanding Additives

A deep concern some parents have about vaccines is the use of additives. Vaccines have a variety of additives for different reasons, all of which are to help make the vaccines as effective as possible.

One concern was about the additive thimerosal, which is actually no longer used. Thimerosal is a form of mercury that was added to vaccines in order to disinfect and preserve the product. Due to controversy over this preservative, although no scientific evidence has proven any harmful effects, thimerosal was removed from the majority of vaccines (all except for one flu vaccine) since 2001 as a precaution.

Aluminum salts are added to vaccines in very small amounts. They are needed to boost the immune response. Otherwise, one would need more doses in order for a vaccine to be effective. The amount of vaccines given to infants is 0.016 ounces (0.5cc). It would require approximately 32 ounces to produce the same immune response.

Formaldehyde is present in vaccines, in only a trace amount, in order to inactivate the germs that are necessary to make the vaccines. We, in fact, have higher amounts of formaldehyde circulating in our blood than what is present in vaccines.

Egg byproducts are in some vaccines. Children who are allergic to egg and egg byproducts cannot receive these vaccines. The flu and yellow fever vaccines contain egg protein, and the MMR (measles, mumps, and rubella) vaccine is produced in chick embryos; However, it can be given to children with allergies under supervision.

Trace antibiotics are also present in minimal amounts and help prevent contamination during the manufacturing process.

The amounts of all these additives are extremely small. We are exposed to more of these substances on a daily basis from our environment. Removing them completely would affect the way the vaccines work and would impact the way children are protected.

Autism and Vaccines

Andrew Wakefield, a doctor in England, published articles in 1998 and 2002 implying that the MMR vaccines cause autism. Although the papers were highly criticized for not being accurate and for not being able to replicate the findings, it was enough to scare parents everywhere. The immediate effect was that many parents refused to vaccinate their children.

The MMR vaccine is given at age one, which is the time when most cases of autism are diagnosed. (The diagnosis of autism is very difficult to make before one year of age.)

Five major international studies were carried out to support the idea that the MMR vaccine does not cause autism. Many ethical issues were found after closely examining Dr. Wakefield's studies, and in May 2010, Dr. Wakefield's medical license was revoked for serious medical misconduct. The entire scientific world hopes that the fear of vaccines will soon dissipate after disproving his theory.

MMR Research

The follow-up studies on the MMR vaccine and autism were performed in the United States, the United Kingdom, and Denmark. The study in Denmark compared more than half a million children. The percentage of autism was the same in the vaccinated and non-vaccinated groups. There was no association between the age at the time of vaccination and the age of the children who developed autism.

The causes of autism and the autism spectrum are not completely understood. New research shows that part of the cause is genetic and due to infections acquired in utero. All of these can damage the central nervous system.

A new study in 2010 showed that there are subtle signs, even in the newborn period (muscle tone and no response to visual or sound stimuli) that may give clues to the emergence and diagnosis of this syndrome down the line. Consistent follow-up of these babies may help shed light on why some children develop autism. Early home videos can help the diagnosis as well.

Many subtle signs appear before the MMR vaccine is given. Unfortunately, since 1998, parents' refusal to vaccinate has caused serious disease—and death in some cases—among the unvaccinated children.

Old Diseases Emerging Again

As a result of the autism controversy, the decrease in vaccinations increased the risk of contracting old diseases for everybody. When all children are vaccinated, the community (or herd) immunity will protect even some unvaccinated children. This means that even in the event of an outbreak, when the majority are vaccinated, fewer people will be getting and passing on the disease. For this reason, it's important to vaccinate as many children as possible.

Following the reduction of vaccines, old diseases re-emerged in the United Kingdom after 1998. A measles outbreak killed many children and left some with serious side effects. Polio, the dreaded disease that is hopefully on its way to eradication, reappeared in some African countries.

In the United States—specifically, in Indiana, Ohio, and New York State—measles, mumps, and pediatric tetanus were diagnosed. In 2009, a large area of Minnesota had an outbreak of meningitis.

Other Consequences of Not Vaccinating

As previously mentioned, the refusal to vaccinate has more consequences. Not only is the infant exposed to diseases that can result in serious illness, permanent damage, or death, but he or she can also expose other children or adults.

If exposed to vaccine-preventable diseases, children or adults who can't be vaccinated due to a weakened immune system, chronic disease, or certain medications could become very sick or die.

Also, new vaccine schedules that spread the vaccine dosages over more time than the regular schedule, in the hopes it will be safer, have not proven to be different in any way than the regular established schedule. The danger is that it delays an infant's protection and therefore the protection of others as well.

Essential Takeaways

- Vaccines save lives.
- Your baby will receive six types of vaccines in the first two months.
- An unvaccinated child is at high risk and poses a risk to others.
- Extensive further research has indicated no correlation between the MMR vaccine and autism.

chapter 11

From a Medical Perspective

How to know when your baby isn't feeling well

Medications and essential items to have on hand at home

Conditions to be concerned about in the first three months

Preventing SIDS

As a new parent, you'll worry about your new baby's health. Truth be known, you will continue to worry for the rest of your life. It's just part of being a parent. Believe it or not, however, although your baby is so young, you'll be able to tell when something is not right. You may not know what the problem is, but you'll know when it's time to call for advice.

Watching for Signs of Sickness

There are signs that can lead you to think that there is something wrong with your baby, and some are more obvious than others. Watch for these symptoms in your baby, because it's likely a sign of sickness that will need the doctor's attention:

Fussiness, not only in the evening

Crying inconsolably a lot of the time

Sleeping more than usual

Difficulty waking the baby up

Heavy eye discharge

Watery stools between feedings

Spitting up more than usual

Projectile vomiting

Stools that look like pellets

Blood in the stool

Less urine

Fever

A fever means that a person is fighting an infection. But in babies, any infection can spread very quickly to the rest of the body. A fever as low as 100.4° Fahrenheit (38° Celsius) can be dangerous for babies younger than six to eight weeks old. Therefore, it's very important for the parent or caretaker to know how to take an accurate temperature.

For infants, ear, pacifier, and temporal thermometers are not recommended. At this young age, they will not give an accurate reading. A rectal thermometer (which is digital) is recommended because it provides the most accurate temperature reading.

Here is how to use a rectal thermometer. Be sure to talk and sing to your baby while you're taking the temperature to keep him or her calm and comforted:

Place the baby on his or her back.

Put some petroleum jelly on the tip of the thermometer.

Take the diaper off.

Lift the baby's legs and carefully insert only the thermometer's tip into the baby's anus.

Remove it when it beeps, or after two minutes.

Read the number on the thermometer.

If the temperature reading is 100° Fahrenheit, call your doctor—and call your doctor immediately if it's higher than 100° Fahrenheit.

Skin conditions to watch for are:

A rash that gets worse after two to three days

Large vesicles (clusters of bumpy red spots)

Peeling skin (other than cradle cap)

Small yellow vesicles on a red base

Bleeding hemangiomas

Medications to Have at Home

It's a good idea to have basic infant-specific products readily available at home, should the need arise:

Infant/children's Tylenol (acetaminophen); not to be used for babies younger than two months of age unless directed by your pediatrician

Infant/children's Advil/Motrin (ibuprofen)

Infant/children's Benadryl (diphenhydramine)

Baby vitamins

Antibiotic ointment

Anti-itch cream or spray

Alcohol pads

Betadine

Bandages (latex free)

Gauze

Saline drops for the nose

Nasal aspirator

Medication syringes or cups for dosing

Because many infant and children's medications have been recalled in recent years, always check online for specific medications at www.fda.gov/safety/recalls/.

For minor ailments, saline drops in the nose, a bath, the right nutrition, and dehumidifiers will help make the baby more comfortable.

Never give cold or cough medication to a child younger than two, and always consult the doctor before giving your baby any medication.

Reasons to See the Doctor

Your baby will be seen at least seven times in the first year. These visits are called "well-baby visits," and they occur at birth, one week, one month, three months, six months, nine months, and twelve months. The doctor will check your baby's nutrition, height, weight, head circumference, and the developmental milestones that he or she has achieved at each visit. Your baby will receive the appropriate vaccines as well.

Besides these standard visits, your baby may need to see the doctor whenever you observe that he or she isn't looking well. Babies can't talk, so keeping a close eye on your baby from head to toe is essential—and if you sense something is wrong, call your doctor. Pediatricians typically have set hours when they take calls during the day. Just talking to him or her can give you reassurance and the ability to know whether the doctor needs to see your baby. Call the doctor (the answering service) after hours if you think it's an emergency or go to the emergency room.

What the Doctor Does at the First Well-Baby Visit

After the weight, height, head circumference, and the vital signs are taken, the doctor (or nurse practitioner) will examine the baby. He or she will watch to see how active the baby is, and let the parents know where the percentiles are for weight, height, and head circumference.

The skin will be checked for rashes, bumps, bruises, and hemangiomas. The head will be checked to ensure it's not flat, that the fontanel is open and flat, and that the scalp has no bumps.

The doctor will also shine a light in the eyes with an instrument called an ophthalmoscope to see how the baby reacts to light.

The nose, the ears, and the mouth are also examined. The neck is checked for any possible bumps, and the collar bone (clavicle) is checked for any possible fractures.

The doctor will look at the chest, then will listen to the chest and the heart with a stethoscope. Then the belly will be touched to make sure it's soft and no masses are felt. The genital area will be checked, then the hips. The doctor will perform some maneuvers with the hips to make sure that they are not dislocated. The hands, fingers, feet, and toes will be checked for their development and position. After the baby has been turned on the stomach, the back and the buttocks will be checked.

Then it's time to check reflexes: Moro (startle), grasp, rooting, stepping, patellar (knee-jerk), and Babinski (toe movement). Muscle tone is determined next.

The doctor will explain everything to the parents that he or she has seen. The doctor will talk to the parents about feeding, sleeping, vaccines, what happens at the next visit, and will answer questions about everything else the parents want to know about. You can always call the doctor when you have other questions.

Concerns in the First Three Months

The first few months are perhaps the most concerning time for most parents about their baby's health. Many of the things your baby may experience are quite common and just part of being a newborn; nonetheless, they can be anxiety-producing for the parents. Here are several conditions that can occur in the first three months and what to expect in each case.

Fever: As we discussed earlier in this chapter, fever is, and should be, a cause for great concern. When a fever approaches 100.4° Fahrenheit in a baby younger than two months old, he or she needs to see the doctor. At this young age, there's a real need to know where the infection is coming from, so the doctors will draw blood, check the urine, and perform a spinal tap. They are checking to see whether the infection has spread to the blood, kidneys, or brain. The baby might be admitted to the hospital to receive medication and for observation for 48 hours. If all the blood work and other tests are negative (no infection reported), the baby will go home. If not, he or she will be treated appropriately in the hospital.

After the second month, the way fever is addressed changes. If a baby has a fever of 100.4° Fahrenheit but looks healthy otherwise, parents can give fever-reducing medication (dosage amount as prescribed by the doctor) and carefully monitor how the baby responds. Also, because vaccines are given in the second month, it's possible for a baby to run a fever for two days in response to receiving the vaccines. If the fever goes higher than 102° Fahrenheit—or if the baby is very sleepy or irritable—contact your doctor.

Baby steps   Never attempt to figure out the temperature just by touching the baby's skin, because at this young age, the skin can be very deceiving. The only accurate way is through the rectal thermometer.

Weight loss: Newborns generally lose 7–10 percent of their birth weight in the days right after birth. They regain it around the first week. If your baby continues to lose weight, the doctor will ask questions about feedings, including the amount of breast milk or formula given to the baby at each feeding and the frequency of each feeding—and sometimes the doctor will even ask to observe a feeding to gauge how well the baby feeds and if he or she is getting enough.

Difficulty waking up: A baby who sleeps too much and is difficult to wake up can be at risk for weight loss, dehydration, or other conditions. Keep track of the amount of time your baby sleeps, and if it's consistently more than what's normal for your baby, talk to your doctor.

Sleep apnea: This means interrupted sleep due to abnormal pauses in breathing. All babies have it for a few seconds without changing color (becoming blue). It happens because the respiratory system is still immature.

There may also be a blockage in the nose, or the brain fails to command the breathing muscles. Premature babies are at a higher risk for prolonged sleep apnea that could be dangerous.

Look at the baby's stomach to see better how well they are breathing. Listen closely to hear the breathing. Touch them to make sure they react. You may see or hear the baby gasping during sleep. If so, touch and move the baby immediately. If she/he continues to breathe normally and the color is fine, it was a short sleep apnea. If, however, the baby fails to respond after being touched and moved, start CPR and call 911. As the baby grows, the condition will disappear.

Jaundice: If a baby's skin is yellow (jaundiced) after six days, he or she needs to be checked by the doctor. This could mean the liver is not functioning properly and the baby will need medical treatment.

Rashes: Rashes on a baby are pretty common and typically not cause for concern unless a rash doesn't go away and gets worse over the course of several days. Whether it's diaper rash or a rash on other areas of the skin, talk to your doctor about it.

Spitting up: Newborns spitting up in small amounts is normal, but spitting up in large amounts—or projectile vomiting—could mean a variety of things (from simple overfeeding to a serious infection or allergy). Talk to your doctor if your baby does either of these.

Watery stools: Very watery stools between meals could mean that a baby has either diarrhea or had a reaction to the feedings. Watch the urinary frequency. If it's less than usual or the baby is not drinking, see the doctor. It's always good to have rehydrating liquids in the house, and follow the doctor's recommendation.

Small stools: Stool that looks like pellets is unusual in the first month and typically means that the baby is constipated. Constipation could be a sign that the baby isn't eating enough or even a disease of the colon. After introducing solid foods, the baby should have fewer bowel movements, but if they're soft and the baby is in no pain, it's okay.

Blood in the diaper: Blood in the diaper could mean a small cut in the baby's anus or an allergy to milk protein. When a baby is dehydrated, you may see pink brick–colored crystals in the diaper, which is not blood. In either case, tell your doctor so the appropriate treatment can be administered.

Not reaching developmental milestones: It's a reason to contact the doctor if a baby hasn't reached a developmental milestone within the standard time period. There's no need to sit and worry when one phone call or one office visit could give you peace of mind and can only help your little one.

Mass in the groin: See the doctor immediately when you find masses anywhere on the baby.

Emergencies: Choking, rapid breathing and panting for air constantly, seeing the ribs and the space above the collarbone while breathing, flaring of nostrils, inability to wake the baby up, rhythmic movements of the head, rhythmic movements of the extremities that do not stop when you touch them, color change, any bleeding, constant vomiting. Call 911 in these instances.

Cleft lip and palate: This happens when the tissue of the lip and palate don't develop and don't grow together. The cleft lip could just be a small opening or a larger one going all the way up to the nose. The cleft palate will show as an opening on the palate. The reasons for this condition are not always known. It could be genetic, environmental, or a result of medication that the mother took during pregnancy. Cleft lip and palate cause feeding problems, so there are special nipples and devices used. These babies are more susceptible to getting ear infections and the position of the teeth could be affected. Cleft lip and palate can be fully repaired by 12–18 months.

Developmental hip dysplasia: This condition, formerly known as congenital hip dislocation, happens when the ball on top of the thigh bone (femur) doesn't sit firmly in the hip socket. Sometimes only the ligaments are loose; other times, the whole bone is out. The hips are checked at the newborn and every well-baby exam. Babies at risk for this condition are those born in the breech position and if there's a family history of hip dysplasia. Many times the cause is not known. All breech babies will have an ultrasound exam of the hips at around three to four weeks. The earlier it's found, the easier it is to treat. The doctors will put a special harness on the baby. If the dislocation is diagnosed after six months, anesthesia and surgery may be required. Consult your doctor if the length of the baby's legs seem to be different, if there is less mobility of one of the legs, or if there is a limp in older infants who are walking.

Seeing a New Doctor

There are times when your regular doctor won't be in the office when you need to bring your baby in for a sick visit or checkup. Rest assured, however, this is a normal occurrence—and doctors' offices are used to accommodating such needs. The new doctor will review the baby's records and be able to give the appropriate guidance and diagnosis.

You may also be seeing a new doctor because you've switched doctors and practices altogether. Be sure the new office requests your baby's medical records in writing from the previous provider and that they are sent to the new office. Also, make sure the new doctor is on your baby's insurance plan before you make the switch.

Make sure that you always have the baby's vaccines updated on a vaccine card.

It's always a good idea to keep your own separate record of all your baby's vaccinations and any other significant medical and developmental information. This way, you always have it in case you move, switch doctors, or need it for travel purposes.

Thinking About SIDS

SIDS (Sudden Infant Death Syndrome) is a frightening thought for all parents. It is the sudden and unexplained death of an infant younger than one year old. Most deaths from SIDS occur in babies up to six months of age, and many babies who passed away this way were healthy.

The cause of SIDS is not known. New studies have shown that some babies who died of SIDS had an abnormality of the part of the brain that controls breathing. Also, there are certain factors that may increase the risk of SIDS, including:

Sleeping on the stomach

Prematurity

No prenatal care

Illegal drugs, smoking, or alcohol during pregnancy

Smoking in the house around the baby

Overheating the baby's room

In the 1990s, the American Academy of Pediatrics (AAP) started the "Back to Sleep" campaign. All parents and caretakers were advised to put babies to sleep on their backs. Sleeping on the side was considered safe at one time, although it's not anymore. Sleeping on the stomach or the side increases the risk of SIDS because the airway is narrowed in these positions. A baby's face can get buried in the mattress, so there will be less inhaled air (oxygen) and the baby will re-inhale the used, expired air that contains carbon dioxide. Then the baby's body becomes deprived of oxygen, and he or she could stop breathing.

After a baby has learned how to turn over on his or her stomach at around four to seven months, he or she will be fine to remain in this position to sleep. Even after your baby can turn over, still try putting him or her down on the back to sleep initially, then check the baby frequently.

Although SIDS occurrence has dropped by 50 percent since the Back to Sleep campaign, it's still the primary cause of death for babies from birth to six months old.

Taking these precautions is the best thing you can do to give you peace of mind that you're doing all you can to prevent SIDS:

All babies all the time (day or night) must be put on their backs to sleep.

The mattress in the crib or bassinet must be firm, the mattress cover should fit tightly, and the bumper should be thin and fit tightly against the sides of the crib.

No blanket, comforter, quilt, pillows, and toys should ever be in the crib or bassinet.

The baby should have comfortable night clothes and should not be over-bundled.

The room should not be overheated.

Check all appliances, and have a smoke and carbon monoxide detector near every room.

Do not smoke in the house, and do not smoke outside if the baby is around.

Do not take the baby into your bed for sleeping.

Giving the baby a pacifier after breastfeeding has been well established may also help prevent SIDS.

Essential Takeaways

- Trust your instincts and call your doctor when you notice that something is not right with your baby.
- Take your baby to all of his or her well-baby checkups.
- Have the appropriate infant medications and products ready at home.
- A rectal thermometer is the most accurate way of taking your baby's temperature; know how to do it properly.
- Have the doctor's emergency numbers readily available, and share these numbers with all caretakers.
- Do everything possible to prevent SIDS.

Part 3

Months Four, Five, and Six

Now we focus on your baby's continuing development. Motor skills have increased as your baby has gotten stronger—kicking, grasping, turning, pushing up from a sitting position, dropping objects, and putting everything in the mouth!

Your baby is becoming a social being—expressing feelings, laughing, imitating sounds, and beginning to make simple vowel sounds. We explain the language of crying—what it means and ways to handle it.

We'll take a look at activities and exercises appropriate for this age as well as new toys and clothing. Also, what to look for in a caretaker and alternatives in child care are important issues for new parents. We'll cover the many questions and challenges in this realm.

By now, your baby is ready for solid food. We'll guide you through what your baby can eat, how to introduce new foods, and how much to feed. Plus, we'll give you some easy recipes to make at home.

Haven't slept through the night yet? We'll offer methods for helping you and your baby get a good night's rest and for establishing good sleep habits for the future.

Finally, we address your medical concerns at this stage and give you some guidelines, should they arise.

chapter 12

This Is the Way We Grow Today

The importance of the sense of touch for your baby

Developmental advancements in gross and motor skills

Becoming more socially interactive

What crying means and what to do about it

The first three months have gone so quickly. There have been so many changes in a relatively short period of time. Your baby has grown a lot, has learned so much, has started to move, and is interacting more.

While the growth from birth to three months was pretty amazing, the differences you'll see in your baby now compared to where he or she was just a month ago is still more amazing. Coming into months four, five, and six, all of a sudden you will have a brand-new little person in front of you.

At this stage, babies' movements are becoming more controlled; there is more purpose to them, and they are more complex. Also, your little person is responding and smiling much more, becoming a real social being.

The World Becomes Tactile

Touching is the way babies learn about the world around them. In the first few months, your touch is what your baby knows and learns to trust. When something is wrong, the mother, father, or caretaker will be there to make it better. Your touch to your baby means concern, care, comfort, and consistency. Around the fourth month, your baby will begin to develop "body-awareness"—feeling and seeing himself or herself as an entity separate from you. Of course, babies won't understand that concept in just that way, but by discovering and exploring their own bodies—such as their ears and feet—through touch, they come to know it.

Soon enough, their world will expand even further beyond their own bodies. Babies soon discover there are so many things to touch and so many textures to feel for the first time. As your baby's movement and mobility increases, there will be many more objects in the immediate environment with which to interact.

Starting to Kick

By now, your baby is likely not sitting still at all. He or she has discovered how to kick the legs and will now kick objects, the swaddle blanket, or just the air. There are many muscles in the legs and hips that contribute to kicking, and they are now being regularly used and exercised. These movements also mean that the baby's coordination is developing. So let them kick!

Pushing Up from a Sitting Position

A four-month-old baby will try, unsuccessfully, to sit up when placed on the back. He or she will be able to bring the head to almost a 90-degree angle when on the back, which fuels the desire to sit up. While being held, the baby will be able to push up strongly with the legs into standing, putting most of the weight on the feet.

A six-month-old will sit with support and be able to sit in a high chair. When helped into a standing position, the baby will put all of his or her weight on the feet.

Turning from Stomach to Back

Rolling over is a major milestone. From four to six months, the rolling will start first going from the belly to the side, then from the belly to the back. When on the belly, the baby's arms and legs will be extended, and the back will be arched with the head raised. This is a great exercise to strengthen the back muscles for the next stage, which is going from the back to the stomach.

At four to five months, a baby can lift the head when on the back and will discover that he or she has feet. This leads to lifting the legs and putting the feet in the mouth while on the back. Also at this stage, the baby's head will not lag or fall to one side when he or she is placed in a sitting position.

Turning from Back to Stomach

Strong back and hip muscles are required for a baby to be able to turn from the back to the stomach. With consistent tummy time in earlier months, by six months old, a baby will be able to turn from back to stomach and stomach to back interchangeably. Tummy time is very important during the day when the baby is awake and should always be supervised.

Once a baby can turn from the back to the stomach, you will find he or she may turn to the stomach to sleep. There are no studies concerning sleeping on the stomach after babies can roll over, but it's still a good idea to put your baby down on the back initially and check in on him or her often.

The Start of Crawling

Some babies attempt to crawl as early as six months. The crawl is not on all fours but rolling from one side of the room to the other, using only one arm or leg to push themselves.

Holding Hands Together

While your baby began to discover his or her hands at about three months, they are now not as much of a novelty as they are starting to be functional. Your baby will bring the hands together with more purpose—to touch and explore, not just to look at them.

Holding Objects

By now, hand-eye coordination is stronger, so your baby will be able to reach for and hold on to objects. Place safe objects within your baby's reach so he or she can reach for them and exercise this ability.

A great accomplishment for your baby is learning to hold on to his or her bottle when feeding, which may start at four to four and a half months (if a bottle is being used by that time). This takes time and is typically driven from the baby's strong-enough desire to drink the bottle but you not holding it up for him or her. Be patient with this developing skill, because eventually your baby will become better adept at holding and manipulating the bottle by himself or herself.

Grasping Objects

Because a baby's vision is becoming clearer and the muscles are becoming stronger at this point, a four-month-old will start to grasp things with the entire palm of the hand. At five to six months, a baby will be able to hold objects in a bit of a clumsy way between the palm and the enclosed fingers. They can also reach and pick up larger objects now. It's the smaller ones that pose more difficulty, although some six-month-old babies can do it.

Dropping Objects Over and Over

A very big milestone at this stage is a baby's ability to see objects in the vertical line as well as in the horizontal. Imagine what it must be like to suddenly discover that in addition to what's in front of you, there's an "up and down," too. So the world just got much bigger for your baby.

Now if you drop something, your baby will follow it dropping down and will enjoy doing this over and over again to both see it and hear it drop. You will pick up the object, the baby will drop it, and it becomes a game. By six months old, your baby will still follow the object, even if he or she doesn't see it anymore, and will try to find it.

Putting Everything in the Mouth

After four months, your little baby becomes a real explorer. Everything is new and interesting. Watching everything, listening, touching, and putting everything in his or her mouth, your baby doesn't discriminate. Everything in his or her reach—and we literally mean everything—will go into the mouth. It's a normal phase of development and yet another way to experience the world.

Be sure not to leave medications, small objects, breakable items, or anything that could cause harm within your baby's reach. This is the time to start child-proofing your home, because it's never too early. We'll talk more about that later, but be aware that this is when it starts.

Becoming More Social

In months four to six, babies will start to interact with you and others more and more. They are learning to express themselves in different ways, whether it's happy or sad, cheerful or angry.

At this point in time, babies are more aware of their surroundings and their vision is more acute. In a playgroup, their interaction may consist of staring more at the other babies. As they exercise their voices, they'll also hear others and will try to imitate them. Because babies may be at different stages of development, some babies may show off their skills, while others observing and imitating may try new ones.

Expressing Feelings

In this stage, your baby begins to more fully recognize you and close family members. You will experience how wonderful it is to see your little one vigorously bouncing, exuberantly moving arms and legs, and jubilantly smiling and laughing with the people he or she knows best. At or after six months, your baby will start to show "stranger anxiety." He or she may not want to be held by any unfamiliar person and may even start crying by just looking at them. Don't let any friends or relatives take it personally; it's just a phase that will pass at about 12–14 months.

Laughing

The warm little gurgle coming from your baby, the "belly" laugh, is considered an important milestone—aside from being so adorable to see and hear. Babies laugh at whatever amuses them and whatever catches their fancy at the time—you, a toy, or even their hands or feet. Try doing some goofy things to trigger the laughter, such as talking in a funny voice, making funny faces, or playing with a stuffed animal and giving it a voice. Your baby will probably think it's funny.

Reacting and Responding

Four- to six-month-old babies react to facial expressions and even moods. If you smile at your baby, he or she will smile back. If you are sad or crying, your baby may very well do the same. They will also turn toward sounds or light and start responding to their name. By six months, a baby can hand clap when he or she has achieved something.

Also, the six-month-old can understand a few commands, such as when you ask, "How big is the baby?" and the baby responds by lifting the arms up in the air. A baby learns to do this by you saying these same words and modeling the raising of the arms over and over.

Imitating Sounds

Your little bundle of joy is becoming a bundle of noise. If you listen to him or her in the morning, you will hear a lot of babbling. The sounds you'll hear are a repetition of vowels, plus some squealing and laughing.

baby steps

Babbling is the baby's effort to experiment with different sounds in order to express himself or herself. It is a mixture of vowels and consonants in various combinations. The origin of the word "babbling" dates back to ancient times. It's believed that the Greeks referred to any language other than Greek as *babble;* in other words, sounding incoherent.

Some Vowel Sounds

Closer to six months of age, you'll realize that the babbling has different tones and gets louder and louder. Some researchers state that by listening to adults' intonations, babies can differentiate among languages. If you say something to the baby, he or she will respond by imitating you. They may not have the words yet, but they are trying to communicate by mimicking intonation. That's the beginning of a conversation.

Speech Development

Researchers Dr. Barbara L. Davis and Dr. Peter MacNeilage, studying the babbling of children from 6 to 18 months, have demonstrated that patterns of baby-babble seem to be common in many languages. This finding suggests that speech patterns may have had a common origin.

They discovered four sequences of sound patterns, each containing a consonant-vowel combination, common to babbling in general, and to first words in many languages. These sequences illustrate the mechanical use of different parts of the mouth—lip, tongue, and the back of the mouth. So, for example, saying "mama" demonstrates the sequence of a lip consonant with a vowel that emerges from the center of the mouth and with a tongue that is flattened. However, "dada" is a tongue-front consonant with a vowel that comes from the front of the mouth. Try making these sounds yourself. Hopefully, this may put to rest the idea that dada or mama is favored. It's rather the sound the baby can make!

The first words of a baby's vocabulary reflect the baby's everyday world—the people and objects that are in their immediate environment.

This research may provide a useful tool to help children who have difficulties in speech acquisition. Awareness of this may help parents identify problems with speech delay faster, and therefore obtain the help that is needed sooner.

The Language of Crying

By this age, a lot of babies have figured out that if they cry, somebody will come and soothe them. You should always respond to crying and examine the situation to figure out the reason for the crying. Make sure that the baby is not sick, hungry, needs changing, is too hot or cold, or any other uncomfortable state.

Consolable and Inconsolable Crying

If the crying continues, the art of distraction is a good way to try to stop it. You can put on some music or give the baby a favorite toy. Talk in a calm voice and change the environment; for example, from the crib to a play activity mat—and soon the baby will forget why he was crying. This is called consolable crying.

Inconsolable crying means that no matter what you do, the baby will continue to cry. The problem could be teething or gas, but there are more serious problems that you may have to consider. Ask your doctor's advice if this continues for any length of time and is unusual behavior for the baby. Many doctors will want to see the baby to figure out the cause of the inconsolable crying.

Alternatives to Giving In

If the baby stops crying but starts again if you put him back in the same place, and everything else checks out to be fine, then let the baby try to soothe himself or herself. In other words, let the baby cry it out. Eventually, the baby will learn to self-soothe, but this process can take a while—so don't expect him or her to figure it out right away. Naturally, your baby wants to be with you but will have to learn to self-entertain for periods of time. Be sure there are safe things for the baby to play with and look at while he or she is learning to self-soothe. Books, toys, and music can come in very handy at this point.

Essential Takeaways

- The baby is becoming more tactile and mobile.
- Start childproofing places that could be potentially dangerous.
- Social skills are more apparent in your baby now, so continue talking, reading, and singing to your baby in response.
- Teach your baby self-soothing.

chapter 13

Play Time

Age-appropriate activities for the four-, five-, and six-month-old

Outdoor activities you can do with your baby

New toys and activities to excite and stimulate your baby

New clothes for your growing child

Now that the world has become tactile and your baby has more strength and better hand-eye coordination, there are many diverse activities that your baby can do now.

Activities for the Fourth Month

Before we talk about activity, keep in mind that babies need some quiet time just like we all do. If a baby is overstimulated or over-stressed, he or she will have a difficult time settling down at night. If you see your baby getting frustrated during an activity, don't continue it any longer. Stop and move on to something more subdued, and try the other activity again on a different day.

Here are great activities to engage your baby and promote healthy development:

Observing: Your baby learns just by watching you. Because you don't have to carry him or her around as much as you did in the first months, your baby can be part of your activities—sitting nearby while you are doing something. Talk to your baby about what you see and what you are doing.

Reaching: Because by now your baby loves to reach, move a toy in front of him or her—up and down and left and right. Your baby will reach for it. Then move a bit farther away and repeat this exercise. This time, your baby will reach but may or may not be able to touch the toy. If the baby does, smile and clap. These movements will help with hand-eye coordination.

Talking: Talking to your baby is important. If your baby says a little sound such as "aaah," go ahead and imitate it. These are the steps toward language. Your baby will be surprised to hear the same sound repeated.

Singing: Sing and listen to music together—whatever music your baby likes. You will know what he or she likes by the reaction to it. Listen to a variety of music to find the sounds that appeal to him or her. Whether it's classical or hard rock, as long as it's not loud, it's fine and is a wonderful activity to stimulate your baby.

Reading: Give your baby a book (a board book or one made of sturdy material), and read it to him or her. Reading is so important from the very first month. It doesn't matter what you read to your baby; just the act of reading and looking at pages is a stimulating activity for him or her. Your baby may not understand what you're reading, but he or she will know that it's an activity that's very soothing as well as social. Also, show him or her pages with images and colors. The four-month-old loves bright colors and will take great pleasure in seeing them.

baby steps

Babies must also learn how to soothe and entertain themselves. Create a place for your baby to be alone to play safely. Put up baby gates around a large space, ideally free of any furniture, with only safe toys and books. Your baby will not feel confined and will learn to entertain himself or herself in the safe place. Don't leave your baby playing alone for too long, though, and let him or her know that you are always there.

Activities for the Fifth Month

At five months, your baby can accomplish two activities at the same time, such as babbling while reaching or turning while grasping. To stimulate these abilities, put your baby on his or her belly and place toys in front within reach. Let your baby reach them and pick them up. Talk to your baby, and clap when he or she does it. Now put the toys a bit farther to the left and to the right. The baby will try to reach—and in the process may turn.

baby steps

It's okay to still use the bouncy seat at this age, but only for a short time. Be sure to have toys attached to it for visual and tactile experiences.

Blowing bubbles is a great activity at this age as well. Babies love them, are amazed to see them float, and will move toward them to reach them.

At this age, babies love to play with their feet. You can gently push their legs toward the belly, or you can make bicycling movements with their legs. Make sure the baby is always safe wherever you're playing, preferably on a mat on the floor.

Activities for the Six-Month-Old

Your six-month-old is almost sitting unassisted, is turning on both sides, is putting his or her entire weight on the feet, and is even attempting to crawl. These activities will further strengthen your baby's achievements and prepare him or her well for what's to come next.

Holding hands: Put your hands in front of your sitting baby and let him or her hold them. Now move your hands to the right and to the left. When the baby starts to lean over, gently push him or her back to the straight sitting position. This will help strengthen core muscles.

Playing peek-a-boo: Making yourself or toys disappear for a moment behind your hands or a blanket is fun for babies. Your baby will look for but will not yet be able to find what's hidden. Playing pat-a-cake is another favorite.

Singing and dancing: While holding your baby vertically, facing you, sing and dance gently to different music. Any music will do; try all kinds of music to experience different rhythms and tempos. Holding the baby while dancing lends a very different perspective for him or her—a new way to see the world—and the movement will be stimulating.

Reaching and turning: Place your baby on the belly and put toys in front, as well as to the left and right. In trying to reach them, your baby will eventually turn from the belly to the back. Just by trying to reach the toys, the exercise will strengthen the back muscles.

Rolling a ball: Encourage hand-eye coordination as well as physical forward motion by rolling a ball toward and away from your baby. Also, when your baby rolls himself or herself from one corner of a room to the other, it's serious exercise—strengthening muscles for crawling and co-ordination.

Baby watch

Don't use walkers. They're simply not safe. They don't teach the baby to walk; on the contrary, babies can trip and even fall down the stairs. Babies can catch a hand or a finger. Safely enclosed spaces, mats, and bouncers are much better and safer choices.

As always, observe for signs of frustration and tiredness in your baby. Make sure you stop any exercise and activity immediately (or ideally, before these set in).

Getting Out of the House

Babies benefit from getting out of the house and being exposed to new environments and experiences. You will enjoy taking your baby out and about as well (which will help keep you healthy, too). With good planning and timing, babies can enjoy a variety of activities and can certainly come along for the ride for the activities you enjoy.

Swimming

Water activities provide great fun for infants and parents. Most babies react positively to being in the water, even if it takes a little time to get used to it. After all, a baby's first home was surrounded by fluid, so it's likely quite a familiar feeling.

If you take your baby to a pool, be aware that an infant does not have the skills or ability to swim or tread water, even if they are taking swimming lessons as an infant. If you decide to enroll in infant swimming lessons, the lessons should familiarize the baby with the water and the parents with water safety and should be taught by a certified swimming instructor. When in the water, even with floating devices, either your baby should be held at all times or there should be an adult at an arm's-length distance away watching them.

The risk for drowning is not decreased if a baby is enrolled in early swimming classes. Beware of classes that promote this idea. A baby needs to be supervised at all times when in water; even one moment can lead to tragic consequences. Most children are not ready to swim until four to five years of age.

Jogging

Getting fit and bonding with your baby at the same time is the best combination possible. If you like to jog or want to start, choose a jogging stroller carefully, because there are many considerations when pushing your precious cargo in front of you. Handle brakes and sturdy air-filled tires are a necessity. The front wheel must be able to lock into a straight/forward-only position. Also, your baby needs to feel comfortable and the straps must be secure and easy to manipulate. Test-drive the jogging strollers before you purchase one, because they can be expensive and you'll want it to be comfortable for you both.

When you're out jogging, try to jog only on smooth and straight surfaces. Even if you're an experienced jogger, remember that your little baby is not—so try to keep your routes simple. Beware of hills, especially when jogging downhill. Also, be cognizant of the temperature outside when you're jogging. While your body will sweat accordingly to keep you cool, your baby's body cannot. Try to jog only when the temperature is moderate and comfortable for the safety of your baby.

Bicycling

There are a number of options available for taking your baby with you on a bike ride. A trailer attached to the back of your bike is the safest option. There are various brands and prices for a bike trailer. As with the jogging stroller, be sure to evaluate them for safety and comfort before purchasing one. The wheels should be large and sturdy to absorb the shock of bumps. The mechanism that attaches to the bike should enable tipping over of the bike without tipping of the trailer. This allows the baby to remain upright in the trailer even if you have a mishap. When biking, your baby should always be strapped in and wear a little helmet. Trailers with a see-through screen are helpful in protecting against small objects that can fly off the ground.

As with jogging, be sure to bike on smooth and straight surfaces, and pay attention to the outside temperature so your baby doesn't get overheated.

Hiking

Taking your baby out into nature is a wonderful activity. If you weren't really a hiker before you had your baby, it's probably not best to start now—because hiking treacherous hills takes a high level of strength and expertise.

For seasoned hikers, use either a back or front pack for your baby. Make sure that the baby is comfortable and his or her head is stable. The front packs have the advantage that you can see your baby. If you use the back pack, make sure the straps are wide and soft so that the weight is well distributed on your back. Remember that carrying the baby will change the feel of your walk or hike. Stop often and attend to your baby's comfort and needs.

Shopping

It's an interesting activity for babies to see new objects and new people, so shopping with your baby is a great activity. Strapping a baby into the shopping cart at this age is not preferable, however, because there are more than 24,000 injuries a year from doing it. It's safer to carry the baby in a carrier or stroller or have another adult with you when shopping.

Use the carts with the special infant seat on them whenever possible, and check the straps before you put your baby inside to make sure they work. The AAP recommends not putting your own infant seat or car seat in the cart. Do not allow an older child to push the shopping cart when the baby is in it.

Yoga

Babies have natural yoga movements: arching the back when on the stomach, lifting the head and chest when on the back, holding the feet, and so on. Baby yoga is very popular in the United States, and there are many places offering classes and many classes from which to choose. It's a great way for the parent to relax, bond with the baby, and meet new friends. Check in advance that the instructor is certified specifically in infant and child yoga.

Many structured classes are not necessary at this age. Free movement and the parent's involvement is what babies need the most at this age. That's what they thrive on.

New Toys and Clothes

By now, your baby is ready for some different types of toys and clothes to go with his or her expanding abilities and interests.

Toys

Your baby will need some new toys in order to keep up with an increasing repertoire of movement, clearer vision, and the love for everything loud, colorful, and moving. When you buy toys, choose some that you can also take with you when you go outside. Please keep in mind that babies at this age also love to tear paper apart, bang boxes together, and feel different textures of fabric. It's fun and less expensive than many toys. An activity mat for this age is more complex. It's bigger and has lights, hanging interchangeable toys, and music and is "kick-activated" for those ever-moving feet. Hand-held toys are enjoyed at this age as well. It can be a rattle, a squeezable toy, or a teething ring. This is the time when teething starts, so a teething ring (cold, not frozen) will accomplish double duty.

Starting around this age, babies will choose a favorite toy or object—another milestone, called the *transitional object.* This is the toy your baby will come to favor and may want to bring along everywhere you go.

At five months, babies are fascinated by mirrors. If the mirror is a toy, it needs to be made specifically for infants (without any sharp corners). You can buy them with or without other attached toys, music, or lights. Roly-poly toys that move and wobble but don't roll are favorites, as is most anything with music.

Your baby will soon understand a cause-and-effect relationship. By pushing a button, something happens. Toys with buttons to push or knobs to turn are good for this age. They also love pushing elevator buttons and cell phone buttons. By six months, action-reaction activities, such as pushing or pulling something and toys with music or things that pop up, are enjoyed, and toys utilizing this concept become absolute favorites.

Your baby can start playing with stacking toys, too. Buy larger, round, and brightly colored ones (red, green, blue, and yellow) that are easier to grab and stack.

As always, do not forget to remove all toys from the baby's crib. Soon, the mobile will have to go, too, because the baby will be able to sit up and grab it.

Clothes

You will notice by now how fast your baby grows out of clothes. Those adorable, tiny newborn clothes are now a thing of the past, and you'll be making room in those drawers for all-new bigger clothes. As always, wash all new clothes before the baby wears them the first time.

For sleeping, say goodbye to the first sleep sacks; the baby has likely outgrown them by now. You can get a larger sleep sack or one-piece pajamas. All night clothes must be flame resistant, and cut the labels out because they tend to scratch the baby's neck. Buy clothes that are not difficult to pull over the baby's head. If your baby is uncomfortable, he or she will protest (loudly). Pants are easiest if they pull on and have snaps in the legs for easy changing. Clothes should, as always, be comfortable for your baby to play and move around in as well.

As your baby becomes more mobile, diaper changing will become more challenging—and speed will be the key. Clothes with snaps in the legs are essential; otherwise, you have to undress your baby each time. Have everything you need at your fingertips and be ready to rush into action, accomplishing the changing task quickly. Remember, your baby's world is rapidly expanding. What used to be a pleasant time on the changing table is now viewed by your baby as minutes wasted from exploration.

A snow suit should be easy to put on and not constrict the baby's movements. Many baby carriers have snuggly baby enclosure accessories that attach for the baby to keep warm, and they are easy to zip for taking the baby in and out. Some type of covering for the head is essential in cold weather. Some babies do not like hats, so a hood may be a good idea.

A baby doesn't need shoes until he walks outside, and socks have to have a nonskid surface. It's best for the baby to go barefoot at home; it's safe and tones the muscles.

Use sunscreen from age three months, and buy one that is made specifically for infants. When it's very sunny, put sunglasses on (if your baby allows it).

Last, don't overdress your baby. Dress your little one as you would dress yourself, with an extra layer.

Ear Piercing

In different cultures, piercing of ears is common for an infant (mainly a girl) and is done at different ages. If you decide to pierce your baby's ears, take the following precautions:

Go to either a pediatrician's office or a reputable place with strict hygiene.

Make sure the person performing the procedure has experience with infants.

Hold the baby in your lap.

Give the baby pain medication before the procedure (infant acetaminophen).

Use only precious metals such as sterling silver, stainless-steel or 14K-gold earrings, and avoid cheap metals such as nickel because they can be irritants to the skin.

Use only studs—no hoops or any hanging earrings.

Keep the studs in the ear for at least six weeks, making sure they are snug to the backing but not squeezed tightly on the earlobe.

Clean the surface of the ears every day, front and back.

Call the doctor if the baby has an allergic reaction, has swollen and red earlobes, or if there is pus or a fever.

It is generally recommended to wait until the baby has had three tetanus vaccines (by six months) before piercing the ears. Do not pierce the ears before six weeks of age.

Essential Takeaways

- Play, talk, sing, dance, and read with your baby. There's never too much of this kind of interaction, at any age.
- Take safety measures for all outdoor activities. What you would do for yourself, do with extra care and vigilance when it comes to your child. Know your environment, understand the "rules" of the activity, and educate yourself about any special equipment you will be using.
- Do not overwhelm the baby with too many activities. Allow the baby to concentrate with focused attention on one activity at a time. Know when your baby needs to stop.
- Toys should be safe and age appropriate. Research and carefully examine all toys before your baby uses them.

chapter 14

Eating and Sleeping

Beginning to eat solid food

The feeding schedule and portion sizes

Preparing food at home

Sleep training methods

Now that you've mastered breastfeeding or feeding with formula, new challenges await. Your baby is ready to start solid food—of course, as an addition to breast milk or formula. Calling it "solid" food is not exactly accurate, however, because it's really food that is very soft or pureed. This stage of graduating to solids is a new one for you and your little one. It's an exciting and fun time, but it could potentially also be a bit stressful—and definitely messy.

You will surely get lots of advice from your parents, friends, and others. It's true that in past generations, infants were fed solids much earlier than six months of age. However, doctors have learned that feeding solids very early can trigger allergies or cause difficulty with digestion. So when faced with everyone's opinions on feeding, be a diplomat: thank everyone for their caring advice, and do exactly what *you* think is in your baby's best interests.

Nutrition for All Babies

Here's what babies need to eat in order to grow well:

Milk (breast milk and/or formula) is essential for the first six months (with some exceptions) as discussed in previous chapters. But as the baby grows, other nutrients become very important: proteins, carbohydrates, fats, and vitamins.

Proteins are made up of substances called amino acids. They are essential in the growth process, but especially in case of illness. Proteins also provide energy. Protein is found in meat, dairy, beans, tofu, soy, chickpeas, lentils, and fish.

Carbohydrates provide energy and fiber. There are simple carbohydrates, such as fructose in fruits and galactose in milk, double carbohydrates such as lactose and sucrose, and complex carbohydrates. The complex "carbs" can be found in legumes or starchy vegetables. Carbohydrates are also found in refined products such as candy, soda, and cookies. While the natural carbohydrates help the body, too many refined ones only contribute to elevated blood sugar levels and increased fat deposits.

Fats are important for energy, and the storage of fat helps prevent loss of heat. The right kind of fats and the right amounts of them are essential. There are saturated fats (red meat, butter, lard, full fat dairy) and unsaturated fats (olive oil, fish, soy, safflower, canola oil, and avocado). Eating too much of the saturated fats will lead to high levels of cholesterol and many other health problems. By using unsaturated fats in moderation, you'll also give your baby extra vitamins that are soluble in fat: vitamins A, D, E, and K.

Vitamins are in formula and most solid foods. Breastfed and vegan babies need vitamin supplementation to get what they need. Babies who are fed fresh and varied foods will usually not need any supplementation. In order to preserve the vitamins found in vegetables, steam or lightly cook them, or have the baby eat them raw (only bananas and avocados in the beginning).

Iron is important for muscle development and for the production of healthy blood. It can be found in meat, eggs, dairy, brown rice, beans, peas, asparagus, dark leaf greens, soy, lentils, chickpeas, fortified cereal, quinoa, millet, and chocolate.

Vitamin A is essential for good vision and growth. It's found in carrots, fish, tomatoes, dark green vegetables (kale, spinach, and collard greens), peaches, squash, eggs, and dairy.

B vitamins are needed for the nervous system, energy, and digestion. They are found in meat, fish, whole grain cereals, dark green vegetables, legumes, and melons.

Vitamin C helps the body to heal wounds and keeps all tissues healthy. It abounds in citrus, fruits, berries, broccoli, bell peppers, spinach, cauliflower, beets, papaya, and tomatoes.

Vitamin D is made in the skin when exposed to sunlight and is important for bone development (along with calcium). It is found in fish, eggs, dairy, and oils.

Calcium is an important mineral that works with Vitamin D to provide strong bones, healthy teeth, and normal growth. It's found in dairy, fish, broccoli, legumes, beans, and flour.

Zinc is a mineral that aids in the efficiency of the immune system. It's also needed for wound healing and helps the sense of taste and smell. It's found in nuts, seeds, legumes, and eggs.

Introducing Solids

Traditionally, starting a baby on single-grain rice cereal has been the way to introduce solids, because this cereal is easy to digest. There are other varieties of infant cereal available today, such as oatmeal and barley, which are suitable to use as well. The cereal can be mixed with water, breast milk, or formula to a smooth consistency for feeding with a spoon.

Don't put any cereal or other food in the bottle. Your baby needs to eat everything in a sitting position, fed with a spoon. Once cereal is being taken, you start introducing stage one baby foods—either buying the commercial brands or making your own baby food. We'll talk more about preparing your baby's food later in this chapter.

Introducing solid food typically starts around six months—and sometimes earlier, in the case where a baby is still hungry, even with enough breast milk or formula. Feeding solids can get very confusing, so we'll take you through the process and give you tips to help your experience be as successful as possible.

Your baby should be ready in the following ways for eating solids:

- The *extrusion reflex* (pushing everything out of the mouth with the tongue) is disappearing.

- Your baby can sit with support.

- Your baby takes food from a spoon and swallows it.

- Your baby is very interested in what you eat.

- Your baby is still hungry, even if fed with the appropriate amount of breast milk or formula.

The Swallowing Process

Do you know how complicated the swallowing process is? Food is pushed around the mouth and then moves to the pharynx, which connects the mouth to the esophagus. This, in turn, is connected to the stomach. There are about 50 pairs of muscles and at least 5 different cranial nerves, as well as other reflexes that all work together.

It's a good idea to have at least one meal a day together with your baby as a family. We understand that people's hectic lifestyles, with different schedules and shifts, may not work toward this goal, but try. Even if you're not hungry, sit at the table together. Television, newspapers, and toys provide distraction from the table and the food. Teaching the baby good habits early on (and maybe breaking habits of your own that are not so good) will stay with your child forever.

Your baby should sit in a high chair with a strap. Remember, he or she will be curious and will reach and grab everything in sight. Try to prepare the meal before your baby gets too hungry and super fussy. It's the same issue as with breastfeeding—knowing the pre-hunger and pre-cry sounds.

You'll need baby eating utensils. The spoon should be small and shallow, and the plate or bowl should be made from a resistant, nontoxic material.

Put a very small amount of food on the spoon. Two things can happen: your baby will eat it fast, love it, and open his or her mouth like a little bird or make funny faces and spit it out.

If the second scenario occurs, stop and try again in a little while. If the response is the same, you may want to wait a few days and try a different food. You can go back to the initial food in a few weeks.

Don't reduce the amount of breast milk or formula you give your baby. You're only at the beginning of adding more food, and you don't know yet how your baby will react. The milk or formula will be reduced when your baby is eating two to three solid-food meals a day.

When Do I Feed Solids?

The first solid foods are given once a day, and the time of day is up to you and your schedule. Find a time that may be less stressful and time sensitive for you, because feeding solids takes a lot of time and patience. You could try mid-morning, lunch time, or dinner time, but keep it the same every day. You can introduce a new baby food every two to three days and give the *same* food for two to three days.

Baby watch

After trying every new food, watch for any signs of allergy: rash, swelling of the lips or face, diarrhea, vomiting, or a runny nose. These are emergencies, and contact your doctor immediately if any of these symptoms occur after eating. Stop giving your baby the offending food, and go back to something you know is safe the next day.

How Much Will the Baby Eat?

Usually, a baby will take two to four ounces of solid food—more or less—per feeding at around five to six months, and more after that. Every baby is different, and it really depends on the individual baby. Chances are that a baby will take a few teaspoons of cereal the first day and more as the days progress. The first few days of solids will be "practice" as the baby gets acquainted with the new texture and flavor, so don't worry if he or she doesn't eat much at first. Formula or breast milk should be given *after* the solid food, not before, so the baby will be hungry enough to try this new food (hopefully). Remember to give the same amount of formula or breast milk until the baby is eating two to three solid meals per day. Also, babies may eat less after a growth spurt or if they don't feel well. They're tiny people, and they'll have their good days and bad days with food.

How Will I Know Whether the Baby Wants More?

Your baby will certainly let you know when he or she wants more to eat. Here are the signs to look for:

- Opening his or her mouth like a little bird when finished swallowing

- Trying to grab the spoon

- Trying to eat from the bowl if you're not fast enough

Make sure the baby has completely swallowed the first spoonful of food before giving the next, no matter how eager he or she may be.

How Will I Know When the Baby Is Full?

As with wanting more, your baby will let you know when he or she has had enough to eat. Watch for these signs, and don't force any more food once you see any of these:

- Closing the mouth as the spoon approaches

- Spitting the food out or spitting up

- Turning the head away

Believe or not, babies know exactly when they're done. Obviously, if a baby refuses to eat or drink for an extended period of time, consult your doctor.

Feeding Schedule

Starting your baby on solids is a process that takes time and patience. Closely observe how your baby reacts to the new food(s), and allow him or her time to get used to it. Don't worry if your baby doesn't eat all the food you make. The beginning is about getting your baby used to eating in a new way and getting used to new flavors and textures.

The following schedule will help you navigate the first few weeks when feeding solids. Before you know it, your baby will be eating solids like a pro.

First Week

First day: If you're starting with baby cereal, it is different than what you might expect cereal to look like. Baby cereal is usually in powder or "dry" form. (You can also buy it pre-mixed.) Start with single-grain rice cereal for two to three days, and then you can try oatmeal and then barley.

Put one to two teaspoons of cereal in a small baby bowl. Add one ounce of formula or breast milk. It will look thin, which is fine because the baby is used to liquids and may like it more than something that is too thick. Feed your baby this cereal from a spoon, being patient as he or she gets to know this new sensation in his or her mouth.

Day 2: Add an extra two to three teaspoons of cereal, which will thicken the consistency a bit.

Day 3: Add an extra two to three teaspoons. Now the cereal will have the granular consistency of oatmeal or farina.

Day 4: Start two to three ounces of a new solid food—either another kind of cereal or a pureed fruit or vegetable (either commercial baby food or homemade). The fruit or vegetable can also be mixed with cereal.

Days 5 and 6: Have the same food as introduced in Day 4.

Day 7: Start another new food. All of these new foods should be given once a day.

Second Week

In the second week, solids are given twice a day—either breakfast and lunch or lunch and dinner, whatever you prefer.

First day: Let's say you're giving food for breakfast and lunch. For breakfast, give a cereal that you've tried before; for lunch, a new pureed fruit or vegetable.

Days 2 and 3: Do the same. You can change breakfast by giving another cereal that you've tried before (vegetable or fruit). Lunch stays the same.

Day 4: Breakfast will be any familiar cereal, fruit, or vegetable; at lunch, give a new fruit or vegetable.

Days 5 and 6: Do the same. Vary the breakfast with a familiar food.

Day 7: Meat isn't necessary, but you can give it at this time if you want. It's also fine to wait until eight months of age before introducing meat.

baby steps

Generally, babies like meat mixed with a vegetable or a fruit (an already-tried one); offer chicken or turkey in the beginning. Most commercial baby foods have chicken, turkey, and beef varieties pureed with fruits or vegetables.

Give four fewer ounces of breast milk or formula. Breakfast will consist of cereal, fruit, or a vegetable. At lunch, meat can be given with a tried fruit or vegetable.

After you've tried a variety of foods for two to three days, you can mix as you please. Don't try more than one new food, and always try them for two to three days. At the same time, you can give the baby all foods that you have tried before.

Third Week

Your baby is ready for food three times a day. An example of a menu is offered later in this chapter. Now you can reduce the amount of fluid to 26 ounces (800–900 ml), because more of their nutritional needs are being met with the solid foods.

Water

You can start giving your baby water at six months. If it's good-quality water, filter it; there's no need to boil it. If not, boil and cool the water. Bottled water, as well as water from other sources, does not contain fluoride. If there is no fluoride in the water, your doctor will prescribe a vitamin with fluoride for the baby. Call your local health department for more information about your water supply.

It's a good idea to give the baby water from a completely different bottle than usually used (or even a sippy cup). Your baby will understand the difference between water and what he or she drank before. The baby may refuse the water in the beginning. Just try again when your baby is thirsty.

Fruit juices are not recommended at this time. In juice form, the good fiber in fruit is removed. Eating a fruit or a vegetable and drinking water is a better choice.

Sample Menu

By now, your baby is getting used to new foods and probably enjoying this variety of new flavors. To keep the consistency of what he or she knows while expanding his or her food horizons, here is a sample menu for the weeks after your baby has gotten the hang of eating solids.

Breakfast

Monday: Rice cereal, applesauce, and water and/or breast milk or formula. You will already have a few ounces of formula in the cereal, so only two to three ounces (60–100ml) in the bottle is needed.

Tuesday: Oatmeal cereal and pears; same amount of fluid

Wednesday: Barley cereal and peaches; same amount of fluid

Thursday: Mixed cereal and apples; same amount of fluid

Friday: Cereal and fruit; four to six ounces of formula plus water

Saturday: Cereal and fruit combination; same amount of fluid

Sunday: Mixed cereal and fruit; same amount of fluid

Mid-morning: Breast milk or formula, four to five ounces (120–150ml)—the same for every day of the week

Lunch

Monday: Chicken and carrots; water, formula, or breast milk (two to three ounces, or 60–100ml)

Tuesday: Sweet potato and a fruit; same amount of fluid

Wednesday: Carrots and green beans; same amount of fluid

Thursday: Turkey with peas; same amount of fluid

Friday: Turkey and fruit; same amount of fluid

Saturday: Chicken and potatoes; same amount of fluid

Sunday: Chicken with a vegetable; same amount of fluid

Mid-afternoon: Breast milk or formula (four to five ounces, or 120–150ml); the same for every day of the week

Dinner

Monday: Fruit and/or vegetable; water; and later, breast milk or formula (two to three ounces, or 60–100ml)

Tuesday: Any familiar fruit or vegetable; same amount of fluid

Wednesday: Cereal and a vegetable; same amount of fluid

Thursday: Fruit and/or a vegetable; same amount of fluid

Friday: Cereal and a vegetable or fruit; same amount of fluid

Saturday: Fruit and/or a vegetable; same amount of fluid

Sunday: A vegetable and/or fruit; same amount of fluid

When Teething Begins

Teething can start as early as two to three months, but for most babies it begins around four to five months. Teething doesn't mean that you'll see teeth right away; rather, it describes the process of teeth emerging (pushing their way through the gums). This process can be painful for your little one. The first teeth to appear are usually the lower incisors (front two teeth).

When teething begins, your baby will produce an increased amount of saliva, will put his or her fingers in the mouth, and will cry. You can give pain medication and/or apply a teething ointment or cream to the gums. It's also helpful to massage the lower gums and give your baby a teething ring. We will cover more on teething in Chapter 18.

Babies may refuse to eat on days when teething is very painful, so don't force the baby to eat. Simply increase the amount of breastfeeding or formula on those days to compensate. Try to remember how you feel when you have a toothache!

Easy First Foods to Make Yourself

Baby food can be bought or prepared at home. With hectic schedules, many modern families may feel that commercial baby food is a blessing. But for some, it's just too expensive. And still others simply prefer to cook their own food. You can always cook more of everything to feed older children or yourselves, as well. Remove the cooked food for the baby first, and use the rest for the family.

Making your own baby food is not as complicated as it sounds. All you need is a small pot, a small steamer, and a blender or chopper. There are also electric baby food makers that you can buy, which steam and puree baby food all in one unit.

Fresh fruits and vegetables, without a doubt, taste the best. If possible, buy seasonal, locally grown produce. Buying organic is purely a personal decision. It is more expensive and can be harder to find depending on where you live. But organic or not, fresh produce is a great choice whenever possible. Frozen vegetables and fruits are fine to use (check the date), but try to steer clear of anything canned. Always peel the produce before cooking, and steaming is recommended because there is less of a chance of losing their nutrition.

baby steps

The general consensus is that baby food needs to be as bland as possible at first. But before long, your baby will desire more depth of flavor. There are ways to make food taste more interesting, aside from adding salt and sugar. While now is not the time to be spicing up the menu, you can use fresh herbs: basil, oregano, parsley, dill, cinnamon (very small amounts), and lemon after six months. As with everything else, try them for at least three days.

Fruit Purees

Applesauce: Most babies love applesauce. Use a ripe apple. Peel and cut it into pieces. Remove the core and all seeds. Steam or cook in enough water, just to cover the fruit, until soft. Remove the apple. Either mash it with a fork or process it in the blender. Add cooking water so it won't be too thick. If this is the first time you're making it, remove one ounce and cool it to room temperature. Add a pinch of cinnamon. Put it in a separate plate or bowl, and feed it to the baby with a spoon. One to three medium-size apples will make a cup of applesauce.

Mix half an amount of cereal and half an amount of applesauce, then add two to three ounces of either breast milk or formula. Discard whatever your baby doesn't eat from the bowl used with the spoon.

You can also bake the apples: after peeling, coring, and seeding the apple, place it in the oven at 350° Fahrenheit for about 30—45 minutes. Mash or blend with two teaspoons of water, breast milk, or formula. Cool. You can do the same thing with pears; they'll bake faster, around 30 minutes.

Pear puree: Two to four pears will make a cup of pear sauce. Peel, core, and seed one to two pears. Cover with water, and cook or steam for around 10 minutes. Check the softness with a fork. Mash or blend with one to two teaspoons of the cooking water. Don't feed the baby from the entire prepared amount. You will want to refrigerate or freeze the rest. You may mix this puree with dried cereal.

Peach puree: Four to six peaches will make a cup of puree. Peel and remove the pit. Cut the peach in pieces. Cook in water for five minutes. Cool, mash, and serve. You can also bake it at 400° Fahrenheit. Add water (one inch) to an oven-proof pan and bake until you see bubbles. Cool, mash, and serve.

Banana puree: A ripe banana can be served before age six months. Mash the banana and serve.

Avocado

An avocado is high in fiber, vitamins, and minerals and contains the good fats (mono-unsaturated). Two avocados will make one cup mashed. Avocado and banana are the only fruits you should not cook. The avocado has a pit, so botanically, it is a fruit.

Peel and remove the pit. Mash and serve. You can mix avocado with bananas, pears, and squash.

Carrots

Use small, young (baby) carrots. The best way to cook them is to steam them. Peel and cut carrots in small pieces. Steam for about 8 to 10 minutes or until tender. Mash them. You can serve them plain or add some fresh, finely chopped thyme or oregano (simmered for two minutes), but be careful with herbs because only a very small amount is needed; otherwise, it will overpower the taste of the carrots. Carrots are great because they can be mixed with other fruits, vegetables, and meat.

baby
watch

Carrots, beets, spinach, and collard greens have natural nitrites, so you should wait until six months to give these veggies. The reason is these root vegetables get the nitrites from the soil, and up to age three months the baby's stomach doesn't produce enough acid to fight them. The nitrites can get into the bloodstream where they affect the oxygen transport. These babies have a bluish color (blue baby syndrome or methemoglobinemia), and the blood is brown instead of red. Such a problem is very rare, but if it occurs, go to the emergency room immediately. By five to six months, when the majority of babies start solid foods, the stomach is well-equipped to digest these vegetables properly.

Peas and Other Vegetables

Peas are steamed or cooked in just enough water to cover them. When they're soft, puree them. Other vegetables that can be prepared the same way are green beans, squash, and zucchini.

Sweet potatoes are often a favorite for babies. They can be peeled, chopped, and steamed, then mashed or pureed in the blender. Or they can be baked in the oven at 350° Fahrenheit until soft when pierced with a fork (about one hour). Cut the baked sweet potato in half, and scoop out the cooked part. Mash and let cool before serving. Regular potatoes can be prepared the same way.

A vegetable can be mixed with fruits and other vegetables to serve your baby; just mix and match as you please.

Baby steps

If you notice that your baby's face, palms, and soles are turning orange after introducing solid foods, there's no need to worry. This happens because the orange and yellow vegetables (mostly favored by babies) contain beta carotene, which can turn into a form of vitamin A. This gets deposited in the skin because there are higher levels of it in the blood. Carrots, squash, and sweet potatoes are all high in this substance. Do you remember the color of colostrum? It's dark yellow, also due to this substance.

All you have to do is give fewer yellow and orange vegetables and more green ones. Your little pumpkin's color will soon return to normal.

Poultry

Start with a boneless, skinless chicken breast. Steam it in water, or bake it (covered) for 30 minutes until the meat is very soft. Cut it into one-inch pieces and put it in the blender with four teaspoons of the cooking liquid. Blend it, then add any fruit or vegetable. You can mix in a very small amount of fresh or dried herbs, such as basil, parsley, dill, or oregano, for a new taste.

Cook turkey as you would chicken. Mix apples, peaches, or sweet potato and squash with it. You can also bake the meat together with vegetables, then puree them.

It's easy to make your baby's first chicken soup.

Ingredients:

½ cup cooked and pureed chicken (or turkey)	A few pieces dill, or a pinch of dried dill
1 celery stalk	4 cups water
1 potato, 1 carrot, and 1 zucchini	

Peel and chop vegetables. Cook until they're soft. Add the meat. Put them in the blender or food processor; mix until pureed.

Food Storage

When storing the baby food you make, use small containers that can easily be pulled from the refrigerator or freezer for one meal. You can refrigerate the food for 48 hours or freeze it for 4 to 5 weeks. Use ice trays in the freezer to portion the food. Try to find small ice trays and cover them well, either with a freezer plastic cover or an ice tray cover. Each cube is almost one ounce, or 32 grams.

Pop out whatever you think the baby will eat, and put the rest back. You can also put all the cubes in special freezer bags and use the tray to make new food. Always label everything with the date.

How much your baby will eat at any given meal will vary somewhat, so it's important to know that whatever food is left over in the bowl at the end of the meal should be discarded and not saved for later. The reason for this is bacteria can accumulate on the food touched by the baby's mouth. Also, baby food that has been thawed should not be refrozen or refrigerated and must be discarded. Bacteria can grow when food sits at room temperature, so only pull out the portion you want to use at that time.

Don't use the microwave to warm up the baby food; it cooks unevenly and can produce hot spots in the food. Instead, thaw at room temperature or overnight in the refrigerator. Don't ever refrigerate or refreeze any portions of food left over after eating.

Meats can be stored for 48 hours in the refrigerator and for 3 to 4 weeks in the freezer, either in small containers, ice cube trays, or freezer bags. Never refreeze, and discard the container from which the baby ate.

The Right Size Portions

Every baby is different, and every baby will eat different foods and in different amounts at mealtime. The following is a general guide to portions, but your baby will let you know what's right for him or her:

> Cereal: ¼–½ cup mixed with formula, breast milk, and/or fruits
>
> Fruits: ¼–½ cup pureed
>
> Vegetables: ¼–½ cup pureed
>
> Chicken or turkey: 1–2 tablespoons; use half of each if you mix them

If You're Vegetarian or Vegan

All breastfed babies are vegetarian, whether you are or not, until you introduce animal products into their solid-food diet. If you are vegetarian or vegan and would like your baby to be as well, introduce cereal and vary all the fruits and vegetables we discussed in this chapter. You'll give your baby soy formula if you are not breastfeeding, and mix it with solid foods if you prefer. We'll talk in an upcoming chapter about meat, dairy, and egg substitutes. The most important thing for vegetarian or vegan babies is that they get enough of the required vitamins and minerals for their growing bodies. Giving them a vitamin supplement may be necessary. Talk to your doctor if you plan to make your baby's diet vegetarian or vegan to ensure he or she is getting all the necessary nutrients.

Types of Vegetarians

All vegetarians are not alike. Different variations in the diet comprise different types of vegetarians. Common types of vegetarians include:

> **Lacto-ovo:** eats dairy and eggs.

> **Lacto-vegetarian:** eats dairy but no eggs.

> **Ovo-vegetarian:** eats eggs and no dairy.

> **Pesci-vegetarian:** eats fish.

> **Vegan:** only eats foods derived from plants.

The vegetarian or vegan mother needs to have a healthy, varied diet supplemented with vitamins during pregnancy and while breastfeeding. The first four to six months are the same for all babies. Breastfeeding is best, and the baby should be given vitamin D supplements. Ask the doctor if your baby needs extra vitamin B_{12}.

When starting solid foods, cereals must be fortified. The diet is considered a healthy choice if a variety of foods (see the list above) and vitamins are given.

An improper diet is noted when there is a deficiency of iron, zinc, vitamin D, vitamin B_{12}, and vitamin B_6. Zinc deficiency is manifested by brittle nails, loss of appetite, and a rash around the mouth and extremities. Symptoms of iron deficiency are tiredness and pale dry skin.

Vitamin B_{12} deficiency is marked by irritability, difficulty sleeping, and numbness. And finally, symptoms of vitamin B_6 deficiency are weight loss and inability to sleep.

When the baby turns one year old, the mom can continue to breastfeed or start soy milk, which is vegetarian (currently only one manufacturer makes it vegan). Goat and rice milk are not good choices for a baby.

Vegetarian-Vegan Recipes

Here's a variety of vegetarian recipes for every meal of the day.

Quinoa with Fruits

Ingredients:

¼ cup quinoa cooked

2 tsp. berries (or any other fresh fruit)

1 tsp. brown sugar

Pinch of cinnamon

Mix and enjoy. It's great for breakfast and is also a great snack.

Tofu Smoothie

Ingredients:

1.5 oz of tofu

1 peach

½ banana

Juice from ½ an orange

Cinnamon (to taste)

½ tsp. cereal

Place all ingredients in a blender and puree. Sprinkle the cereal on top and enjoy.

Veggie Stew

Ingredients:

1 onion, cut into small slices

1 tomato, sliced

1 bell pepper, seeded and sliced

½ tsp. olive oil

Pinch of dill, parsley and thyme

Heat the oil in a pan and add the onion. Let it lightly brown. Add the bell pepper and tomato. Add dill, parsley, and thyme.

Cook until all vegetables are soft.

For variation, cook brown rice or potatoes and mix them with the vegetables.

Tofu with Veggies

Ingredients:

1 oz tofu	½ onion, chopped
½ celery stalk, chopped	Parsley and dill
½ carrot, peeled and diced	½ tsp. olive oil (or you can omit this and steam if you prefer)

Heat the oil in a pan, add the onion, and let it brown. Add the carrot and celery. After 2–3 minutes, add the tofu and mix well with the vegetables. Add dill and parsley.

Fruit Compote

Ingredients:

1 apple, cored and sliced	1 slice of lemon
1 plum, sliced	Pinch of cinnamon
1 peach, peeled and sliced	2 tsp. brown sugar
	2 cups water

Boil water with the sugar and cinnamon. Add the fruits and cook until they are soft. Squeeze the slice of lemon over the mixture. Cool. Serve as is or on top of a pancake or waffle. (This can be used for breakfast.)

Sleep Training

By now, when it comes to sleeping (among other things), things have changed. You should be able to have a few uninterrupted hours of sleep at night because the number of night feedings will be fewer. Most babies will sleep a stretch of five to six or more hours, which is heaven compared to two or three!

Continue to reinforce the bedtime routine you have established, such as quiet play, dinner, a bath, reading, and changing into night clothes.

By now, your baby's afternoon naptime can experience a shift as well. Try to have the afternoon nap a little earlier, if possible, to leave more waking hours between the end of the nap and bedtime. The baby will be tired come bedtime and will likely sleep well for a longer stretch.

When it comes to sleeping, consistency is most important. Everyone who cares for the baby needs to understand that and stick to the bedtime routine.

Your baby is old enough now to begin the process of teaching him or her how to sleep for longer stretches through the night. There are two theories about how to accomplish this task—the crying-it-out method, otherwise referred to as Dr. Ferber's method (he is the director of the Child Sleeping Center in Boston), and the noncrying method.

The Ferber Method

This method of "crying it out" means that you will have to be up a lot for a few nights in a row before your baby gets the hang of going back to sleep on his or her own in the night. After about four or five nights, most babies will get it. Don't try this method before four months of age.

If you try this method, keep in mind your baby will cry a lot. You also have to remain consistent every night or you'll have to start over from the beginning. The idea is that babies will learn that they need to soothe themselves after a few days and will be able to fall back asleep on their own in the night.

Here's how you do it. Put the baby in the bassinet or crib while he or she is still awake but drowsy. If the baby wakes up and cries, wait and go into the room after five minutes. Talk to and touch the baby, but *don't* pick him or her up, and don't turn the light on. The second time the baby wakes up, go into the room after 10 minutes. After the third time and throughout the night, go in only after 15 minutes.

The second night, start waiting 10 minutes before going into your baby's room. Increase to 15 minutes and then 20 minutes for subsequent cries.

Every night, you'll increase the going-in time by an extra five minutes. By the third night, go into the room for 15 minutes, then 20 minutes, and then 30 minutes. Many babies typically sleep for long stretches by the fourth or fifth night.

Pros of this method are that after a few nights, your baby will learn to soothe himself or herself and you can get some more sleep.

Cons are that you will likely have to repeat the cycle several times, and it's difficult for parents to hear their baby crying for a long time. Plus, the parents have a loss of sleep.

The Noncrying Method

For this method, do your bedtime routine every night, and have a transitional object for your baby. In the night, you'll get your baby every time you hear him or her crying and either stay in the baby's room or bring the baby into your room to get him or her back to sleep. You can rock and sing to the baby to pacify him or her, and eventually, the baby will go to sleep knowing that you are there. Once the baby goes back to sleep, you can put him or her back in the crib, and if all goes well, everyone goes back to sleep.

Pros of this method are that the baby is reassured that the parent is always there before going to sleep, and there is no long-term crying in the night.

Cons of this method are that the baby will get used to somebody always being there and will become dependent on it, so it takes much longer to get a baby to eventually sleep on his or her own.

Try each method and see what works best for you and your baby. Remember to have patience and ask your partner to help in the night.

Essential Takeaways

- Starting solid food typically occurs at six months.
- Try a new fruit or vegetable for three days in a row and only one new food at a time.Solid foods should be fully cooked until soft, then pureed and fed with a spoon.
- Always discard what is left over in the bowl used for feeding.
- Stay consistent about the bedtime routine, and choose the sleep method that works best for you and your family.

chapter 15

From a Medical Perspective

Well-baby doctor visits: checking milestones and receiving vaccines

Common medical conditions and symptoms in the four-, five-, and six-month-old

When to call your doctor

What to do in an emergency

Your baby will have regular well-baby visits at the pediatrician's office at four months and six months. At the physical exam, the baby's height, weight, and head circumference will be checked, and the doctor will let you know how the baby is growing. The doctor will enter these measurements on your baby's growth chart and explain how they translate in terms of percentiles.

With percentiles, what matters is that they remain consistent for the height, weight, and head circumference of *your* baby. For instance, if your baby started at the 50th percentile or lower and is growing the same in all parameters, that's fine. There's no reason to compare your child with the baby who was born at the 95th percentile and stays there. The time to be concerned is if the percentiles change or become different for the different parameters; for example, 30th percentile for weight and 80th percentile for height, or vice versa.

Your baby's development and milestone achievements will be checked as well. There'll be a discussion about feeding and whether or not the baby is ready for or already eating solid foods.

At four months, your baby will receive the following vaccines: diphtheria, tetanus, pertussis, pneumococcal, HIB, Rotavirus, and Hepatitis B.

Baby steps

There are two Rotavirus vaccines that your baby could get. One is given in a series of two, at two and four months; the other is given in a series of three, at two, four, and six months. Make sure you know which Rotavirus vaccine your baby receives.

There are no vaccines given at five months of age unless your baby missed previous ones. At six months, he or she will receive the same vaccines (with or without the Rotavirus, depending on the vaccine type). When the baby gets the flu vaccine at six months, it's a very good idea for parents, caretakers, and older siblings to get the flu vaccine as well.

You can relax now. The next set of vaccines will not be given until 12 months of age. There's nothing in between unless the baby missed any vaccines. Just as before, be aware of possible vaccine side effects: pain, fever, redness and swelling at the site, and crying or sleeping too much. Call your doctor if any of these symptoms don't disappear within 48 hours.

Common Concerns at Four Months

The newborn days are now gone, and now you have a new little person with different abilities and curiosities. New health issues will present themselves as the baby becomes more and more mobile and social and exposure to the world increases.

Sunlight: First, remember to keep your baby's exposure to direct sunlight to no more than a few minutes at a time. Even with sunscreen (which is permitted now), it's still advisable for the baby to wear a brimmed hat and try to be in the shade as much as possible. In hot weather, babies need to drink more. Remember that breastfeeding and formula are still the only fluids the baby should be drinking at this stage.

Viruses: Now that your baby is more social, other infants and children are likely around more. While the social interaction is great and everyone is having a good time, there are uninvited intruders lurking everywhere—germs! Especially at this stage, babies' natural tendency is to "mouth" everything—whatever is around, including their own hands. There's a very good chance that one or more of the children that your child is hanging out with may be a bit ill. While learning to share is important, playing with the same toys and sharing germs is also the way that viral disease, the common cold, is transmitted to your baby.

It's scary for parents to see their little ones getting sick. Babies will be exposed to all the viruses in the environment and through contact with other children and will come down with about 9 to 10 viral infections a year. Although unpleasant, these mild illnesses run their course and actually confer immunity. It's a rite of passage.

Fever: As frightening as fever is in babies younger than two months, now a low-grade fever—less than 101° Fahrenheit—is the body's way of fighting infection. As long as your child looks good, eats well, drinks well, and there are enough wet diapers and normal stools, don't worry. Always call your doctor to seek advice about any medication, homeopathic remedy, and so on that you want to give your baby.

Do not use over-the-counter medication for colds. The FDA has taken many of these off the market.

The common cold is, well, common at this age and even more so in the months to come. The baby may have a low-grade fever but looks good and is eating and drinking as before. The nose may be running, and there may be a short-lived cough. Again, this is a viral infection, and no medication is needed.

Make your baby comfortable. In particular, a stuffed nose makes the baby really uncomfortable, so use saline drops and the nasal aspirator to relieve the pressure and to help the baby breathe better. (There'll be a lot of protesting, and you may need two people to do it, but be persistent.) Have a humidifier in the room. In two to four days, all will hopefully be back to normal

MISC.

Teething

The teething process begins around this age and may cause a low-grade fever. The baby will have bouts of crying, will drool a lot, and will attempt to put the fist in his or her mouth.

Visit the doctor's office if the fever is more than 102° Fahrenheit and if the baby is coughing.

Coughing: Pay particular attention to the quality of the coughing and see your doctor if the cough:

Is present mainly at night and makes the baby vomit

Sounds like a little barking puppy

Has a long, musical sound on inspiration (taking air in)

Causes the baby to breathe too fast or gasp for air

Causes the baby to have a bluish color

Makes the baby refuse to drink

Causes nasal flaring, seeing the ribs and the space on top of the collarbone, panting for air.

Again, watch the belly since it's easier to see how frequent the breathing is.

These symptoms could include signs of *croup,* a viral infection of the airways, *whooping cough* (he or she only received two vaccines and is not fully protected yet), *bronchiolitis* (infection of the small airways of the lung), or *pneumonia* (infection of the lung tissue).

If these symptoms happen at night, know your doctor's emergency number and/or bring the baby to the emergency room. Know the insurance provider's emergency policy.

Baby steps	**Croup** is a viral infection (parainfluenza virus) of the baby's airways. It starts as a cold, but the cough gets worse. It's a distinctive cough that sounds like barking and gets worse at night. On inspiration (taking in a breath), there may be a gasping sound, called stridor. Sometimes steam helps loosen the congestion and relieve the discomfort, or bundling the baby up to breathe in cold air, but always consult your doctor if these symptoms are present.

Whooping cough results from the bacteria Bordetella. Pertussis is reemerging due to unimmunized children and adults who are infected. All parents and children older than 10 should have the new tetanus, diphtheria, and pertussis vaccine. The cough is continuous, with a deep inspiration at the end. This could become serious very quickly for babies of this age.

Bronchiolitis is a viral infection of the small lung airways. (Adults have bronchitis, an infection of the larger airways.) This can be a short illness or can produce respiratory distress in the baby.

Pneumonia is a viral or bacterial infection of the lung tissue. Long ago, before antibiotics, the mere mention of pneumonia meant serious and sometimes fatal illness. However, now recovery is fast if diagnosed early.

Vomiting: At this stage, the baby shouldn't be spitting up that much. The stomach is growing and is able to accommodate and tolerate most everything. If there is a small amount of spitting up that happens regularly, or if there is real vomiting, the baby can become dehydrated. Have rehydrating fluid on hand at home. Consult with your doctor first before you give it to your baby. Don't give water or juice.

Diarrhea: Diarrhea means frequent green or watery stools, sometimes with mucus and blood. A baby who has diarrhea, with or without vomiting, can become dehydrated. See your doctor before this situation becomes a serious emergency.

Constipation: Even if the baby hasn't had a bowel movement for a few days, if the stool is soft and he or she is comfortable, there's no reason to worry. You need to see the doctor if the stool looks like pellets and there is blood in the stool.

Rashes: A small, red rash on the neck, face, and diaper area is nothing to be concerned about. But if the baby's body is covered in a rash, if it looks infected, or if there is scaling or the rash has vesicles, the baby needs to see your doctor.

Inconsolable crying or sleeping too much are also causes for concern. If you think your baby is not meeting the milestones—not smiling or laughing, not wanting to be hugged, not holding the head up well, and not making usual baby sounds—consult with your doctor.

Common Concerns at Five Months

All the same concerns and illnesses discussed in four months apply to five-month-olds as well.

Ear infection: This is a new issue at this age. Babies will pull their ears out of habit, because of teething, or because there is an infection brewing. Ear infections can start as a cold that doesn't go away after seven days. If your baby has a fever of 102° Fahrenheit, is pulling his or her ears and crying, and is noticeably more uncomfortable and distraught at night, it's likely an ear infection—and it's time to see your pediatrician. For older children with ear infections, the doctor may wait with treatment, but with a baby of this age, the doctor will treat it right away.

Choking: Now that babies can reach, hold, and put everything in their mouths, the risk of choking increases. Check all toys—make sure there are no small parts and no dangerous toys or pieces of toys or games left around by older children.

All of your medication—including ones that appear not to be dangerous, such as vitamins—should be locked in a medicine cabinet. Cosmetics, jewelry, batteries, coins, and cleaning products—anything to be explored by those curious little hands—should be put away and secured.

If the baby chokes, put him or her in your lap or on your arm, and pat the back vigorously four times. Call 911 immediately if the choking continues.

From the beginning, it's a good idea for all caregivers of your baby to take a CPR (cardiopulmonary resuscitation) course. Call the American Red Cross or your local hospital to find out where and when these courses are given. Also, know the poison control number, 1-800-222-1222, available 24 hours a day, 7 days a week.

Common Concerns at Six Months

Your worries will increase exponentially with the baby's mobility. At six months, your budding explorer is starting to crawl. The world is so new, interesting, and bigger than ever—and what better way to learn about it than by touching everything and putting these finds into the mouth, just to see what it "feels" like.

On top of the list of things to worry about now, other than the illnesses already covered in months four and five, are accidents.

Choking: Some small, smooth objects could be swallowed—and if they're not dangerous, they'll be passed and eliminated. But others, such as batteries or any chemical or acid, can put the baby's life in danger.

All "solid" foods you're introducing into the baby's diet at this stage need to be pureed. Don't give the baby finger foods yet or large amounts of food at once, because these still pose a choking hazard.

Burns: These can happen anytime, anywhere—touching the hot water faucet during bath time, an iron or a curling iron, reaching and pulling down something hot in the kitchen, or putting fingers into an electrical socket.

If a burn occurs, immediately put ice on the burn (not oily liquids). Call 911 for an electrical burn, which needs follow-up in the emergency room (even if you don't see the burn on the skin). For other burns, call your doctor.

Strangling: This can happen with any hanging cords. Anything hanging—blinds, drapes, curtains, and appliance cords— needs to be put high up and away from the baby. If the baby gets entangled, immediately cut the cord off and disentangle the cord from the baby. If the baby has become pale, has turned blue, or has breathing problems, call 911 immediately.

Falling or being hit by a large object: Being hit by large, unstable objects or falling off a bed or sofa may cause serious injury. See your doctor or call 911 if the baby has lost consciousness or is bleeding badly.

Cuts: Babies can readily crawl into a sharp furniture corner or cut themselves with any sharp object. If it's a small, very superficial cut, clean it with water only (not betadine or alcohol), and cover the area with a non-latex adhesive bandage. If there is a larger cut and the bleeding continues, call your doctor.

Fractures: Babies can also break bones. If the baby is crying, if the arms or legs are swollen or bluish, or if the baby can't move or seems distressed when trying to move an arm or a leg, go to the emergency room.

"Nurse-maid elbow" can happen if you pull the baby by grabbing his or her arm. The arm won't move and may be limp. If this happens, see the doctor immediately. Most pediatricians will be able to treat this condition by performing two movements with the arm. Be aware that if it happened once, it may happen again. Advise all caretakers to hold the baby under the armpits and not to pull the arms.

baby watch

Child-proof your home by covering all electrical sockets with special plugs and all sharp corners with protective padding. Put out of baby's reach all electric appliances and hanging cords, and child-proof the faucets in the bathrooms and kitchen.

Essential Takeaways

- Short-lived colds, rashes that go away, and low-grade fevers will happen frequently. Keep your baby comfortable, and don't become overly concerned.
- Call your doctor when coughing is persistent at night, causes vomiting, and sounds like a barking puppy.
- See your doctor between well-baby visits if you observe any developmental lags.
- Take a baby CPR class to learn how to handle a choking situation effectively.

chapter 16

Childcare

How to prepare to return to work

Different child care options, including daycare

Child care in your home

Keeping an eye on those who care for your baby

As parents, you have the immense responsibility of taking care of, feeding, cleaning, and clothing your baby—as well as making sure your little one is safe, healthy, and developing well. For many of you, there's another issue as well: going back to work and trusting all of that to someone else.

Making Your Decision

Two things happen to you when you become parents. Along with the intense love that you feel for your baby, you also often feel worry and guilt. Going back to work can be very difficult when you finally feel comfortable with the baby and the everyday routine you two have established together.

These are not easy times. Going back to work or staying home are very personal choices and depend on a variety of factors:

- Financial needs

- The baby's needs

- Investment in your career

- A job you love

- Lifestyle choices

- Finding the right childcare

You're not a better or worse parent if you stay home or if you go back to work. Parents who stay home may feel that they are sacrificing a lot personally, while parents who go back to work may feel guilty about leaving the baby.

Try not to be hard on yourself for whatever choice you make. Make your best decision after you've really considered all aspects of your individual situation. Don't be influenced by family, friends, or societal pressure. Although well intentioned, other people's ideas are simply that— their ideas—and ultimately, these opinions usually have little or nothing to do with you and your family.

Going Back to Work

If you're returning to work after maternity leave, make sure everything is in place in an adequate time frame before your leave is over. Research your child-care options, which we'll discuss in detail in a minute, and try them *before* you make the decision about the caregiver. Have the new caregiver spend time with you for a few days or more to learn everything you need to teach him or her about your baby. This way, you can also observe how your baby and the caregiver relate to each other. The younger the baby, the less stranger anxiety he or she will have.

If you are breastfeeding and want that to continue, make a plan for how you will be able to pump and store enough milk for the hours you're away. Check with your employer about where you will be able to pump during your work hours, the time you will need to do it, and how you can properly store the milk. Also, make sure your baby will drink from the bottle (given by the caregiver) if he or she is not used to drinking from a bottle.

Your first day back to work is sure to be packed with emotions: sadness, guilt, and worry—but maybe also excitement to be back at work, to be using your work skills again, and to be seeing co-workers again. You may find that you've changed during your time away. Your perspective will likely be different now. You may be more understanding and more organized, and now you may be able to ask for help more than you did before.

It may take a while for your emotions to even out and for you to feel that you can separate your-self emotionally to really be present at your job. After a while, the emotional patches and nega-tive feelings will ease and slip away. But if that doesn't happen and you find that the sadness, worry, and guilt continue—and you feel that you just can't do it—it's time to talk to your doctor and your family. Your work decision must be one that will be best for you and your baby.

Some companies allow new parents to bring their babies to work, and some companies provide childcare on the premises. The advantages of this are:

- You could go back to work earlier.

- It may make it possible for you to afford to have a family earlier.

- You can be with or near your baby while at work and not feel guilty and worried.

The disadvantages are:

- You and your co-workers may be distracted from work.

- Your co-workers may resent this arrangement and create a stressful environment.

- Unless there is a specific place for the baby, it's difficult to create a safe environment in a small workplace.

- If the baby is younger than two months old, he or she could be exposed to a lot of infections.

Talk to your employer about what the childcare options are, and see whether something offered might work for you.

Child-Care Options

If you know you plan to go back to work, or even if you are unsure, research your child-care options ideally before the baby is born or months before your start date back at work. There are many options and considerations, and you'll want enough time to think them all through and investigate each one. You'll have to decide which type of care to use: family, other relatives, daycare, nannies, baby sitters, or the like.

Relatives

A trusted family member or close relative is, of course, a likely choice. If you are thinking about this type of arrangement, and as much as you trust them, talk to them, have many discussions, talk about your expectations, and show them extensively exactly what your baby needs.

The relative should be at least 18 years old. If the relatives are from an older generation, they should know that baby care has changed quite a lot. Even if they have experience, they need to do whatever you as the parent ask them to do, whether it's tried and true or new.

Daycare

Day-Care History

In the nineteenth century, day-care centers were charitable groups for children and families with problems, not working parents. It wasn't exactly an orphanage, but close to it. Later on, the centers were open to other families. The first one in the United States was in Pennsylvania.

During World War II, when women joined the workforce in high numbers, day-care centers were the only acceptable place for children of working mothers. Still, they weren't licensed, and even in the 1960s The Child Care Bureau stated that, "Any child who needs day care has a problem."

Once the idea of "educating" infants was raised in England, many day-care centers sprang up in Europe. And in the United States, the philosophy surrounding these centers was more fully embraced. This time, the centers excluded the impoverished population, until 1942, when federal funds were granted.

Today, there are many types of day-care centers: public, private, group child-care homes, and Early Head Start for infants who have special needs. There are also respite daycares for parents who take care of children with serious diseases.

Here are the essential questions to ask and evaluate when considering a daycare center in which to place your baby:

- Is it reputable?

- How long has it been functioning?

- Is it licensed?

- Can you afford it?

- What is the adult/child ratio?

- Can you visit?

- Does the center communicate regularly with you?

- What happens if the baby gets sick?

- Is the center hygienic? Is cleanliness a priority?

- Does the center follow strict safety measures and required protocol?

- How do you rate the quality of toys and activities?

- Are the caretakers CPR certified?

- What happens in case of an emergency? What procedures are in place?

Tour the day-care center and take notes about your likes and dislikes. Talk with the staff and get all your questions answered. Also, take your baby to the day-care center for a few visits before you go back to work to ease him or her into the environment. (This will also give you some time to make preparations of your own and to be close by if needed.) Start with just a couple hours one day, then a little longer the next, and a few more the next. Spend time also observing your baby's interactions with caregivers and how your baby is responding.

In-Home Childcare

Many people offer childcare in their homes. It may be a mother with a child or two of her own who takes in additional children to watch, or it may be someone with a child-care business run from their home. However it's structured, in-home child-care centers must be state certified and have no more than the legally specified ratio of number of children per caregiver.

Parents should meet and get to know all caretakers working in the home. In addition to all the questions listed previously for day-care centers, other important questions to ask in-home child-care providers are:

- Are there pets in the home? If so, what are they, how many, and are they in the same area as the children? Also, do they have the necessary vaccinations?

- Are the children ever taken out of the house, such as to a park? If so, where, for how long, and what is the means of transportation?

- Is there smoking in the house?

When it comes to pets, it's important to know that children and pets will be kept separate—or if they are permitted in the children's immediate environment, make sure that pets have had all the appropriate vaccinations. If your baby has any pet allergies that you know of, a home with pets will likely not be an option.

Regarding smoking, it goes without saying that smoking is prohibited both inside and outside the home during hours of operation. Ideally, there should be no smoking at any time. For children who have allergies or asthma, a totally smoke-free environment is essential.

Also, do a background check on the caregiver and anyone that lives in the home.

Babysitters

Babysitters help parents on a temporary basis, evenings or weekends, or in case of emergency. Many teenagers and college students are available for babysitting. You need to interview these young people and watch them interact with your baby, unless you know and trust them from before. It's preferable to have referrals from friends and family.

Sometimes, older adults are interested in spending time with children—especially if their own children are out of the house. Again, references from reliable sources are preferable.

Nannies and Au Pairs

Nannies spend time with babies when the parents are at work or are spending time away. A nanny can live with the family or come in every day. Some nannies sleep over during the week and leave on the weekends.

Nannies need to have experience and must be qualified in childcare. They can transport the children wherever they need to be and can even take them to the doctor with the parent's consent.

The main ways to find a nanny are either word of mouth (through people you know who have had one), through a placement service that prescreens all candidates, or through your local classified listings. When looking for a nanny, it's important to thoroughly interview the person, check the references and work history, discuss each other's child-care philosophies, see how your baby takes to the person, and have the person spend some trial time with you to see whether it'll be a fit for you and your family.

If cost is a concern, a "shared nanny program" allows families to get together to share a nanny. This means that the nanny will take care of several infants, preferably the same age, in one of the parents' homes. The cost is shared by the families, and the babies have playmates.

An au pair does the same thing a nanny does; the only difference is that an au pair refers to young people from abroad who take care of your child in exchange for room and board in your home. Au pairs can be found the same way as nannies and should be thoroughly screened as well.

The essential point to keep in mind with childcare is that after you've thoroughly researched it, visited day-care centers and other facilities you're considering, interviewed perspective caregivers, and done your homework obtaining references from a caregiver's former employers, if for any reason you are uncomfortable with a potential caregiver or facility, no matter how glowing and effusive the references and recommendations are, follow your gut instinct and do only what you feel completely comfortable with. Don't feel foolish if others think you're being too cautious, too picky, or too unrealistic. It's your child and your instinct will guide you to your best decision.

Help at Home

It's perfectly okay to ask for help. Involve family members, especially fathers or partners who can do errands such as grocery shopping and picking up and taking siblings to school or activities.

You can also hire a mother's (parent's) helper. This person will work together with the parent to help take care of the baby and household needs. They are not usually left alone but are around the house to help. Just having an extra pair of hands feels very supportive, and having someone there to take care of things you don't have the time or energy to do otherwise is very helpful.

A babysitting co-op is a unique way to get some time away without costing money. Several mothers (and fathers) can get together and barter hours. Instead of paying with money, you pay with hours. This way, too, you know that the people watching your baby are reliable and trustworthy.

Remember, you need time to rest, time to go out or just be alone, and time to spend with your spouse or partner—working on your relationship or just enjoying each other's company.

When Parents Separate

Childcare becomes more challenging, and often more necessary, if the parents or partners have separated, or are separating.

In this situation, the best thing for the baby is to share the same caregiver if at all possible in order to ensure continuity of care. As much consistency as you can keep is important for the baby's well being. The routines of feeding, naps, playtime, and bedtime should remain firmly fixed in the separate households.

Babies feel their parent's moods, and if the parent is upset or rattled, the baby may react with crying and fussiness. Work to maintain a calm and loving disposition toward and around your baby. No matter what feelings you have elsewhere, the baby you brought into the world and are helping to raise is innocent and needs your love, care, and respect.

Monitoring a New Relationship

It's nerve-wracking to leave your baby with a stranger, either at home with a new babysitter or nanny or at a daycare. If the person or facility is familiar already through your other children, it'll be much easier.

One question you will constantly ask yourself is, "How do I know that everything is okay?" Coming home or picking up your baby and finding him or her happy, full, and clean is a good sign. It's a good sign, too, if the caregiver is readily in touch with you and you know you can always call him or her.

But other things can happen. Your baby could always be cranky, crying, or acting unusual when you come home or pick him or her up. If you have any worries or suspect that something is wrong, talk to the caregiver about your concerns. Because your baby is too young to tell you, you must be keenly aware when something doesn't seem right with your child-care situation, and you must do something about it. One thing to try to make your own assessment of the situation is to drop in periodically unexpected and see how your baby is doing. You can also ask your spouse or partner to do the same. You can also ask for a time line of events during the day and what your baby's mood was at different times. If any caregiver is not willing to allow you to drop in or take the time to make a report for you, you may want to start looking at other options.

When to Be Concerned

Be very concerned and take action in your child-care situation if you observe any of the following:

> There are "accidents."

> There are suspicious bruises.

A baby is crying and unhappy (especially if this is very different from the way the baby usually is).

A baby is kept in dirty clothes.

A baby isn't growing well.

A baby is left in the crib without any stimulation.

Immediately contact your baby's doctor for even the slightest suspicion of abuse or neglect.

This situation can be more difficult to deal with if it's somebody with whom you've already worked. A confident caregiver with a clear conscience will be happy to accommodate whatever you ask, but be prepared to start looking for someone else if you receive excuses. These are clear warning signs that someone is not putting the care of your baby first.

Essential Takeaways

- The decision to stay at home or go back to work is solely yours to make after careful consideration of your and your family's needs.
- Research and plan for childcare well before you go back to work.
- Make sure all caregivers are consistent with your baby's routines.
- Don't hesitate to let anyone go who you believe is not giving your baby the best possible care or is not the right fit for you and your baby.

Part 4

Months Seven, Eight, and Nine

Here, we talk about how your baby's movements continue with the accomplishment of more complex tasks. Gross motor skills develop: sitting with help, then sitting alone, bouncing, and for some precocious kids, crawling. Fine motor skills become more refined: transferring objects and grasping with fingers. We'll also talk about the baby-proofing that is absolutely essential by this time.

Language and cognitive skills continue to increase. Your baby can "play" with new friends now, and there are lots of new educational toys to discover and stories not to be missed.

There's still more about sleeping and eating (but more about eating). Hopefully, you and your baby are getting more sleep now.

As we've done before, we'll address your concerns about your baby's well-being, discuss when you need to see the doctor (other than for well-baby visits), and talk about basic first aid and what to do in case of an emergency.

chapter 17

This Is the Way We Grow Today

Further development of motor, cognitive, language and social skills

New toys and activities

Adjusting furniture and equipment for baby's changing needs

Baby-proofing the home

Your baby will change very quickly from this time forward. He or she will become more mobile, will react and understand more, and will even start misbehaving.

At this stage, your baby will start the steps toward moving independently. You'll notice rolling over easily in both directions, the ability to sit with or without support, and a number of other new skills that will make every day a new adventure for you and your baby.

Sitting Up

Generally, at about seven months old, babies can sit up with support. The back muscles have become much stronger, the head is now perfectly stable, and the back is almost straight. Babies are now able to look in different directions.

Your baby may still be unstable and fall forward in the sitting position. But it won't be long before he or she will be able to sit without support. From the sitting position, the baby will also learn to turn and then will be able to return to a sitting position after lying on his or her back.

Typically, by the end of the seventh month or beginning of the eighth, babies can sit on their own. But don't leave the baby without some kind of support at this point (for example, a pillow at the back).

If you hold your baby, he or she will quickly push himself or herself up. But this is not enough; now babies start bouncing up and down, sometimes even following a musical rhythm (which is a lot of fun for everyone).

Transferring Hands

Another milestone is transferring, which begins at about seven months. As eye-hand coordination improves, your baby will grab a toy with one hand and transfer it to the other hand, with or without a stop at the mouth.

At first, babies may use two fingers and the thumb to accomplish this task, then quickly evolve to using the forefinger as well. Your baby will be fascinated by this newly discovered ability. Having small objects or toys in reach that can easily be grasped by your baby's small hands will facilitate this activity even more. Of course, don't put objects in reach that are so small that the baby could choke on them.

Enjoying Peek-a-Boo

Your baby will now discover that objects exist even when they can't be seen. This is an important milestone called *object permanence*. You can show an object, then hide it—leaving a small part uncovered. The baby will be able to find it. Also, he or she will continue to figure out the cause-and-effect relationship—push something, it will move or fall; touch something, it will make a noise; hide something, it can be found.

Because of object permanence and because the brain can now make associations it couldn't make before, one of the most favorite games and enjoyable playtimes at this stage is peek-a-boo. Your baby will be entertained for a long time by just pretending to appear and disappear. And he or she will really understand that you're there, even if you "leave" for a while.

Seeing and Hearing

Vision is becoming clearer, and hearing ability is increasing. Babies will watch objects moving in all directions. They'll drop objects to watch and hear them fall—and so you'll pick them up! Babies will hear sounds all around them and will turn their heads in that direction and listen.

Babies can now laugh and shout very loudly. They understand when you call their name. They'll react with real emotion to what is happening around them and will imitate you. You may even notice your baby imitating your cough!

When Your Baby Starts Crawling

When your baby is sitting up and a toy is placed in front of him or her, your baby will likely lunge to get it. While lunging, the baby will discover stability on the hands and feet, which eventually leads to crawling. The baby will first learn to rock back and forth on the hands and knees. He or she may tumble, but eventually the baby will start moving forward. This is called crawling—the first big step on the road to walking.

Be aware that there are babies who don't ever really crawl. Instead, they just stand up and walk, skipping crawling altogether. It's perfectly normal. Once upon a time, it was theorized that a baby who didn't crawl might have learning problems. However, no studies have shown this to be true. Crawling typically comes before walking, but if your baby decides to skip it, there's nothing wrong with that.

Since the 1990s, when parents were told to put babies to sleep on their backs, more and more babies have stopped crawling. Many researchers think that back sleeping may be the cause for less crawling than before. Instead of crawling, some babies sit and move by scooting; others will roll from one side of the room to another.

Crawling Styles

At first, some babies may be apprehensive about beginning to crawl while others can't wait to get moving. Either way, they'll learn the movement and their own style and become proficient at it and will eventually become very fast. There are many styles of crawling. The "classic" style is on all fours, the hands and knees. The "bear walk" is on the hands and feet. Pushing forward with one arm and leg, or on one side, is often referred to as "combat style."

Some babies will stand and take a few steps while holding on to furniture. This is called *cruising,* and it will be perfected later on (from 8 to 12 months).

Once crawling begins, safety becomes a major issue because the baby can now get into many more things. It's a serious topic for discussion covered later in this chapter.

See the doctor if the baby can't sit, if the baby's muscles are too stiff or too soft, if he or she can't grasp, or if the baby has no interest in toys or people.

Cognitive Development

Cognitive development—your baby's thought process—is progressing rapidly now. Your baby will be doing and figuring out new things every day through some reasoning and intuition. At this stage, your baby will start to understand what's going on around him or her and begin to become familiar with the environment. This is also the stage when *stranger anxiety* is in full bloom.

Stranger anxiety is when babies will refuse to stay with or be held by anybody other than the parents or caregiver. They may also show this "anxiety" toward the parent who spends less time with them or grandparents. Others shouldn't take it personally; it's just a phase. The more time other significant people spend with the baby, the more the baby will get used to everyone.

Reacting to emotions is happening even more now. Your baby may laugh a lot and even squeal in happy surroundings. He or she may even start crying if somebody else is sad or cries, which is a major milestone—the beginning of your baby's ability to show empathy. The baby may touch a person's face in an attempt to make him or her feel better. From now on, you can teach your baby to become a gentle, understanding, and compassionate human being. Don't think for a moment that it's too soon.

Your baby will start imitating not only moods but even some gestures. Your voice, your actions, and the way you react and solve problems are all being observed—even now. Your baby may not understand the words but will certainly understand the tone of your voice. If possible, don't yell, talk loudly, or speak in an angry voice around the baby, because he or she is taking it all in.

Your little one is becoming proud of his or her accomplishments—and for good reason. If you clap when he or she does something, the baby will learn to clap as well. By eight to nine months, your baby will understand that clapping (the effect) is a response to a positive achievement, and he or she will clap for himself or herself. Always respond in a positive way.

The Discipline of Distraction

Distracting babies to help stop them from being upset or to steer them away from something dangerous becomes the best way to "discipline" at this age. Saying no is important in order to set some boundaries. By nine months, babies understand a stern "no" but won't necessarily stop doing what they started. That type of logical thinking necessary to stop an action or behavior is simply not possible until a child is much older, which is why distraction is important. Say no only if it's really necessary and done in a soft but stern voice. Your baby may look at you and cry because he or she can't get what's wanted, but that's okay. Give your baby a hug, and distract him or her with something else. He or she will soon forget.

Make sure to tell all caregivers to do the same thing. There's a saying: "Repetition is the mother of mastering." It's true even at this very young age. We'll add consistency to this wise saying. It's important also to be consistent with what is and what isn't okay. For instance, if you allow your baby to play with something one day, then tell him or her "no" to playing with it the next day, this will be confusing to the baby. Be consistent with your discipline.

Screaming at your baby, threatening with consequences that a little one couldn't possibly understand, or punishment of any kind simply will not work and will only cause harm, fear, and frustration. Hitting a baby or a young child is absolutely out of the question—not even on the hands or the buttocks. It will not solve the problem. Rather, it teaches a child early on that violence solves problems. He or she will not listen, and your baby will only become frightened and distrustful of you. Ask for help from another caregiver if you get frustrated or angry.

Language

Language will not be moving along as fast as cognition, but rest assured your baby is working on it even if you don't hear it yet. Double consonants will be used, such as "gaga," "baba," and sometimes "dada." (Moms, don't feel hurt if the baby doesn't say "mama" yet. It's a more difficult sound to make, but by 9 to 10 months your baby will master the sound "m.")

Just a short time ago, your baby was babbling incessantly, mainly to herself or himself. Now, your baby starts to understand that people don't talk at the same time and will begin to start and stop, depending on the conversation. Talk to your baby; show objects and name them. Don't use DVDs or television for language development; you and other caregivers are the best teachers of language.

Also, your baby can become bilingual or multilingual. Babies have a natural ability to learn any language. You can begin teaching a second or third language while you're teaching the native language. The theory is that there is a common origin for speech patterns in many languages. Just as you would help your baby acquire their native language by talking to them, singing songs, playing games that stimulate speech, and reading books, you or others can do the same with a second or third language. Exposure is the key to acquiring language.

If parents or caregivers speak other languages, it's a good idea for one person to speak to the baby in one language while the other speaks in a different language. Even if no one around speaks another language, there are resources to draw upon: classes, videos, audio CDs, and computer programs. Research shows that being bilingual or multilingual doesn't delay speech. Be consistent and your baby will pick up the second language. Remember, there's a window of opportunity for acquiring language when a child is very young, so take the opportunity while you can.

For the last few years, American Sign Language (ASL) for infants has become very popular. The American Association of Pediatrics (AAP) is not against it but cautions parents to still use speech and other ways of interacting to encourage language development.

Social Development

At seven to nine months, babies become more interested in other babies. They want to touch others like themselves; they may want to look at other babies, but they're not really interested in "playing" with them yet. Still, getting babies together is important so they are exposed to others besides adults.

Playgroups

Participating in playgroups continues to be an important source of social development for your baby at this stage. The get-togethers of babies and their caretakers in a relaxed environment are good for both your baby and you. Playgroups provide many new experiences for little ones, encouraging them to acquire new social skills while learning to share and be together with their little peers.

You can often find a local group by talking to other new parents, or by investigating what schools or religious institutions may have to offer along those lines. If you can't find an organized playgroup in your area, why not start one? Playgroups don't have to be formal, you can simply invite other new moms and their babies you've met over to your house, or meet in a clean, safe public place where you can all spread out and chat.

There are also other organized playgroups as well for music, sports, arts and crafts, and outdoor activities for babies. Check your local community centers, schools, and churches for what's available in your area.

Parallel Play

At this stage, when babies are around other babies, they will continue their own play—crawling and sitting in a non-interacting, parallel way, which is why it's called parallel play.

Some babies, however, may be up for trying some simple games. Because they have a slightly longer attention span, they can roll balls or toys to each other, can crawl after each other, and can try out their own language.

Some babies may be more aggressive toward others and even bite, especially if they're teething; others may pull someone else's hair. When this happens, say "no," distract and separate the little troublemakers, and hope that all parents in the group have the same approach and understanding.

Educational Toys and Activities

A variety of books and even common household objects can be educational toys for babies. Baby books with images that he or she can relate to are good ones to use at this point, such as pictures of toys, fruits, vegetables, babies, and so on. In books with animals, show the baby the animals and make the animals' sounds. Show books with different textures, and name and describe them. Read as much as you can to your baby. Make up fun stories and use different sounds. But be careful at bedtime, because you don't want to excite or stimulate them too much. Easy poems such as *Goodnight Moon* and Dr. Seuss's books are good at night. The words will not be understood, but the rhythm will help the baby become sleepy.

Let your baby play with wooden utensils and use pots and pans as drums. Also, babies love balls, especially soft ones. Roll one to and from your baby, playing a baby version of catch. You can also place toys in different locations and have the baby move toward them. This is a great exercise to strengthen muscles for crawling (and eventually walking).

By nine months, even before they like stackable toys and rings, babies love big puzzles with three to five different shapes. Mirrors and toys that move are other favorites.

Music classes for babies are great now, too, and babies may even make their own "musical" sounds. Little "gyms" with soft obstacles, balls, and a large crawling area are good at this age as well.

Baby-Proofing's Next Phase

Your little one is growing. There are some baby things you've been using that you'll want to remove, but store them away for your next baby (if you plan to have one!). You can also donate furniture or gently used clothes and toys to women's shelters, houses of worship, the American Red Cross, hospitals, or anywhere else they're needed in your local community.

Bathing

The little baby bathtub will not work and is no longer needed once your baby can sit up. It's time to graduate to the family tub. Place a non-slippery mat in the bathtub (or large sink if you don't have a tub), and always keep one hand on the baby during the bath. Bathing together with your baby in the bathtub is not a good idea. The baby is slippery, and if there's too much water in the tub, it's possible for mishaps—even drowning—to occur. It only takes two inches of water for a drowning to occur. Buckets are not safe, either.

When you put your baby into the big tub, make sure that the water is very shallow—less than 2 inches (6 cm). Test the temperature of the water before you place the baby in it, as you've done before. Have safety devices covering the faucets.

You can place a bath seat designed for infants in the tub to support the baby during the bath, but still keep a hand on the baby at all times. A bath seat is better than a bath ring because it's more stable. Research consumer product reviews for bath seats, and be familiar with recalled products before purchasing one.

The baby can play with toys and splash in the tub, which he or she will enjoy. Place a mat on the floor underneath you so you don't slip while bathing the baby or lifting him or her out. Do not, under any circumstances, leave the baby alone in the bathtub—even if he or she is sitting in the bath seat.

Equipment and Furniture

You can now retire the changing table if you desire, because the baby likely won't lie still anymore. (It can now become a shelf for toys or books). Also retire the mobile, because your baby can reach up and grab it.

Lower the crib mattress all the way down because your baby can sit up now, and before long he or she will be able to pull up to standing. Soon, your little athlete will try—and succeed—at climbing over. Still, there are no pillows, blankets, or toys allowed in the crib.

Check and adjust the car seat to make sure the belts are at the right shoulder height. Because your baby is growing, check these often to ensure proper safety. Also check your stroller to make sure it's still sturdy, because babies move around a lot at this age. Use an umbrella stroller for short walks and on even surfaces.

The Home

Babies are so quick now—moving one way or the other—and touching and putting everything in their mouths. You may want to try to do something silly but helpful: explore your home on all fours to see what you find.

The kitchen and bathroom are dangerous places. There should be a safety gate in front of the doors of each of these rooms and definitely in front of all stairs.

Ideally, the baby should not be in the kitchen at all due to all the dangerous things in it. But understandably, that's practically impossible. Therefore, have safety devices on the faucets and the stove and oven knobs. All cleaning products should be locked away. The garbage bin should be out of the baby's way. Anything sharp or breakable should be removed. All cabinets (as well as the refrigerator) should have latches.

In the bathroom, the toilet should be latched, faucets should have safety devices, and cabinets should have latches.

In other rooms, cover all outlets, don't have any cords exposed, and don't run cords under the carpet. Door knobs should be covered, use edge and corner bumpers, and don't have glass tables if possible at this stage.

Have tassels and cords wound up and out of reach, a safety net for the deck and balconies, and window guards on all windows.

Lamps should not be placed near curtains due to fire potential. Have and know how to use a home fire extinguisher. Make sure smoke and carbon monoxide detectors are appropriately placed and in good working order.

If you have a pool, fences need to be at least four feet high around it, with slats less than four inches (1.1 cm) apart, with self-closing and latching gates. If you have a hot tub, don't take the baby into it because he or she can become overheated.

More than one third of households in the United States have firearms. If you keep firearms in your home, take the ammunition out and keep it separate from the firearms. Keep everything locked, out of sight, and far away at all times from any child. Firearms cleaning solutions should be out of sight and locked away as well. BB guns are also very dangerous and should be handled the same way. Teach all children firearm safety rules.

Essential Takeaways

- Sitting up and learning to crawl are milestones typically reached in the seventh and eighth months.
- Distraction is the best form of discipline, never hitting or screaming.
- Playing peek-a-boo and having the baby find partially hidden toys helps teach object permanence.
- Playing games and making up stories of your own is just as good, if not better, than buying toys, games, and books.
- More baby-proofing of your home is needed now, especially latching cabinets, gating off stairs and certain rooms, and protecting table corners.

chapter 18

Sleeping and Eating

Changing of sleep patterns as the year progresses

Food allergies and foods to avoid

More great recipes

A well-rounded food guide for your baby

As you are learning by now, during the entire first year of life, activities surrounding sleeping and eating take up a large portion of a 24-hour period. Therefore, an important goal is to regulate your baby's schedule according to his or her needs—but to meet your needs as well.

Sleeping

As time passes and babies mature, their patterns eventually start conforming to a "day/night" schedule. They learn that sleeping takes place mostly during the night, with some sleep breaks during the day for a little timeout.

At 7 to 9 months, most babies sleep at least 6 to 7 hours at night and a total of 12–15 hours a day (naps included). Most babies take two to three naps during the day—typically one mid-morning, one early afternoon, and one late afternoon. Having the last nap before 5 P.M. is a good idea so the baby is tired before bedtime.

Continue the bedtime routine with quiet time an hour or two before bedtime.

baby steps It's difficult for the working parent to come home to a baby who is already in the pre-bedtime zone. Understandably, the two want to spend time playing and being together. As hard as it is, understand that altering the bedtime routine too much inhibits the baby's ability to achieve relaxed sleep, and putting the baby to sleep if he or she is overtired becomes a difficult task for everybody. As tempting as it is to play with your baby when you get home close to bedtime, you can make your time together quiet with books and lullabies. Just being with you is what's important to your baby, no matter what you're doing.

Try to put the baby in the crib before he or she is asleep. The routine doesn't have to be complicated or long. As always, don't leave pillows, toys, or blankets in the crib. You can use a transitional object, such as a toy, a small towel or little blanket square, or a rattle. Remove the object after the baby falls asleep.

Waking Up in the Night

There are situations when a baby has been sleeping well and starts to awaken again during the night. This could be due to teething or to the excitement of great new achievements. Some babies are trying to crawl or even stand up in the crib. After "exploring" for a while in the crib, babies may just not be able to get themselves back into a comfortable position for sleep and start to cry.

When this happens, go into the room, gently settle the baby on his or her back, say "good night," and leave the room (as hard as it may be). If everything is fine, wait a few minutes to answer the crying the next time it happens. Go into the baby's room, but don't pick the baby up and don't turn the light on. Talk softly, rubbing the baby's back or head to help him or her fall back asleep.

If you see your baby trying to climb out of the crib, your next step is to replace the crib with a low toddler bed. Chances are this won't happen until 12–15 months of age or even later. But be aware that some babies can climb out of the crib by 9 to 10 months.

In all instances of waking up in the night, go into the room initially to make sure the baby is fine. As it happens sometimes, babies get sick with fever and discomfort, so crying inconsolably in the middle of the night is normal and needs your attention.

Sleep Training … Again

By now, you're probably using a method to sleep-train the baby (discussed in Chapter 14). If not, it's never too late to start. If you used a method before and it worked but the baby is waking up again, use the same method to get your baby back on track. If you used the Ferber method, try it again—checking to make sure nothing is wrong with the baby first. Or you can pick up and rock the baby, holding him or her until almost asleep, then placing the baby in the crib. If the baby continues to cry, continue soothing the baby by rubbing the back and singing soft lullabies, but don't pick the baby up. If the baby is used to having a night light on, leave it on. Babies like routine and need everything to be the same, in the same order. Also, with object permanence, as opposed to earlier months, the baby will eventually understand that even if you're not in the same room, you're still around.

baby steps

The use of a sound machine can help a baby sleep by providing soft background noise. Sound machines typically play the soothing sounds of ocean waves, rain falling, crickets, and even heartbeats. Choose a sound that your baby seems to like, and turn it on every night at bedtime. Your baby will get used to hearing the sound at bedtime and begin to associate it with bedtime and sleep.

Eating

Your baby is eating more and trying more new things. You are also likely becoming more aware of the foods your baby likes and dislikes.

Food Allergies

Before we start talking about food at this age, we'd like to review a few issues regarding food allergies. In the United States, 6 percent of children younger than three years of age are allergic to certain foods. The foods most often associated with allergies are:

- Milk

- Eggs

- Nuts

- Soy

- Wheat

- Fish

- Peas

- Shellfish

Egg, soy, and wheat allergies tend to be outgrown earlier. Around 70 percent of children outgrow allergy to milk by 15–16 years of age. Only 15–20 percent of children allergic to peanuts outgrow this allergy. Allergies to tree nuts (almonds, cashews, walnuts, and pecans) and shellfish are seldom outgrown. Symptoms of food allergies, listed below, may include hives, which are itchy, raised, red blotches on the skin.

Anybody can have an allergy to anything and at any time. Recently, studies demonstrated that a lot of additives and artificial colorings in foods are responsible for allergies. (It's important to note that babies may be allergic to medication or the colorant that is added to them as well.) The typical signs of a food allergy are as follows:

Runny nose

Itching

Coughing

Wheezing

Hives

Vomiting

Diarrhea

Once a baby has been diagnosed with a food allergy, the parents will be instructed to always carry an antihistamine or even an injection to counter the potentially dangerous effects of the allergy.

A very serious allergic condition called *anaphylactic reaction* is the swelling of the lips or face and difficulty breathing. This is an emergency, and a baby needs to be taken to the hospital immediately when this happens.

baby steps

Why do allergies happen? The body essentially makes a "mistake" by recognizing a certain part of the food as harmful. Antibodies (against the harmful substance) will be released, which in turn will trigger the release of histamines. These are responsible for allergic reactions, from mild ones to anaphylaxis.

If necessary, your doctor will refer your baby to an allergist. This doctor will perform either a skin allergy test or a blood test and give you instructions about using anti-allergy medication.

If there is a strong family history of allergies, wait until introducing that food(s). Tell your doctor about your family history of allergies, because the doctor may recommend having an antihistamine on hand just in case. Even after following all recommendations, there's no guarantee that a baby will not develop food allergies.

The same rule for introducing new foods still applies: only one new food every three days, and never more than that. As your baby gets older and is eating most foods, there will be times when meals are served out of your home. Be careful when eating out or ordering food. Even if the food itself doesn't contain an allergen (for example, peanuts), it may have been processed or cooked where peanuts were processed or cooked. Make sure you ask. Sometimes even peanut dust is enough to elicit the allergy. The same issues apply to every canned or packaged food. Many have a written warning that the food was manufactured in a factory that may handle other allergens. To be absolutely sure, call the manufacturer.

Celiac Disease

Celiac disease is an allergy to gluten (found in wheat, barley, rye, and oats) that inflames and destroys the lining of the small intestines. The first line of treatment is total elimination of those foods from the diet.

Eczema (Atopic Dermatitis)

Eczema derives its name from the Greek, meaning to boil. It's a form of allergy, and many times is associated with allergies to food. It can also come about through contact with chemicals, although in many instances, the reasons for its appearance are unknown.

Eczema manifests as a disease of the skin with a red, scaly, itchy rash. In infants, the rash is on the cheeks, behind the ears, and on the thighs. Babies with this condition are uncomfortable, irritable, and have loss of appetite. Scratching of the affected areas can cause infections. Keep your child well hydrated. The doctor will give you a cream and may test for allergies.

Never give a baby younger than two years of age raw honey. Raw honey can cause a very serious disease in infants called botulism, a severe kind of food poisoning. Botulism spores found in honey are benign, except to babies and children up to two years of age whose immune systems haven't yet matured enough to handle them.

Risk of Choking

Choking can easily happen in babies and little children. Babies simply put anything and everything in their mouths, and they have no understanding about size or texture. It's up to parents and caregivers to ensure that babies only eat foods and the piece sizes they can handle.

These foods should be totally avoided until a later time, when your baby has the ability to properly chew and swallow them:

Raw pieces of carrot or any hard vegetable

Popcorn

Whole grapes

Hot dogs

Peanut butter

Any nuts

Hard candy

Raisins

Any dried food in clumps that are hard to chew

Eggs

Egg whites have four proteins that can cause allergies. Allergy to the egg yolk is very rare. The safest way to introduce eggs to a baby is to only feed him or her the yolk at first—either hard-boiled or scrambled.

To hard-boil an egg, place an egg in boiling water for 10 to 12 minutes. Remove the egg and cool it in cold water, then peel off the shell. Remove the yolk, making sure no parts of the white are included. Mash the yolk with a fork and add two teaspoons of either formula or breast milk. You can also add fruits or vegetables to the egg yolk.

For scrambled eggs (yolks), separate egg whites from the yolks by cracking the shell in half and moving the yolk back and forth from one shell half to the other, letting the clear egg whites fall away. Place only the yolks in a small bowl and beat them. Warm up half a teaspoon of vegetable oil in a pan; add beaten egg yolks. Stir the eggs until completely done—about three to five minutes. Remove the pan from the heat. Leave the eggs standing for another five minutes to cool, then mix with any favorite fruit or vegetable.

Poultry

Continue to use chicken and turkey at this age. It's not necessary to feed red meat to your baby yet. But if you want to feed red meat, choose very lean, tender cuts, and chop it into very small bites or puree it to mix with a fruit or vegetable.

Here are some good, basic chicken and turkey recipes that are packed with nutrients for your baby.

Baked Chicken or Turkey and Vegetables

Ingredients:

One chicken or turkey
  breast, sliced thinly

Vegetable oil

Oregano

Lemon juice

Vegetables of choice

Brush meat with a drop of vegetable oil and season with oregano and a drop of lemon. Do the same with tried vegetables (squash, carrots, and peas, for instance).

Bake meat and vegetables at 375° Fahrenheit for 14 minutes on each side. Turn vegetables over earlier, when soft. Cool and blend.

You can give your baby more texture now by using coarser pieces of meat and vegetables, but be careful they are not too big.

Baked Chicken Fingers

Ingredients:

2 boneless, skinless
  chicken breasts

¼ cup nonspiced bread-
  crumbs

2 egg yolks

¼ tsp. lemon zest, dill,
  parsley, or basil

¼ cup water

Vegetable oil

You can boil the chicken in advance to cut down on the baking time. Boil two pieces of chicken breast in water or broth for 20–30 minutes. Cut them into long and narrow pieces.

Preheat the oven to 375° Fahrenheit. Brush a baking pan with vegetable oil.

Combine the nonspiced breadcrumbs, egg yolks, lemon zest, dill, parsley, or basil, and water. Mix well; coat the chicken strips.

Place the pan of chicken strips in the oven. Bake seven to eight minutes on each side.

Cool and cut into pieces that are the size of half your pinky finger nail. Make sure the chicken isn't pink anywhere. If it is, bake the chicken a little longer. Serve with any fruit or vegetable.

Meat and Veggie Stew

Ingredients:

1 cup chicken, turkey, or
  lean red meat

1 carrot

1 celery stalk

2 potatoes

1 green or red pepper
  (only the sweet ones)

¼ cup onion, chopped
  (optional)

1 small garlic clove,
  minced (optional)

½ cup water

Cut up the meat, carrot, celery stalk, potatoes, and green or red pepper into small pieces. Warm up one teaspoon vegetable oil in a pan. Cook meat for five minutes, then the vegetables. Use oregano, basil, dill, or parsley for seasoning. Mix everything well. Add water. If it looks too thick, add more water or turn it into soup.

Cook until meat is very soft (around 30 minutes). Blend or chop cooked meat and vegetables coarsely. Serve with any cooked and cut-up pasta.

This dish can be cooked for the entire family, but remove the baby's portion before you add salt, sugar, or heavier spices.

Dairy

Give only pasteurized dairy products to your baby. Whole milk is not recommended until after 12 months because of its fat content and because it's more difficult for babies to digest. But dairy products that are safe at this age, as long as there is no allergy to dairy, are yogurt, cottage cheese, and mild cheeses (in moderation).

Yogurt can be mixed with fruits and cereal. You can mix cottage cheese or grated cheese with scrambled eggs for added flavor and protein. You can also grate mild cheese onto vegetables and bake at 350 degrees Fahrenheit for 15 minutes.

Yogurt Smoothie

You can also use soy-based yogurt, if necessary.

Ingredients:

1 cup yogurt	½ cup cereal
1 cup fruit (a single fruit or mixed fruit)	½ to 1 cup formula or breast milk, depending on desired thickness

Mix all ingredients in a blender and serve as is, or blend it with cottage cheese and fruits for a great snack.

Fish

You can introduce fish at around eight to nine months. Use mild, white fish such as cod, sole, or flounder. Make sure the fish is fresh, and it should have firm, shiny flesh. If you press the skin, it should spring back. The smell should be very mild, not fishy or strong.

Baked Fish Sticks

Ingredients:

1 lb. fish	½ tsp. lemon juice
1 cup water	½ onion (optional)
½ tsp. oregano, dill, basil, or parsley	

Boil all ingredients until fish is completely white (15–20 minutes). Remove from the heat but leave fish in for another five minutes.

Blend, adding cooking water if necessary to make it less thick. Serve with mashed rice and vegetables.

How Much Will the Baby Eat?

If you're using commercial baby food, you can now start stage two. Stage two is still pureed but contains combinations of foods. Make sure the baby has tried every food in the combination. If not, you'll try that particular food for three days. If the combination has one or two known foods and only one unknown food, it's okay to give the combination. But give that combination for three days, because you're testing the new food.

You can start stage three after eight months. The same rules apply. The following is only a guide. A baby can eat more or less until he or she is full. One day, your baby may love a food; the next day, he or she may not touch it. That's fine; try the food another time.

Food Guide

Cereal: ¼ cup with 2–3 ounces formula or breast milk, once or twice a day. The consistency is similar to farina or oatmeal for adults. Serve with or without fruit.

Fruits and vegetables: ¼–½ cup 2–3 times a day

Meat or fish: a few teaspoons to ¼ cup once a day

Eggs: one, two to three times a week

From seven to eight months and on, your baby can have three meals a day: breakfast, lunch, and dinner. You can give him or her a spoon now that coordination is so much better, but don't expect the baby to actually feed himself or herself independently yet. Do expect an amazing mess, and don't get angry. Just wash the baby's hands and continue feeding. This shouldn't be considered playtime, though. Gently guide the baby to use the spoon properly.

Finger Foods

Your baby is becoming more independent and will want to eat more and more on his or her own. Finger foods are perfect for this stage. The proper size of a finger food is half of your pinky finger nail.

The best finger foods are:

> Boiled carrots or other root vegetables
>
> Potatoes or sweet potatoes
>
> Pieces of avocado
>
> Pieces of banana
>
> Boiled peas
>
> Cheerios

Offer only one piece at a time. Be sure that the first piece has been swallowed, not still sitting in the mouth, before you give the next piece. Giving finger foods should always be supervised. Pay attention to when the baby is full, then don't force another bite.

Drinking

By this age, you can introduce a sippy cup—a cup with a built-in straw—or a tiny regular cup. It will likely take a while for your baby to get used to drinking from something other than a bottle or the breast, so be patient. You will need to try different types of cups to see which one your baby prefers. There are several varieties of sippy cups and cups with straws, so if your baby doesn't take to one, simply try others until you find one that works.

Water or milk can be put in the cup, but juice is not recommended at this time. Put ½ to 1 ounce of fluid in the cup, and be sure the baby drinks slowly. You can give water immediately after food, but wait a while after eating to give formula or breast milk. If the baby eats three times a day, the amount of total fluid should be around 24 ounces. Bottles are still okay to use and will likely still be an important part of your routine. Remember not to put the baby to sleep with a bottle, though, and not to put any solid food, including cereal, in the bottle.

Getting Protein

Babies will get enough protein from fish, eggs, dairy, and tofu. These are considered complete proteins. On their own, vegetables, legumes, and grains are incomplete proteins, so be sure your baby is getting enough protein every day.

Tofu is a nonfermented type of soy that's very high in protein and calcium. You can start giving tofu around eight months.

A combination of vegetables, grains, and legumes can also make up complete proteins; for example, cheese and avocado, rice and beans/peas and barley, or lentils and vegetables.

baby steps

The body produces substances called amino acids—essential and nonessential. Proteins are made from these substances. Ten essential amino acids need to be ingested every day for correct nutrition and energy because they're not produced by the body. A diet rich in eggs, meat, dairy, nuts, grains, legumes, and rice provides what is necessary.

Vegetarians and Vegan Babies

If you're vegetarian and eat fish and want your baby to follow this diet as well, follow the recipe guidelines in this chapter and substitute the meats with tofu or fish.

Use soy-milk formula instead of formulas based on cow's milk. Don't give soy milk or tofu to babies who are allergic to soy, however. If a baby is allergic to soy at 12 months, you can use rice milk, but make sure it's fortified. Don't use goat's milk (it can produce a very serious type of anemia).

If you're vegan and want your baby to follow this diet as well, substitutions for one egg when cooking include:

1 tsp. baking powder plus 1 TB. water plus 1 TB. vinegar

1 TB. cornstarch plus 3 TB. water

2 TB. seltzer (carbonated water) plus 2 tsp. flour

¼ cup applesauce

¼ cup tofu

Any of these substitutions can be used for baking.

Use tofu in all egg recipes (for example, scrambled tofu instead of scrambled eggs). You can substitute tofu in the chicken fingers recipe and the meat stew recipe as well. Also, gluten-free flour for the breadcrumbs can be used for infants with celiac disease (intolerance to gluten). Tofu can also be combined with fruits and yogurt or with vegetables.

Essential Takeaways

- Sleep training may need to be started again, and the bedtime routine is important to continue.
- Diversify the diet by continuing to introduce new foods for three days at a time.
- Give solid foods three times a day.
- Watch for allergic reactions, and know what to do in case one occurs.
- Start the baby drinking from a cup.
- Reduce the amount of fluids as you increase the solid food.

chapter 19

From a Medical Perspective

How to help your baby through teething

When the healthy baby needs to see the doctor

What to do in an emergency

Concern about developmental issues or delays

Your baby is growing and developing in so many ways. Along with teething and the well-baby checkup, you'll learn here about other conditions to watch out for and how to handle emergency situations.

Understanding Teething

Teething is the process that results in the appearance of the baby's first teeth. These first teeth are called primary teeth because they'll fall out and be replaced by the secondary or permanent teeth.

By three years of age, a child will have 20 primary teeth. After 12 years old, a child will have 32 permanent teeth. The third molars, or wisdom teeth, will erupt in adulthood.

The roots of the teeth are present from birth. In some rare cases, babies are born with teeth. Unless they're loose, they don't need to be removed.

Teeth Order

The first teeth to come in are the lower-middle teeth, called the lower incisors. Teething can start as early as three months but usually begins at four to six months. The upper incisors appear one to two months after the lower ones, at about age seven to eight months.

Next are the lateral lower incisors at 10–16 months, followed by the upper lateral incisors at 9 to 13 months. The first molars will come in around 13–19 months, the canines at 16–23 months, and the second molars at 22–30 months.

Because all babies are different, teething will happen at various times for every child. Expect a lot of fussiness, drooling, sometimes mild diarrhea (due to the swallowed saliva), and a low-grade fever of 100.5–101° Fahrenheit. If the symptoms appear to be getting worse and the fever is higher, it's probably not because of teething and you may need to see your doctor.

Ways to Help with the Discomfort

Some babies will go through teething without anyone even knowing it—and let's hope your baby is one of them. But typically, a baby will experience some discomfort during the process of cutting teeth.

To alleviate the pain of teething, you can gently push your finger on the baby's gums; the compression makes it feel better. Somehow, babies know this, and that's why they put their fingers or their entire fist in their mouth. You can also give your baby a teething ring or a teething toy. This should be cold but not frozen.

Putting topical teething gels, lotions, or creams on the gums to numb them is controversial. It may help temporarily, but the increased amount of saliva from drooling will dilute it in seconds. Also, these topical applications can only be used four times a day at most.

Teething biscuits or large pieces of bread to chew can alleviate the pain of teething, but it needs to be closely monitored to make sure the baby doesn't try to swallow a big piece and then be in danger of choking.

Hold off on giving pain medication for teething pain until it's absolutely necessary. The baby will be uncomfortable no matter what you do. Consult with your doctor about medication for teething before you give your baby anything.

You may notice a bluish color right on top of a tooth that's about to erupt through the gum. This is called a teething hematoma (bruise). The tooth will usually cut through, but if it doesn't, you may need to see a pediatric dentist.

Now that the baby has teeth, even if it's only one, the teeth have to be cleaned morning and evening. Cleaning the baby's teeth in the evening can become part of the bedtime routine. Use a soft toothbrush designed for infants or a finger brush. You can just use water because toothpaste isn't really important yet. But if you want to use toothpaste, be sure it's infant toothpaste that is fluoride-free (extra fluoride isn't needed now), doesn't foam, and has a good taste.

Consult with the doctor if the teeth have strange shapes, if they're colored (bluish or dark) other than what's normally expected, if they fall out, or if there are no teeth by 15 months. These situations could be signs of certain diseases.

The Well-Baby Checkup

Your baby will be seen for a well-baby visit at nine months. There will be no vaccines unless the baby needs to catch up or didn't get the flu vaccine at six months.

Flu Vaccine
Since 2009, the vaccine for the "swine" flu, caused by the virus H1N1, is given together with the seasonal flu vaccine. Two vaccines are necessary, separated by at least one month, for all children up to age nine receiving the vaccine for the first time. It's recommended that parents, caregivers, and older siblings receive the flu vaccine as well. The vaccine is given once a year because every year there's a new vaccine made against the new yearly flu strain. Visit www.cdc.gov for the latest information on flu vaccine.

Your baby's height, weight, and head circumference will be measured. The doctor will check the baby head to toe. You'll talk about developmental milestones and sleeping. So much has happened since the baby was last seen at six months, so you'll have a lot to catch up on. You'll also talk about nutrition, teething, and safety. The next well-baby visit will be at 12 months.

Common Concerns

It's hard to separate what happens from one month to the next in this age group—seven to nine months—as far as symptoms and illnesses are concerned.

The more social your baby becomes, the more infections he or she will be exposed to from other children. You'll treat the common cold at home with nasal drops, a warm bath, and a humidifier.

If the baby has a fever and still looks well, you can wash him or her (sponge bath) with cool (not icy-cold) water. If the baby refuses to eat but is still drinking well, increase the fluids. Don't force the feeding of solid foods.

Other Conditions and Diseases You Should Know About

As babies become more social and are spending more time in the bigger world, it's possible for them to catch or be exposed to other things as well.

Lice: Babies may get lice from older siblings, another infected baby, or by the use of infected objects (comb). The condition of head lice is the result of an insect that lives in hair. It's highly contagious, but fortunately, not as dangerous as it is annoying.

Babies will be uncomfortable because the scalp will itch. Only older babies are able to scratch their scalp but the younger ones will be very irritable. The open wounds from scratching can get infected if constantly touched.

You may see a small insect moving on the scalp or small white lice eggs that attach to the hair shaft. Lice will not hurt the baby. Although unpleasant to deal with, having head lice is not a sign of poor hygiene.

If the baby has hair, get a fine-tooth comb and try to comb out the hair lice and nits (eggs). Talk to your doctor, who will recommend nontoxic substances to use on the hair. Don't share towels or combs. Wash the bed (crib) linen well in hot water as well as towels and articles of clothing that may have been infested, and thoroughly vacuum carpets and furniture.

Insect bites: Most insect bites will only cause a small, red pimple. If the baby is allergic to the specific insect, however, there could be a large itchy, painful area. Clean the area well with cold water, give an antihistamine, and see the doctor.

Snake bite: Be familiar with snakes that live in your area, or any area you will be staying in for a length of time. Know how to distinguish the venomous from the non-venomous ones. Usually the round-headed snakes are non-venomous. If the baby is bitten, clean the area immediately and take him or her to the closest ER. Don't apply a tourniquet, don't suck out the venom, and don't rub the area. The best thing you can do is get to emergency care as soon as possible.

Lyme disease: This disease is named after the town in Connecticut where it was first described in 1975. There are a few areas in the United States where Lyme disease is more endemic: the Northeast, the Pacific Northwest, and some areas of the northern part of the Midwestern states.

The disease comes from the bacteria *Borrelia burgdorfi,* which is found in small animals. It's transmitted to humans through a small tick called the deer tick. People are only at risk for the disease if the tick is embedded in the skin for 48 hours.

Some patients demonstrate a rash that looks like a bull's-eye: a red spot surrounded by a clear area and a red circle. After the initial symptoms, one may feel tired, aches and pains, fever, and headaches. A baby won't show all of these signs. Consult your doctor right away if you discover a tick on your baby.

Poison ivy, oak, and sumac: Familiarize yourselves with these plants. Poison ivy either grows as a vine or as a small shrub. Poison oak is a shrub with oaklike leaves and poison sumac is either a tall shrub or a small tree.

If the baby touches this plant, he or she may develop a very itchy rash. This occurs because the plant contains an oil called urushiol, which is extremely allergenic.

Wash everything well that was in contact with the plant. Clean the area with cold water and soap or you can use ice cubes. Give a bath with lukewarm water and baking soda or oatmeal two to four times a day. Apply a paste made with equal parts of baking soda and water on the rash.

This condition usually clears within 7–14 days. See the doctor if the rash is on the face or scalp, the eyes, or genital areas.

Impetigo: This is a rash that looks like it's crusted with honey, derives from *Staphylococcus* and *Streptococcus,* and is contagious. It appears mostly on the face or around the nose and mouth. See your doctor for treatment.

Ringworm (tinea corporis): Ringworm is a highly contagious fungus that your baby can contract from another just by touching. The lesion appears red with white scales in the middle. This condition is easily treatable with a cream. If the ringworm is on the scalp (tinea capitis), the baby needs to take medication by mouth.

Pinworms (*Enterobius vermicularis*): This is a contagious condition that is a result of parasites that live in the intestines. One may not know that they're infected, and children can have extreme itching around their anus or vagina. Children can acquire pinworms from sandboxes or dirty hands. There are many other parasites, but they're rare in this age group.

With a flashlight, look at your child's anal area or put a transparent tape on the anus. If you see very small white worms, you've made the diagnosis. You can bring the tape to your doctor, who may look at it under the microscope. Pinworms are treated with medication and some doctors recommend that the whole family be treated as well.

Scabies: Scabies are very small mites that can infest the skin. This can cause itching, especially at night. Babies can have a rash anywhere on the body, while older children have them in between the fingers. It's highly contagious, and you'll need to wash everything in the house and see the doctor.

Bed bugs: These are small parasitic insects that like to live in homes—in mattresses, curtains, frames, wallpaper, etc. (Their existence is not a sign of uncleanliness.) A rash develops and looks red, either linear or in groups of lesions and is very itchy. The rash is usually seen on the face, arms, and legs. Talk to the doctor, who may prescribe a cream and/or an antihistamine.

Vacuum everything, wash linen and bed sheets in hot (120° Fahrenheit) water, or you can leave them outside in freezing temperatures. You may have to discard a very infested mattress.

When to See the Doctor

Any number of conditions and symptoms can arise in your baby that will require a visit to the doctor:

Fever above 103° Fahrenheit can indicate an infection. The doctor will determine whether further treatment or medication is necessary. Of course, if your baby doesn't look well to you, that's a good enough reason to see the doctor.

A **persistent cough** with fever, increased fussiness, or sleepiness with or without fever can be alarming and a cause for concern. Also, a cough with labored breath and a whistling sound or stridor (a short, high-pitched sound). If there is a **rash and fever**, it could be anything from a simple viral infection to meningitis or chickenpox (the baby will receive the first chickenpox vaccine at 12 months).

Rapid, labored breathing is very worrisome, especially if you can see the spaces between the baby's ribs. This means that the baby is working too hard to breathe.

If there are any **color changes**; the baby is too pale, too red, or jaundiced. A bluish coloration of the lips and nails may indicate that the baby is in respiratory distress; he or she may not be getting enough oxygen.

If the baby's stool looks like grape or currant jelly, you must see the doctor immediately. At this age, *intussusception* becomes more common. This means that part of the baby's bowel can be obstructed. The baby needs to be taken to the emergency room immediately.

Intussusception happens when one part of the bowel is pushed into another part. It telescopes, or folds in on itself. This will cause the bowel to stop functioning, resulting in severe abdominal pain, vomiting, and infection.

If you observe a bump in the inguinal area (the groin) in girls or boys, or if one side of the scrotum is much larger than the other, this could indicate the presence of a **hernia**.

Vomiting and/or diarrhea that doesn't stop within a period of 24 hours, especially if the vomit is dark yellow, green, or contains blood, may indicate a more serious condition.

If the baby stops drinking or drinks very little and has fewer wet diapers, you need to be concerned about **dehydration**. Your doctor will assess the severity and advise you about fluid replacement or other treatment.

If the baby's eyes still can't focus and the child remains "**cross–eyed**," it may be time for a referral to a specialist. If the baby is tearing all the time, it may indicate a **blocked tear duct**—a condition that while not serious may need attention.

Swelling of the eyelid with surrounding redness may indicate **conjunctivitis** (pink eye), a contagious condition that can be easily treated with medication prescribed by your doctor.

Babies will have **ear infections** more often, indicated by pulling on the ear. But ear-pulling could also be a sign of teething.

After eight to nine months of age, if the baby has **thrush** (from *Candida albicans,* a yeast infection of the mouth), it could be a sign of a weak immune system. (Up until five to six months, this condition is considered normal.)

Although bruises may become more evident as the baby becomes more mobile, the sudden appearance of **a new, large bruise** on the baby's body needs immediate attention by your doctor.

First Aid and Emergencies

The more mobile your baby becomes, the more vigilant you have to become about the dangers in the immediate environment. This is not meant to frighten you. The idea is not to try to impose unhealthy and unrealistic limitations on your baby's movements in order to keep him or her out of harm's way but rather to make you aware of how to safely monitor your baby's actions. So if a problem comes up, you'll know what to do about it.

As babies become more adept at negotiating their environment and their movements become more and more refined, they also become very fast! You turn your back for literally a second and they're somewhere else.

It's recommended that parents and caretakers take a class in first aid. This will give you basic information and skills in case of an emergency—enough to be able to make good decisions and if necessary spring into action.

If the baby is **choking**, first observe whether the baby is coughing. The piece of food or object can become dislodged on its own, but if not, put the baby on your arm and give four firm swats on the back. Do not put your finger in the mouth to try to dislodge the object. If there is any change in the baby's color, if the baby's lips are turning blue, or the baby is having difficulty breathing, call 911.

Babies will inevitably fall and hurt themselves. Most of the time, the only problems are a little bump and a bruised ego. If the baby falls or hits the head but is crying and seems fine otherwise, talk to your doctor for further advice. If the baby is **unresponsive** (unconscious) or is vomiting, this is an immediate emergency. Call 911.

If the baby sustains a **burn** over a small area and it's just red with no blisters, run cold water over the area and place a clean gauze or adhesive bandage over the site. If the burn blisters or if it covers the face or a larger part of the body, call the doctor or 911. **All electrical burns are emergencies.** They don't cause burns on the skin as much as serious damage to the body (especially the heart).

Cuts that are superficial, small scratches can be washed well with water, followed by applying an antibiotic cream. When a cut is deep or bleeding can't be stopped, that's an emergency.

Broken bones need to be checked as soon as possible. If the mobility of an arm or leg is inhibited, if an arm or leg is limp, if the baby appears in pain, is limping, or refuses to put any weight on the legs, you need to see the doctor.

For potential **poisoning**, if you suspect that the baby has swallowed something, call Poison Control immediately (1-800-222-1222). Give as much information as you can about what you think the baby ingested. They'll tell you what to do and whether you need to go to the emergency room.

If you observe rhythmic movements of the arms and legs, if there is head-bobbing, or if the baby's entire body is shaking, this is a **seizure** and is an emergency. Call 911 immediately.

Developmental Concerns

It's important to continue to note your baby's development to ensure that it's on track within a reasonable range. Talk with your doctor if you observe any of the following in your baby:

At seven months: isn't turning, isn't babbling, or isn't sitting with support

At eight months: isn't sitting, isn't attempting to crawl but doesn't try to cruise, and doesn't transfer

At nine months: the baby doesn't sit, crawl, babble, or still has the grasping reflex

At all ages: doesn't appear to see, doesn't follow objects, or doesn't look at you; doesn't respond or react to sounds; doesn't play and doesn't enjoy being hugged; the muscles are too stiff or too soft; the baby can't swallow solid food or chokes when attempting to eat

Essential Takeaways

- The common signs of teething include fussiness, drooling, and low-grade fever.
- Take a first-aid class to know the treatment procedures for burns, cuts, poisoning, and choking.
- Consult your baby's doctor if you're concerned about any developmental issues.

Part 5

Months Ten, Eleven, and Twelve

You're almost there. Almost a year has passed since you brought your brand-new baby home. Here, we'll discuss your baby's exploration of new things and the making of so many discoveries. Some babies will be crawling by now, and some will just skip the entire thing.

We'll cover baby talk, new sounds, and words as well as eating, new toys and clothes, and new equipment.

Finally, we'll talk about milestones and potential concerns. As always, we'll help you understand and guide you through if conditions or problems come up that need attention.

chapter 20

Going Mobile and Interacting

More milestones: standing, cruising, and taking steps

Understanding your baby's temperament

New activities you and your baby can do together

Updating furniture, equipment, clothing, and toys

The good news is that you won't need to exercise too much at this point. You'll be kept on your toes by a very curious and fast little one. In months 10–12, babies are extremely active with exercising their new mobility and can get into trouble within a second, so be sure to watch your baby constantly.

Cruising

By this stage, babies are typically cruising, which means they are standing up and moving around with support from you or other stationary objects, such as tables and chairs. This is an exciting time in your baby's growth, and your camera will be working overtime.

Climbing Out of the Crib

Believe it or not, many babies at this age can climb out of their crib (or at least, they will try). If bumpers are in the crib, they help boost the baby up to do it. So remove the bumpers and lower the mattress to the lowest possible level. After many attempts, some babies just get frustrated, cry, and give up; others, however, will actually succeed and climb out.

If the baby can still climb out after you've lowered the mattress and taken out the bumpers, it's time to move the baby to a toddler bed with sides that will still hold the baby in the bed if he or she rolls over. Don't use crib tents because the baby will still try to climb out, and tragic accidents can happen.

There's no set time for switching to a bed; it can happen out of necessity, such as in the case of being able to climb out of the crib, or later when you feel it's time to switch. There are cribs that can convert to beds as well. When you do switch to a new bed, the baby may be fine with it and comfortable, or there may be a lot of protesting.

Your baby will slowly get used to the new bed in time. Don't bring the baby into your bed, and don't put them to sleep on an inflatable mattress or waterbed. These are not safe for babies. Also, be sure that the baby's room or area is completely childproof—outlets covered and so on. Then, even if the baby does get out of the new bed, the surroundings will be safe—a much better alternative than falling out of the crib.

Holding On and Taking Steps

By now, the baby has likely mastered crawling. Remember, though, some babies won't crawl at all and will just stand up. First, the baby figures out how to stand up from sitting. In the attempts to stand, he or she will probably fall down many times back into the sitting position.

After that, the baby will hold on to anything that's sturdy (mostly furniture). At the beginning, it'll just be standing, holding on, and looking at the world from a different perspective. Then, the baby will slowly start taking a few steps while holding on. By 10–12 months, babies get confident holding on to furniture, so now you can try to have him or her take a step while holding on to your hand. Don't force it if the baby gets scared or upset. Just let the baby reach this milestone at his or her own pace; it will happen soon enough.

While it may be tempting to put your baby in a walker at this stage, don't. Walkers are very dangerous and shouldn't be used under any circumstances. Let your baby learn to take his or her first steps with your helping hands.

Walking

Some babies will walk early. It's thought that the time of walking may be genetically linked; an early-walking parent will have an early-walking baby. There's no set early time, but if there are no steps taken by 15–16 months, it may be cause for concern. Walking requires coordination of the brain, eyes, nerves, and muscles. When it happens, it's a major milestone.

Timeless Wisdom

Fall seven times, stand up eight.

—Chinese proverb

Babies will take a few hesitant, small steps. This reflects the immaturity of the brain that's sending commands to the muscles. You can hold both of their hands (and later, just one). Babies will fall a lot, usually on their buttocks. They will be okay; they don't have far to fall. Just help your baby stand up and try again.

Most babies walk with a broad-based gait (legs wider apart) and with an exaggerated curvature of the spine (called normal lordosis). In the beginning, the baby's feet and toes will be turned a bit inward, and many babies will walk on their tiptoes. This is normal at first, but if it continues after two to three years, it's a reason to see your doctor. Bowed legs, knocking knees, and flat feet are normal at this age and are no need for concern.

We take walking for granted, but it's a very complicated movement and function of the human body. The normal gait is heel to toe. Walking involves more than 200 muscles and many bones, joints, and nerves.

Buying Shoes

Before your baby started walking, the cute little booties were fine—but now the baby will need some real shoes. At home, the baby can walk around barefoot. Going barefoot is actually very good for the feet because it increases their strength and flexibility. But don't let the baby walk around in just socks, because slipping and falling is possible. Socks with rubber soles are okay. For safety, always carefully check all the areas where you think your baby will cruise or walk to make sure the floor is clean and clear of any potential hazards.

When the baby goes outdoors, he or she will need shoes to protect the feet. You don't need to spend a lot on shoes because they'll be outgrown in no time (probably every two to three months). Just because a shoe is more expensive doesn't mean that it's better.

What's most important is that the shoe size is right. With the baby standing, bend the front of the shoe. It's not the right shoe or fit if it's too stiff and doesn't bend at all. Push down on the front of the shoe gently when the baby tries the shoes on. Your thumb should be between the toes and the end of the shoe.

The shoe has to be wide enough not to hurt the toes but should not fall off while the baby is walking. They should have nonslip soles and be made of material that is able to "breathe" (nothing too thick). The first shoes should be closed-toe (no sandals).

Once your baby feels secure in the shoes and sees that walking is great fun, he or she will take off and need to be watched, because they can still (and will likely with new shoes on) fall or slip.

No parent will ever forget their baby's first steps!

Fine Motor Skills

Fine motor skills are improving at this stage. The baby is mastering the fine pincer grasp. He or she can push buttons and will be able to bend and pick up objects while standing.

At this age, the baby may discover that it's fun to throw things. If this gets out of hand (and someone could get hurt), tell your baby "no" and show him or her how to play properly with the object or toy.

The baby will begin to show preference for the right or left hand by now, but left- or right-handedness isn't definitively determined until two to three years of age.

Cognitive Development

The baby can now find objects that are completely hidden, will point at pictures, and will even start "pretend" play— pretending to brush hair or talk on the phone. They'll imitate everybody, so pay attention to your habits!

Social Development

At this stage, babies like to be with people even more than with toys. They take more interest in other babies, but little ones still don't play together. They explore by touching other babies, saying words, and showing emotion. Playgroups help many babies overcome stranger anxiety.

Games for 9–12 months old are more interactive. Sports, music, and arts and crafts are popular activities.

Babies understand simple commands. They'll shake their head "no." They understand the word "no" but still won't stop doing what you're asking.

Again, consistency is the most important discipline. Say "no" and take the baby away from the place or situation you don't want him or her to be in, or give the baby another toy (distraction). If you allow your child to touch something today but not tomorrow, there'll be confusion. Be sure all caregivers are consistent as well.

Discipline

Discipline is teaching, not punishing. Actually, by being consistent and having a routine with your baby, you're performing a type of discipline. As the baby becomes more independent, more mobile, and more understanding of people and the environment, the way you discipline will change.

As previously discussed, saying "no" may stop the baby for a second, but don't expect that the baby will understand. Don't use "no" all the time, only when absolutely necessary. Babies will challenge you.

The "out of sight, out of mind" method works much better at this age. Always offer an alternative for the object you are taking away. By talking and repeating what you mean, your baby will eventually understand certain boundaries.

Practice positive reinforcement. You don't want your baby to think that you react only when something is wrong. Clap and smile and hug your baby often.

If you get angry, it's very important not to allow your anger to escalate. If you need to count to 10, then do so. If you need to leave the room, it's okay. Yelling is not a method of discipline; neither are derogatory words that an older infant may understand (if not the meaning, the tone). Don't imitate your baby when they're crying or being fussy.

Physical punishment is not discipline—it's just violence, and is teaching the child aggressive behavior. Although over 90 percent of parents say they spanked their child at least once, the AAP wants parents to find other ways to discipline. A baby under 18 months will not understand spanking. The baby will notice, however, that hitting is allowed. If the baby is spanked once, the parents will likely do it again and more forcefully. And eventually with other objects other than the hands. If a baby stops misbehaving after being yelled at or spanked, it's because they're scared and shocked.

The theory that some people may ascribe to that says, "This is how I grew up," no longer stands. Times have changed and so have parenting and discipline. If a child is hit on a regular basis, it becomes child abuse. *Time-out*, which is putting the child in a place that is removed from the problem area, doesn't work at this age, either. The baby won't understand why he or she is put there, nor will he or she remember what they did to begin with. Most 12-month-old children won't stay in place for more than a few seconds.

The best ways to discipline at this age are by:

- Explaining why something is wrong

- Practicing consistency

- Ignoring certain behaviors

- Distracting the child

Your Baby's Temperament

You'll probably have figured out by now that all babies aren't the same, don't do things in the same way, and don't do things in the same time frame. Beyond genetics (the traits that are inherited) and environmental influences, each of us comes into the world with our own inherent temperament.

Temperament or disposition describes the level of activity, the way a person responds to different stimuli and other people, and how he or she adjusts to new environment and change. Temperament describes the traits that are persistent and stable within an individual.

Temperament Theory

definition

The Greek physician and philosopher Galen (130–200 C.E.) developed a theory postulating that temperament is determined by the different concentrations of fluid within the body: *blood-sanguine* (extroverted, active, and social), *black bile-melancholic* (creative and kind), *yellow bile-choleric* (energetic and passionate), and *phlegm-phlegmatic* (dependable and affectionate). Which do you think your baby will be?

Babies' personalities have been studied for decades. In a landmark longitudinal study in the 1950s, child psychiatrists Stella Chess and Alexander Thomas found that certain personal traits could be seen as early as four weeks old.

Because every baby is unique, no comparisons should be made to any other child. That being said, there are certain general categories that describe the way babies behave. These descriptive categories are simply meant as a guideline to understand different types of temperament. Chess and Thomas described four categories of temperament: easy, difficult, slow to warm up, and mixed.

Easy babies are generally in a good mood, calm, and adjust quickly to change. There's regularity to their routines; for example, they have no problem eating and going to bed on a fairly set schedule. Parents need to remember to spend a lot of time with these babies, even if they feel they seem pretty self-sufficient.

Babies who are very shy are slow to warm up and often fearful. They have trouble calming themselves. They don't respond well to change, tend to withdraw from new situations and people, and can easily become overstimulated. These babies respond to hunger slowly. Parents need to know the signs of overstimulation, learn to make changes slowly, be calm, know their baby's signs of hunger, and respond quickly to their baby's needs. Introduce new situations and people slowly and gradually because these babies need more time to feel comfortable interacting.

Difficult, fussy, and feisty babies are restless and respond to hunger vigorously. They're generally light sleepers. Bottom line: these babies have trouble establishing a routine. It's hard to soothe them, and it's hard for them to soothe themselves. At times, they can become inconsolable.

It's difficult for parents to take care of these babies. The often unsettling environment creates a lot of anxiety, self-doubt, and stress for the parents. For these types of babies, try to establish a calm environment. Most importantly, parents should not expect a routine or pattern of behavior. Parents should make as few changes as possible (and only gradually). They need to know the early signs of hunger, not allow overstimulation, and be consistent at all times.

Mixed temperament refers to babies who fall into more than one category. Sometimes they're easy and sometimes they're difficult, depending on the situation. The key here for parents is to be attentive and flexible.

In the 1950s, a scale of nine temperamental characteristics of babies was created. Perhaps this scale will help you better understand your baby's temperament and to better respond to his or her specific needs:

1. Activity level

2. Regularity (of sleeping and eating patterns)

3. Adaptability

4. Initial reaction (approach or avoidance)

5. Sensitivity (reaction to change in the environment)

6. Intensity (emotion or reaction)

7. Distractibility

8. Persistence and attention span

9. Mood (positive or negative)

We waited until now to talk about temperament because it's really one of those things you need to discover about your baby on your own. Having a preconceived notion about what to expect might easily color the way you treat your baby and behave around him or her. You've certainly had enough on your plate up until now without information and theories that could easily confuse you.

But now, your baby is on his or her way to becoming a healthy youngster, and who he or she is inherently is a good thing to know. Although the temperament doesn't reflect one's ability to parent, the parents' influence is enormous. The environment you create and your capacity to love and be there for your child is what will stay with him or her for life.

Language

Your baby's language is developing quickly now. Babbling seems more organized, and consonants tend to be different than they have been. It seems that your baby is speaking a foreign language that only he or she can understand. It's actually called jargon. If you listen, you'll hear that the intonations are different as well. There's a lot of conversation going on with questions and answers—and it sounds adorable.

When you talk to your baby, he or she will listen and respond in his or her own baby language. Now, your child understands that "talking" and responding to talk provokes a positive reaction. Here and there, you may hear "mama" or "dada," but maybe not directed toward the right person. There may be other words your baby can say as well, such as "up" or "bye."

The baby shakes his or her head at "no." This is a good time to begin to teach good manners. Repeating "please" and "thank you" will teach the baby to use these words appropriately very soon. It's never too early to begin. The baby understands so much more than he or she can express.

Calming Frustrations and Anxieties

Emotions are now running high. Your baby will express feelings by laughing out loud, "talking" a lot, or being really fussy and crying when he or she can't get his or her way.

Throwing toys or other objects may become part of the frustration. You can help by talking to your baby. Is he or she going to understand? Probably not, but your baby will know that you're there during those moments of frustration. Don't make the situation worse by reacting negatively toward your baby; use the word "no" only when absolutely necessary. Otherwise, it will lose its meaning.

Always react positively to any accomplishment, and respond when the baby wants your attention. This in no way means that you have to constantly entertain your baby. He or she knows you're there, but your baby also needs some quiet time to learn how to entertain and soothe himself or herself.

Be aware of your emotions around your child. Raised voices should be reserved for your own private time, away from the baby. Parental anxiety, depression, inconsistency, and even hostility can make the baby insecure, frightened, and unable to adjust.

Always strive to maintain calm. Remove the baby from a difficult situation and quickly give him or her a toy, put music on, or walk around with the baby. If you give in to your own anger or frustration and try to take something away from the baby with force or shout at him or her, it can create a bad situation where both of you may end up crying and feeling even more frustrated.

Alleviate the baby's anxieties as much as possible—mainly, stranger anxiety. For example, if you go to work, ask the sitter to come earlier. Don't create a big "good-bye" scene. A short hug and kiss is enough. The baby will stop crying shortly after you leave (even if you don't).

Your baby may be frightened of loud noises, such as a telephone ringing, an operating vacuum cleaner, thunder, or outside noises. Calm the baby down, and after some time, bring your baby to the offending object and let him or her touch it. You can even get a toy phone or vacuum to help show the baby it's not something to be frightened of.

If the baby is accustomed to having a light on in his or her room at night, continue to leave the light on. You may decide that it's time for lights out at night, but the baby won't understand about suddenly being left in the dark and may become frightened and anxious. It's easy enough to just leave the light on.

We know it's not easy. Being calm requires a huge amount of energy, but this is what being a parent is about. The capacity to put aside your feelings and look out for your baby doesn't mean that boundaries shouldn't be established. Consistency and distraction will help the most.

Sometimes, parents remember what their own parents did. Now that you have your own child, take a moment and reflect. A lot has changed since you were a child. Use your own instincts and feelings and ask for advice, but always choose to do what you feel is best for your little one.

Make your best effort to understand your baby's ups and downs, don't take things personally, and learn how to defuse difficult or uncomfortable situations. The time you spend now on your relationship with your baby will help ensure a good and solid relationship moving forward.

Age-Appropriate Activities

You can now sit on the floor together and play more interactively. You can toss a ball back and forth or place toys all over and have the baby find and pick them up. You can also roll and pull around toys for the baby to follow and chase. Of course, be sure that the baby's play environment is safe. If there are objects that the baby can pull down or anything that's breakable, remove them.

Name everything you pick up or see, and repeat the words as much as you can. Help the baby identify a favorite toy. Show colors, and show animal pictures and imitate the sounds. Playing peek-a-boo, finding hidden toys, and putting toys back together are other great activities.

Give the baby safe utensils and pots and pans to bang together. Going in and out of a safe, three-walled, large box can be entertaining for hours. You can also sing ("Head, shoulders, knees, and toes") and show the body parts at the same time. Dance to different rhythms, and watch your baby imitate you.

If you like arts and crafts, make your own simple toys, such as a sock puppet. Take a clean adult sock, fill it with cotton balls, and tie a string around the "neck." Paint eyes, a nose, and a mouth with a nontoxic marker. There should be no small objects on the doll that the baby could pull off and swallow. You can place something inside that makes noise, like a small bell.

Make a caterpillar by cutting one leg of an old pair of tights, filling it with cotton balls, and tying it in three or four places. You can also make a fun, busy box. Cut different shapes into the sides of a large box, sew or stick on toys, other soft, safe objects, bells, or cut-out animal pictures. These toys are fun and inexpensive, and your baby watched you and even helped you make them.

Playing Outdoors

The sandbox is an easy and fun place in which babies can play. It may be hard to control the environment for your baby in a public playground with a sandbox. Instead, if possible, create a sandbox at home:

> Buy sand that is labeled for play and is crystalline silica-free (this is a harmful substance).

> Before the baby starts playing in it, check the sand with a rake for any sharp objects, animal feces, insects, etc. Change the whole box if you find any.

> Cover the box so animals can't get in.

> Make sure the sandbox is not too close to a pool or any landing areas (swing, monkey bars, etc.).

> In very windy areas, wet the sand.

> Make sure there are no pea-size pieces of gravel.

> Don't feed the baby while playing in the sandbox.

> Wash hands after play in the sandbox is over.

If the sand gets in the baby's eyes, place the baby on one side, and pour water gently on the eyes. Don't allow the baby to rub his/her eyes. If there's a great deal of discomfort, see the doctor or go to the ED.

Doing Things Together

Aside from playing together, reading is the next-best pastime. Read together at least once during the day and definitely at night. Now you can interact, so you can show a picture and tell the baby or ask him or her what it is. He or she may say something that sounds like the answer or make an animal sound.

Different colors, textures, and pop-up books are all fun. Talk a lot, ask questions, and name everything that you see and do. Sing together; you'll be surprised to hear musical sounds from the baby in response. Dance and hold the baby in your arms, or let him or her imitate your movements.

You can go to a museum—either a children's museum or a regular art museum. There are so many colors, different people, and everything that the baby likes. Go to the botanical gardens, the park, or wherever there are flowers and trees. The zoo may be a bit frightening, but it's worth a try.

The best classes at this age are music classes, baby gyms, and baby yoga. Many of them are interactive with the parent or caretaker.

As always, know when your baby is getting tired. Don't overstimulate, and let the baby have time to play on his or her own.

What You Need Now

Time flies—and before you know it, your baby will grow out of and into new equipment, toys, and clothes. Be sure to pay attention to your baby's evolving needs and desires.

Equipment

It's time to recheck all equipment. Child-proofing of your home should be completely finished.

Crib: If the baby can climb out of it, it's time for a bed or "converting" the crib into a bed. The bumpers, mobile, and changing table should have been retired a while ago.

Car seat: If the baby weighs 20 pounds at age 12 months, you can use a front-facing car seat—always in the backseat with no airbag device. (Or you can continue with a rear-facing seat up to 30–45 pounds.) The same rules apply to the five-point seatbelt; the baby should not look or feel uncomfortable. Be sure that the seat is perfectly stable. If you were using a small infant seat, it's time to change that now, but you can continue to use a convertible one.

Stroller: The baby is moving around a lot and may even try to climb out of the stroller, so the seatbelt needs to be safe—perhaps doubled—and the stroller wheels should be sturdy. Car seats that fit into a stroller are too heavy now and shouldn't be used. You don't have to spend a lot on a stroller. If you need to be on a subway (underground) or on buses, you may need a second (much lighter and collapsible) one. If the stroller you use meets all criteria we described (sturdy and collapsible), you don't need another one.

Shopping carts: The baby can ride in a shopping cart only if there's a safe baby seat with a belt.

Baby packs: You can now carry the baby in a backpack or a front carrier, but no more slings.

Jogging and bicycling: Take the same safety measures you did as before for these types of exercise with your baby. If you bought sturdy, solid equipment the first time, it should work for you for several years.

As always, check for recalls frequently at www.cpsc.gov.

Toys

Babies love toys that move (pushing and pulling anything). Musical and sound-making toys are also favorites. Toys that pop up generally surprise and delight babies and reinforce the cause-effect relationship.

When the baby plays with toys that have letters or colors, make sure to repeat what the letters or colors are. Simple puzzles with a few different large shapes and anything that has buttons that a little one can push are big hits.

Babies like stacking toys—either construction blocks or stacking rings. Toys that let the baby put things in and take them out are fun and help eye/hand coordination.

Little ones learn by imitating. They enjoy toy phones and will pretend to talk; they may also use toy brushes to pretend to brush their hair.

Balls can be tossed, kicked with the foot, or rolled on the floor. They'll help the baby's physical development.

Clothes

The amount of clothing you need depends on how many times you can do laundry. You should try to at least have the following items on hand at all times:

- Three to five comfortable jumpers or outfit separates

- Three to four sets of night clothes

- One or two "special occasion" outfits

- Five to six pairs of socks

- One sweater or light jacket, plus one warm coat if it's the season for it

- Five to six onesies

- One hat (either a sun hat or winter hat, accordingly)

- One or two pairs of shoes

At this age, clothes and shoes are outgrown very quickly, so you don't need a lot of anything. Dress by season as you dress yourself, plus one extra layer. Don't forget to buy larger diapers as you see the fit becoming tighter and more difficult to fasten. Always take one or two extra clothing changes with you whenever you leave home.

To save money on new clothes, check department store sales and discount stores. Sometimes yard sales and second-hand stores have nearly new things to offer. Make sure that night clothes are flame-resistant and that all clothing is free of hazards (strings and so on) that the baby can swallow.

Essential Takeaways

- If the baby climbs out of the crib, it's time to change to a toddler bed.
- The furniture needs to be sturdy when the baby is cruising.
- Babies need real shoes once they are walking.
- Get to know your baby's temperament so you can work best with it to help your baby respond to his or her environment.
- Spend time playing with and reading to your baby every day, and be consistent with discipline.
- Maintaining a calm demeanor around your baby and in response to his or her needs is most important for instilling a sense of security and safety.

chapter 21

Sleeping and Eating

The importance of maintaining a sleep routine

Feeding: new foods, baby utensils, and encouraging self-feeding

Introducing milk

A sample menu and great recipes

By now, hopefully you have a very respectful baby who's sleeping eight to nine hours a night. You did a great job sleep training, and your baby can actually put himself or herself to sleep. Some babies, though, still wake up at night, so you and your baby may not be getting a full night's sleep yet. Don't despair. Be diligent and consistent, and soon enough both you and your baby will be getting a good night's rest without interruption.

How to Handle Waking Up in the Night

After four to five months of age, you don't need to—and shouldn't—feed the baby at night. You may think you're doing the right thing by giving your baby food in the night, just in case he or she is hungry or because you feel feeding will comfort your baby. But this is a big mistake. You can actually make your baby a trained night-feeder!

Many babies wake up at night after achieving major milestones, and this is normal. In the night, you can find the baby crawling or standing up in the crib. These new skills are too exciting to not use at any given opportunity. But there's no need to panic (unless your baby has also figured out how to crawl out of the crib). Go into the baby's room, but don't pick the baby up and don't change the baby unless it's absolutely necessary. Talk to your little one, reassure him or her, give a hug, lay him or her back down, and leave. Your baby will likely protest some, but he or she will understand by now that you're still around, although you're not in the room—and will eventually soothe himself or herself back to sleep.

Sometimes babies just cry in their sleep. Wait a few moments before going into the room, because your baby may stop the sleep crying soon. If the baby wakes and continues to cry, go in to check on him or her just to make sure there are no health or safety issues.

Continue to keep pillows, blankets, and toys out of the crib. A transitional object is fine as long as you remove it after the baby is asleep.

The bedtime ritual should remain simple and consistent. Have quiet play one to two hours before the baby's bedtime, then a bath if you wish, followed by reading and singing. You can give the baby a transitional toy or object in the process. After your baby is in the crib and you leave the room, music of lullabies, gentle or classical music, or even a recording of your own voice can be left on to play. You can even have this music on repeat to play the entire night if this soothes your baby.

Make sure the last nap of the day is earlier in the afternoon to ensure a tired baby come bedtime. It's also helpful if the schedule during the day remains as consistent as possible.

Many new parents are sleep-deprived, dazed, and walking around with dark circles under their eyes. Why? They simply can't allow their baby to cry himself or herself to sleep. For some parents, hearing their child sobbing alone in the crib is heart-wrenching. So night after night, the parents give in to the same routine.

Do yourself a favor. Resist your immediate impulse to help and the guilt you feel about being a bad parent if you let your baby cry, and allow your baby to work it out on his or her own. Your baby will still love you in the morning.

Eating and Drinking

Eating and drinking at this age should really be considered a milestone. There are so many changes. Your baby can now eat finger foods and even hold a spoon. He or she is trying new foods, and at 12 months, your baby can start drinking regular cow's milk.

Mealtime Expectations

More than ever, it's important for your baby to sit at the table with the family at mealtime. You'll soon realize that the baby is just not interested in baby food anymore. Your baby will want what you have on your plate.

Put cut-up food on the baby's tray, not on a plate. At this age, babies want to feed themselves. It's part of their healthy development. Everything you place on the tray needs to be cut to half the size of your pinky nail.

You can feed the baby with a spoon and teach him or her how to eat with utensils. Be prepared for a mess. Put a large bib on the baby, and protect the floor.

The baby may start throwing food. Obviously, you don't want this to become a habit. Immediately say "no," be stern, and pick up the food. You can explain to the baby that this is not a good choice: "We don't do this." You can demonstrate the kind of behavior you want from the baby by placing food in the mouth, saying "yes," and then making a movement that imitates throwing food and say, "no."

Babies will explore by touching the food as well. This is fine as long as the baby's hands are clean and he or she ends up eating the food. Remember that all feedings still need to be done under supervision, because the baby can put too much in his or her mouth and choke. The rule is that there should be no distractions during feeding and definitely no toys or TV.

How Much Will the Baby Eat?

All babies are different, so the amount they will eat at this stage will vary. If a baby started solid foods earlier than six months, he or she may eat more at this point. A baby who is teething will eat less but is able to drink more. Babies will eat approximately two to three ounces per meal (some more, some less).

What to Feed at This Age

At this stage, your baby can eat almost everything. Avoid foods that have the potential to be a hazardous choking risk, such as candy; dried fruit; clumped food; nuts; whole grapes (cut them in half or quarter); big chunks of apple, pear, or carrots; and chewy meat (grind it instead).

You can try stage three foods and see whether your baby is interested. If not, there are easy recipes at the end of this chapter to make for this age. If your baby doesn't have any teeth (or fewer than four), continue to puree everything.

If you buy canned or frozen food, be very careful about the amount of salt and chemicals. Cold cuts, such as salami, bologna, and so on, also contain a fair amount of salt and chemicals. If you choose to feed them to your baby, look for natural, low-sodium varieties if possible. Also, don't give the baby any raw meat or fish.

baby steps

Taste buds have developed since about 15 weeks in utero. They peak at around 25–26 years, after which they decline more and more as one gets older. There are about 10,000 taste buds that are grouped into four categories: bitter, in the back of the tongue; salty at the side; sour in the middle; and sweet at the front of the tongue.

You can now start feeding the baby a whole cooked egg (the whites and the yolk), honey, all fruits and vegetables, and all meats. Any new food needs to be tried for three days to introduce it and to watch for any adverse reaction. Don't give more than one new food at a time.

Nuts and shellfish can wait until after 12 months. If there is a serious food allergy in the family, talk to your doctor about the best time to introduce those foods and how to introduce them.

Always have an anti-allergy medication at home and know how to use it. Ask your doctor's advice about what medication to have on hand in case of a reaction.

Your baby can breastfeed or drink formula until 12 months. Drinking water, permitted at six months, is still an important liquid, and it's still preferable not to give juice. A real fruit and water are much better choices.

Moms can breastfeed for as long as they choose, but if you decide to wean your baby at this point, do it slowly. Weaning abruptly will result in a very unhappy baby and a mom with extremely painful breasts.

Give up one breastfeeding a day or every other day. Instead, give the baby a favorite meal or snack, and increase the amount of water the baby drinks. The evening breastfeeding is the most difficult and will be the last to go.

If the baby has previously used a bottle, you can give one with either formula—before 12 months—or milk (after 12 months). There's no reason to introduce a bottle now if the baby has never used one before. Give your baby a sippy cup, a built-in straw cup, or a tiny baby cup. Put a small amount of fluid in the cup at first, and have the baby take a few sips. He or she may drink immediately (or not). If the baby doesn't seem to like this, wait and try again another time. It's a good idea to give the baby the cup when he or she is thirsty. If the baby doesn't want to drink, don't force it. Instead, you can add more formula or milk to the food.

Starting Milk

When the baby reaches 12 months, he or she can stop drinking formula and start drinking cow's milk. Use regular, whole milk. Babies need the fat for normal development. Never use unpasteurized milk or any other unpasteurized dairy products.

You can finish up whatever amount of formula you already purchased, and start cow's milk after that. Mixing formula and milk is not necessary. Babies can make the switch in a short time, and you want the baby to get used to the new taste. Offer milk in a cup as well. You don't want the baby to think that milk only comes in a bottle. This will make bottle weaning easier in the long run.

You want your baby to eat solid food three times a day, plus two snacks, so the amount of milk you give should be about 18–24 ounces. More than that isn't necessary because there will be too many calories and it'll be harder to digest. Continue giving vitamins, and if the water you use doesn't contain it, supplement with fluoride.

If you're still breastfeeding and produce enough milk, you can add your milk to the solid food. Milk protein–allergic babies should not be given cow's milk at this stage. Vegan babies can have soy or rice milk, but make sure these are enriched. Do not use goat milk because it can cause a serious anemia.

Childhood Obesity

Obesity means extra fat tissue and higher weight percentile compared to height. In older children and adults, the BMI or body mass index is used as a measurement. The prevalence of childhood obesity is high in the United States. Obesity in childhood predisposes to heart disease, diabetes, and early atherosclerosis.

In a recent study (David McCormick, "Infant Obesity: Are We Ready to Make this Diagnosis?", *Journal of Pediatrics*, 2010) it was shown that the diagnosis of obesity can be made at as early as six months of age, and that 16 percent of six-month-old babies were obese. The obese two-year-olds studied were found to be obese at six months.

If weight management through good nutrition and exercise is addressed early on, obesity can be prevented and it will be much easier to develop a lifetime of healthy habits.

Older infants and toddlers have a tendency to eat a high calorie-poor nutrient diet. Just replacing fruit juice with a whole fruit and drinking water is already a step toward healthy eating. Breastfeeding was shown to be the best in healthy feeding and reducing the risk of obesity.

Parents should know the hunger signs and feed the baby at that time. By feeding an infant whenever they cry, you'll be giving them too many calories. Introducing solid foods too early poses another risk.

When it comes to sweets, an infant can eat fruits and good-quality sweets in small amounts, such as a homemade pancake, fruit-based cookies, and smoothies.

Parents and caretakers should watch the baby's nutrition now, while you can easily control it. Hopefully, even with later temptations, through a good early start, and by setting a good example, your babies will grow up happy, healthy, and well nourished.

And contrary to the way we were raised, an unfinished plate is okay.

Breakfast

For breakfast, babies may like scrambled eggs, mini pancakes or French toast, or cereal. Your baby probably won't like baby cereal anymore. He or she will like the kind of cereal that they can actually grab. Give dry cereal with separate formula or milk.

For variation, you can put cottage cheese or cut-up veggies in the scrambled eggs. Put fruit on top of the mini pancakes or French toast, or give cut-up fruit with the dry cereal.

These recipes are made for more than one serving and can be kept in the refrigerator for 24 hours (and in the freezer for two weeks, at less than zero degrees). Don't freeze anything with eggs, fresh vegetables, or yogurt. Never refreeze anything.

French Toast

To make French toast, use only the yolk before 12 months and a whole egg after that.

Ingredients:

1 egg or egg yolk	2 slices bread
½ cup formula or milk	1 tsp. vegetable oil

Mix egg with milk and add a pinch of cinnamon. Heat vegetable oil in a frying pan to medium heat. Drench bread in egg and milk mixture; place in the pan for one to two minutes on each side. Serve with fruit (banana, peach, or berries).

Cheese Omelets

Ingredients:

1 egg	Thyme (optional)
1 tsp. cottage cheese	½ finely chopped tomato (optional)
1 tsp. formula or milk	1 tsp. vegetable oil
¼ cup very finely chopped small onion (optional)	

Mix egg with milk, cottage cheese, and thyme. Add vegetable oil to a frying pan over medium heat. When it's hot, add onion and tomato (if using). Let them brown for one to two minutes. Pour in egg/milk mixture and let them cook together for another two minutes. For vegans, use tofu or another egg substitute and soy or rice milk. Let cool thoroughly and cut into small pieces before serving to the baby.

Mid-Morning Snack Ideas

Cut up apples, pears, and bananas. Put a pinch of cinnamon or vanilla on top. (Be careful when you use vanilla because of the alcohol content.) You can serve the fruits on their own as finger food or with plain yogurt. (Be careful with commercial mixed yogurts; they contain a lot of sugar.)

Cut up vegetables—carrots, peppers (sweet), tomatoes, cucumber, and whatever else the baby likes. Spice them with dill, thyme, oregano, or basil (choose only one) and grated cheese (or tofu) sprinkled on top.

Lunch

Lunch is the time to get some vegetables into your baby's diet, along with more protein.

Vegetable Soup

Ingredients:

2 small potatoes

1 carrot

½ small bell pepper

4–5 green beans

Tomato

Celery stalk (about 4 inches long)

Pinch of dill and thyme

Vegetable oil

Peel and cut up vegetables into small pieces. In a small pot, add 1 cup water. Bring it to a boil; add cut-up vegetables. Add dill and thyme and 1½ tsp. vegetable oil. Cook until all veggies are soft. You can use less water for vegetable stew.

Rice with Cheese and Vegetables

Ingredients:

1 carrot

1 tomato

1¼ cup peas

½ red or green bell pepper

⅓ cup rice

Pinch of basil

2–3 tsp. cheese or tofu

2 oz. cooked, chopped meat (poultry or beef, optional)

Chop vegetables. Cook rice per the instructions on the package. When five minutes are left to cook, add finely chopped vegetables and basil. When finished cooking, add cheese or tofu. Mix well; serve. If using meat, mix it with the cooked rice and vegetables, and don't use the cheese.

Healthy French Fries

Ingredients:

2 small potatoes (or sweet
  potatoes)

Vegetable oil

1 TB. lemon juice

Pinch of dill or oregano

Peel and cut potatoes into half-inch pieces. Dry very well. Place in a baking pan greased with 1 tsp. vegetable oil. Squeeze lemon juice on potatoes
and sprinkle with dill or oregano. Sprinkle with another teaspoon oil.
Bake at 375° Fahrenheit for 35–40 minutes until the potatoes are golden
brown and crispy. You can use other root vegetables instead of potatoes.

Mid-Afternoon Snacks

Use half a carrot and one broccoli floret. Cut up veggies thinly (at 12 months they can be raw,
but before that you should cook or steam them first). Serve them plain, or have them in two
ounces cottage cheese or yogurt. Serve this in addition to milk and water.

Dry cereal with cut-up fruit is always a great snack.

Dinner

The baby should only eat meat once a day. Decide whether you will serve meat at lunch or
dinner.

Pasta with Vegetables

Ingredients:

⅓ cup cooked pasta
  (small pasta is best)

3–4 celery stalks

½ tomato

¼ bell pepper

1 broccoli floret

Pinch of basil or oregano

Cook pasta following package instructions. Don't overcook it. Pour out
water. Cut up celery, bell pepper, broccoli, and tomato into very small
pieces. Add vegetables to pasta. Add basil or oregano; serve.

Fish and Veggies

Ingredients:

4 oz. white fish	½ tomato
1 zucchini	Dill
A few slices onion	½ tsp. lemon juice
½ potato	1 tsp. vegetable oil

Pour oil into an ovenproof baking pan. Peel and cut up vegetables. Place fish, onion, and dill into the baking pan. Bake fish for 20 minutes at 350° Fahrenheit. Pour lemon juice on fish. Cook the tomato, potato, and zucchini separately for 15 minutes in the oven until soft but not mushy. When fish is done, add vegetables and serve.

Desserts

The following are healthy, yummy, and quick deserts.

Yogurt parfait: Place cut-up peaches and strawberries into a baby bowl. Top them with dry cereal topped with yogurt. Repeat for layers.

Yogurt with mashed banana and avocado: Use ½ banana, ¼ avocado, and 2 TB. yogurt. Blend everything. This makes a great smoothie. You can use any soft fruit with or without the avocado. They have different colors and are fun to eat.

Baked bananas or peaches: Slice one banana. Pour 1 tsp. baked honey (not raw) over top; add cinnamon. Add ½ tsp. vegetable oil to an oven-proof dish. Cover and bake at 350° Fahrenheit for 10–12 minutes. Serve with yogurt or just as is.

A Word About Birthday Parties

Happy birthday! (And yes, Mom and Dad, partners, and caretakers, we mean *you* too.) You and your baby have arrived at a great, truly unforgettable milestone: one year. Your baby is becoming a toddler, and you're a seasoned parent. It's time for celebrating.

One-year-old parties can be a small family dinner topped off with a cake to a party with many children and adults to a theme party. Choose the way you wish to celebrate. You've looked forward to this day for a long time, so do whatever makes you happy. But keep in mind that children get bored easily.

The party shouldn't be longer than one or two hours, if possible, and if you notice that your child is getting too tired, try to say goodbye earlier—or retire your child earlier than the party is over.

If you're buying a ready-made cake, a lot of them may have ingredients that the baby hasn't tried yet, so keep this in mind. Making the cake and frosting is always a safer bet if you have the time. Try to accommodate your guests as well as babies with special diet needs.

No-Bake Cheese or Tofu Cake

Ingredients:

1½ cup toasted graham crackers or rice cereal

1 cup brown sugar or honey

1 tsp. vanilla

⅓ cup vegetable oil or melted butter

8 oz. cream cheese or tofu

Zest of ½ lemon

2 tsp. lemon juice

1 pint plain yogurt or soy-based yogurt

20 oz. any fruit (berries, peaches, or apple) cut into small pieces

Prepare fruit by peeling and cutting, then mixing with 1 tsp. lemon juice and ⅓ cup sugar. Set aside. (You can use store-bought pie filling if you wish.)

Mix crackers or cereal with ⅓ cup sugar, ½ teaspoon vanilla, half the lemon zest, and oil. Press mixture into a pan. Chill until firm.

Beat cream cheese, half the lemon zest, ½ tsp. vanilla, ⅓ cup sugar, and 1 tsp. lemon juice. Add yogurt and mix well. If it's not sweet enough, add more sugar or honey. Pour crackers on top; top with fruit.

Different topping ideas are raspberries or blueberries mixed with sugar, vanilla, and yogurt. Raspberries will turn out as a pink topping (good for girls), and blueberries will turn out dark blue/purple (good for boys).

Essential Takeaways

- Babies will wake up in the night again when they have reached new milestones.
- Eat dinner together as a family—baby included—as much as possible.
- The baby will be interested in what you're eating, so allow the baby to try new foods—and remember the rule of three (any new food tried for three days).
- At 12 months, a baby can start drinking cow's milk.
- Let the baby drink from a cup, and teach the baby how to use utensils (starting with a spoon).

chapter 22

From a Medical Perspective

The 12-month well-baby visit

Vaccines and testing for tuberculosis, lead, and anemia

When to see the doctor and emergency situations

Alternative or integrative medicine for babies

The 12-month-old well-baby visit will bring lots of changes. All of a sudden, your baby is not an infant anymore. Your baby is now officially a toddler.

There are so many new milestones, words, behaviors, and foods and drinks! There are also new vaccines. You'll feel a little bit of sadness that your tiny baby has grown up so quickly, but you'll also experience a great deal of pride as you look forward to more growth and new adventures.

Your doctor will discuss your baby's weight (it probably tripled since birth) and height (he or she will have grown around 10 inches). After a head-to-toe examination, you'll talk about the milestones: crawling, cruising or taking the first steps, understanding simple commands, talking lots of "baby talk" and even some words, and being curious and getting into everything. Nutrition and how feedings are going will also be discussed.

If you're still breastfeeding and want to start weaning, you should talk about the process as well as for weaning from the pacifier and introducing the baby to drinking from a cup.

Twelve-Month Visit Vaccines

There are a few vaccines that your baby will receive at this age that he or she has not received previously.

MMR—Measles, Mumps, and Rubella

You may recall from Chapter 10 that the MMR vaccine was implicated as a potential cause of autism. The originator of this theory, Dr. Wakefield, had his license revoked for serious medical misconduct. But unfortunately, the damage had already been done, and many parents around the world had refused to give their child this vaccine. Very sadly, three nearly forgotten diseases resurfaced and killed many children.

Measles (rubella) is caused by a virus. It starts with a bad cold, rash, and eye infection (everything seems to be running) but can progress to *pneumonia* and *meningitis*. The occurrence of meningitis and encephalitis (an irritation and swelling of the brain) is very rare—0.5 per 100,000 children. A relatively small percentage of those who contract this condition will not survive, and those that do will probably have serious neurological problems.

Measles can also manifest later as a condition that infects the entire brain (*sub-acute sclerosing pan-encephalitis)*. There's no cure for this disease.

Mumps (*parotitis*) is a viral disease as well. It causes very painful swelling of the salivary glands (parotid glands), which are located in front of the ear (close to the jaw). It hurts to eat or drink, and children can become dehydrated very fast. In older boys, it can cause an inflammation of the testicles, called *orchitis,* and can cause inflammation of the pancreas in both males and females.

Rubella (German measles) is also caused by a virus. It's called German measles because it was first described by German physicians in the middle of the eighteenth century. Although it's a relatively easy disease with fever, painful lymph nodes, and a rash, the reason this vaccine is given is to prevent the congenital form of rubella.

Congenital rubella can occur when a pregnant woman contracts rubella during the first trimester of her pregnancy—therefore likely affecting the fetus as well. The baby will stop growing and will have *microcephaly* (a smaller head than usual). The brain won't be able to grow, and severe developmental delay will result. The eyes and the heart are affected, and the baby can be hearing impaired as well.

Chickenpox

Another vaccine given at 12 months is for chickenpox, or *varicella,* which is viral as well. The symptoms are fever, a rash, and discomfort due to itching of the rash. There may be some scarring of the skin after the disease has run its course.

The vaccine is given to prevent the serious effects of the viral and highly contagious diseases—varicella pneumonia, meningitis, and other neurological diseases. The vaccine is repeated at four years of age.

These vaccines may cause pain and redness at the site. Fever may come on in 10–14 days. At that time, the child may have a rash and a fever as high as 103° Fahrenheit that may last up to 48 hours. Treat the fever, and make the child comfortable.

Both vaccines are given under the skin (subcutaneous) in the arm if the baby is crawling well, cruising, or taking steps. If the vaccines cause pain, the baby may associate that with his or her motor skills and become hesitant.

Hepatitis A

Another vaccine at 12 months is for Hepatitis A, a viral disease. It is contagious, so a person can become infected from another person or from contaminated food or drink. This is important for everyone and especially if you travel.

The virus causes fever, muscle pain, tiredness, abdominal pain, loss of appetite, and yellow coloring of the eyes and skin (jaundice). It can cause liver failure (when the liver stops functioning).

Two vaccines are given 6 to 12 months apart; the second is given typically at 18 months. The vaccine is injected into the muscle (intramuscularly) and has very few, if any, side effects and mild pain at the site.

Additional Tests

Testing is done at 12 months for tuberculosis (TB), lead detection, and anemia.

Tuberculosis

TB still exists worldwide. Amazing as it may seem, there are around nine million people infected every year and up to two million deaths from TB each year. Due to extensive global travel and immigration, the cases of TB have increased in the United States since the 1980s.

Also called "consumption" or "the white plague," tuberculosis existed in antiquity. The disease is caused by bacteria, produces lesions in the lung that become infected, and lung cells die. The patient coughs up blood, can't eat, and sweats profusely. There is also tuberculosis of the lymph nodes, kidneys, bones, and the lining of the spine and brain (meningitis).

TB History

Hippocrates called the condition *phthisis,* which means consumption (weakness until death). There was no cure, and it wasn't known that the disease was highly contagious. In the seventeenth century, Italian doctors made the connection, assumed the possibility of contagion, and recommended strict hygiene around the patients.

The first treatment for TB was the sanatorium. The idea behind this was that a patient with TB would get better if they were exposed to clean, healthy air and nutritious food.

The bacteria were observed for the first time in 1882 by Dr. Robert Koch. The first medication for it, called actinomycin, cured the patients but caused serious side effects. With the discovery of X-rays, damage to the lungs due to the disease now became visible to doctors.

Later in the 1940s, the antibiotic streptomycin successfully treated the disease. Despite some side effects, it's still used today in cases of resistant, active TB, but many other medications are now available.

The test for tuberculosis is referred to as the PPD (Purified Protein Derivative) skin test or the Mantoux test. The Mantoux test replaced the "Tine" test that was used previously and administered as multiple punctures into the skin.

In the PPD test, a very small part of the killed TB bacteria (0.1cc/ml) is injected with a small needle just under the skin, usually on the forearm. Within 48 hours, the doctor or nurse can read the result. It's positive only if the skin is red and raised. If there's only redness and the skin around is flat, the child may be just reacting to a substance in the PPD. If the PPD is positive, the doctor may wait and repeat the test. If the second test is positive, the doctor will order a chest X-ray and start a medication called isoniazide. It doesn't mean that your child has TB; rather, it indicates that he or she was exposed to it. The medication is given as a preventative measure.

If the baby was born abroad, he or she could have been already given a vaccine called BCG (Bacilli Calmette-Guérin, named after the two French scientists who researched it). It's a TB vaccine that's given in many countries but not in the United States. The vaccine is not standardized; it has been shown that it doesn't offer complete protection from TB. More research is needed on it for this age group of younger than two years.

The BCG vaccine will give a positive PPD reading. If the red, elevated area is larger than 10 mm, if the baby was in contact with anyone who had TB, or if the baby lived in a country where TB is very common, then the baby will have to take medication. For older children and adults, there's a blood test that distinguishes the difference between a positive PPD given by the vaccine or by the TB bacteria. For children younger than two years old, research is being conducted to study the efficacy of this new test.

Lead

Lead is a metal that is used in many industries. Children younger than six years of age are at high risk because they touch and put everything into their mouths. Children who are exposed to high levels of lead can become very ill, with the lead attacking every organ. Many children don't have immediate signs. This is why screening and checking for lead levels is very important. If there are signs, they're generally not specific: behavioral changes, irritability or sleepiness, constipation, lack of appetite, and abdominal pain.

Before 1978, there was lead in all paints, but since then it has been banned. However, lead dust can persist. Very specific regulations are in place for the renovation of homes containing old lead paint. During renovation, pregnant women and children shouldn't be in or around the house.

Parents or caretakers who work in high-risk jobs for lead exposure (welders, scrap metal workers, and glass manufacturers) need to change their clothes before they come home to make sure they're not bringing in lead dust. In your home, check all pottery and ceramic plates, all toys, and children's furniture. They should all be labeled lead-free. The U.S. Consumer Product Safety Commission (CPSC) website is the place to check for recalls involving lead paint and any unsafe products: www.cpsc.gov.

To prevent lead dust from accumulating, wet mop on a regular basis because vacuuming is not enough. Let the children play in a sandbox rather than in outdoor soil that can contain high levels of lead. Don't use unregulated herbal medicine. Food colorants from abroad may contain lead. Call your local health department for information about how to check for lead in your home. Don't move into a new place until this check is done.

At every doctor visit after six months, the doctor will screen for lead poisoning risk by asking you questions. Either a finger stick or a venous blood test will be done at one and two years of age. If a baby has high levels of lead, the treatment could be as easy as removing the source of lead or cleaning the dust. Or the child may need to be hospitalized for chelating therapy. Chelation is a treatment for heavy metal poisoning (lead, iron). A chemical substance is given that attaches to the lead, reducing its activity and increasing its elimination from the body. It's called DMSA (dimercaptosuccinic acid).

Anemia

Anemia comes from the ancient Greek meaning lack of blood, but it actually means a deficiency in red blood cells. At 12 months, along with the test for lead level, there'll be another test called the CBC, or complete blood count.

This test checks all the components of the blood: the white cells, which can be high or low depending on different diseases; the platelets, which give information about the way the blood coagulates; and the red blood cells, which if low indicates anemia.

How does a child get anemia? The most common reason is a lack of iron, as might be the case if the child doesn't eat enough iron-fortified foods. Vegetarian and vegan children will need extra iron. After another one to two months, the test will be repeated. If it's still low, the doctor will investigate other reasons for anemia.

These reasons could include: the baby had a viral disease when the blood was drawn, high lead levels, sickle cell disease, vitamin B_{12} deficiency, other types of anemia, and many other chronic diseases. The doctor will tell you the results and what you need to do.

Common Concerns from 10–12 Months

As we've discussed in previous chapters, you'll need to see the doctor for the following:

Fever: If it's higher than 102° Fahrenheit, if the child doesn't look well (too irritable or too sleepy), and if the fever continues for more than three days, visit the doctor. Infectious diseases are very common at this age: common cold, flu, vomiting, and diarrhea. The fever could indicate other diseases as well, such as pneumonia, a urinary tract infection (UTI), or meningitis.

Ear infection: These are seen more often than before. The doctor will look in the baby's ear and tell you whether you need medication and for how long.

Hand, foot, and mouth disease: Caused by the coxsackievirus, this disease is especially prevalent in the summer months. There are small lesions in the mouth and on the palms and the soles. Sometimes you'll see them only in the mouth. There's no medication for it because it's caused by a virus. The big problem is that children can become dehydrated easily because they refuse to drink due to the mouth lesions. The doctor will give you a liquid to apply to the mouth lesions that will alleviate the pain. Use a straw or even a medication-measuring syringe when giving fluids in an effort to keep the baby well hydrated.

Respiratory Infections

A constant cough during the night, especially if it sounds like "barking" or if it's continuous, may be a sign of a lung infection such as bronchiolitis, pneumonia, croup, or whooping cough.

If the fever is 102° Fahrenheit and the baby is eating, drinking, and playing as usual, give medication to reduce the fever, make sure the baby drinks well, and don't force food if he or she refuses.

Wheezing, the noise that sounds like a whistle, is another reason to see the doctor. Not all children with wheezing have asthma, which is usually not diagnosed until later. If there is a strong family history of asthma, if the baby was premature, or if there's wheezing after every viral disease, then the diagnosis could be made earlier. You may have to use a nebulizer at home.

Allergies

Babies mostly 10 months and up are susceptible to different allergies. Food allergies are covered in Chapter 18. **Seasonal allergies** are to pollen, molds, grass, and trees. **Environmental allergies** include allergies to animal dander and chemicals or products used in the house or outdoors.

Babies can have a stuffy or runny nose, watery and itchy eyes, and sneezing. If you've been outside and you observe these symptoms, change the baby's clothes when you come indoors, wash their hands, or give the baby a bath. Avoid areas, inside or out, where you observe that the baby seems to be uncomfortable.

When it comes to allergies, it's preferred to have area carpets instead of wall to wall. Dust and vacuum regularly, and use an air purifier if possible. As nice as they are, avoid down and feather pillows and comforters in the house. Remember that dust mites can be everywhere. Curtains and upholstery should be cleaned as well.

Eventually, the baby can be tested by an allergist, but usually not before 18 months. Antihistamines need to be given with a lot of precaution, and always consult with your doctor if you suspect your baby has an allergy.

Off-Limits Medications

Aspirin: Aspirin should never be given to a child younger than 19 years. Giving aspirin to children is associated with a serious disease called Reye's syndrome, which affects all organs of the body and can be fatal.

Over-the-counter medication: There was a massive recall of liquid over-the-counter (OTC) medications for infants and children in 2010 for a variety of issues. Medications included Tylenol, Motrin, Zyrtec, and Benadryl.

Acetaminophen and Ibuprofen can be used for symptoms of fever and pain. Consult with your doctor for the correct dosage for your child's age and weight. However, the AAP strongly recommends that infants and small children not be given OTC cough and cold medicines.

Herbal remedies: These are not FDA-approved and may contain harmful ingredients. You can talk to your doctor and get a referral for a certified herbalist physician if you want to use them.

Medications for nausea and diarrhea: Usually, diarrhea and nausea run their course in children. By giving medications for them, you can mask the symptoms of other diseases.

Any medication not prescribed for your child: Just because your child's friend may have had the same symptoms, it doesn't mean that the medication prescribed for that child will be good for your child.

Chewable medications: These should not be given yet.

Medications from other countries: Medications from abroad are regulated differently than medications in the United States and therefore should be avoided.

Any medication for adults: Many adult medications are very dangerous for children, and dosages are much higher in adult medications.

Expired medications: Old products are subject to contamination and becoming ineffective.

Baby steps It's a very good idea to check all your medications, including over-the-counter ones, vitamins, ointments, and creams, at least once a year (if not more often). The efficacy, how effective they are, may be compromised by how long they've been hanging around on store shelves and in your medicine cabinet. At times, products may actually be harmful if they're too old to use.

Taking Care of Problems at Home

You can take care of many of the following medical issues at home—those that are not considered emergencies. But remember, if you as a parent or caretaker feel something needs a second look, then trust your instincts and call the doctor.

A fever lower than 102° Fahrenheit with no changes in the baby means that the baby is fighting an infection. It'll probably run its course in a few days.

A cold or a cough that goes away and doesn't bother the baby can be treated with nose drops and a humidifier.

For minor scratches and cuts, clean them well and apply antibiotic cream or ointment.

For a diaper rash or a small pinpoint rash that lingers beyond a few days, call the doctor for advice. Your doctor will tell you which cream to use.

Constipation can be waited out as long as it only lasts a few days and the baby is content. The doctor may tell you to pretend to take the temperature rectally, which will provide rectal stimulation to help.

For an insect bite, try to pull out the stinger (if there is one) and apply a cold, icy compress to the area. Watch it carefully. If the baby starts to have an allergic reaction, that's an emergency.

Emergencies

It's important to know what conditions indeed constitute an emergency and immediate care. Because your little one at this age has become so active and adventurous, you never know when one might occur.

What to Watch For

Fever: A temperature higher than 104° Fahrenheit accompanied by any strange movements, convulsions, or seizures. Don't put anything in the baby's mouth if these happen. Make sure there's enough air around him or her, and call 911.

Hitting the head: If the baby has lost consciousness, and/or is vomiting, or is irritable or too sleepy. A loss of consciousness at any time could be a sign of a heart, brain, or other organ disease.

Severe pain: Pain from any source is an indication to see your doctor immediately.

Color changes: Blue coloration or jaundice (turning yellow) can indicate heart, blood, or liver disease.

Refuses to move or has a limp (with fever): This could indicate a virus or another type of bone or joint infection.

Rash with a high fever: Could indicate an infection of the covering of the spine and brain called meningitis.

No urinary output: If it has been for eight hours despite drinking fluids or if the baby is unable to drink, it's a cause for immediate medical attention.

Bleeding: Bleeding from any source could be an infection, a coagulation problem, or other blood diseases.

Burn: One that covers a large part of the body needs immediate care, as well any electric burn—even if there are no external signs.

Choking: If the baby cannot breathe and/or is turning blue, call 911.

Ingestion of any poison: Especially if Poison Control has directed you to take the baby to the emergency room.

Deep cuts: Continued bleeding and that need stitches.

Severe allergic reaction (anaphylaxis): If it persists, even after you've used an Epi-pen (an epinephrine injection).

Breathing difficulties: Require immediate care.

Injury to the eyes: Necessitates seeing an eye doctor.

Tooth injuries: You'll need to see a pediatric dentist.

Insect bite: Causing an allergic reaction with swelling of the lips, difficulty breathing, and loss of consciousness.

Near drowning: This is defined by survival after saving the baby. Call 911 immediately. Keep the baby warm. If he or she is unconscious, start CPR.

Going to the Emergency Room (ER)

It's never easy taking your baby to the emergency room. If you have to, make sure that you have all your baby's vaccine records and any allergy and medication information. Be familiar with the pediatrician's office policies (do you have to notify them?) as well as your insurance policy in case of an emergency.

Be very clear in communicating with the emergency room staff about what happened. If you can remember, try to bring a familiar object (toy or blanket) for your baby. Being taken from the familiar to unknown surroundings with a lot of strangers isn't easy. If you're there, comfort your baby; everything will become more bearable. Try to keep your calm, no matter what you feel. Children react to their parent's mood and emotions.

If the baby needs to be admitted to the hospital, one parent, family member, or caretaker can stay in the room at all times. Talk to your baby and have toys from home. Again, try to keep calm and don't be afraid to ask questions of the hospital staff. Understand the diagnosis, medications, or any procedure they may need to perform. You'll need to give consent, so be sure that you're clear about everything.

It's necessary to have a written consent and signature, allowing the caretaker to bring the baby to the doctor or to the emergency room in case you're not around. You need to leave a phone number or an alternative way to reach you at all times.

Alternative Medicine for Children

We'd like to mention a few words about complementary and alternative medicine (CAM) for children, because these practices are becoming more and more prevalent in our society today. It is rather hard to define because it changes all the time. The National Institute of Health (NIH) defines CAM as medical products and practices that are not the standard in Western medicine. But these practices and methods have existed for centuries in other cultures (among them

Chinese, Japanese, and Indian). The approach is holistic, meaning that it takes care of the entire body—the emotional component as well as the physical.

To help understand the makeup of CAM, the NIH has established four categories for CAM:

Biologically based: This term refers to herbs, food supplements, and tea. As opposed to medication, these are not regulated by the FDA. An example is the use of Ephedrine (used as a decongestant, for example), which has been around for a long time. It was banned in 2003 after it was shown that it can cause damage and a few cases of death resulted from its use.

Body-based practices: These include therapeutic touch, massage, and chiropractic medicine.

Energy-based practices: Qigong (China) and Reiki (Japan) both promote mental and spiritual practices for healing.

Mind-body medicine: This technique uses prayer, music, yoga, and meditation to heal the spirit in order to enhance the physical body.

There are overlapping practices, such as homeopathy (healing remedies), *Ayurvedic medicine*, and acupuncture, that combine parts of all four categories mentioned here.

Ayurvedic Medicine

Ayurvedic medicine is the world's oldest medicine. *Ayurveda* in Sanskrit means "the science of longevity." The principle is based on universal interconnectedness: the human body and life forces.

Diseases arise when the body is out of harmony with the other elements. Other valued issues are hygiene and decreasing toxic physical and spiritual elements. The patient is examined from 10 points of view: constitution, fitness, diet, abnormalities, stability, essence, body measurement, digestion, psychological stability, and age.

The treatments are based on plant-derived medication, meditation, praying, chanting, alignment, breathing and yoga, and stress reduction.

Ancient Healing Principles

Some principles of Chinese medicine can be traced as far back as fifth-century China. The main principle of early healing is that the universe is made of energy. The human body is a small universe also made of energy. The diagnosis of any imbalance is made by observation (hearing, smelling, and touching) and questioning.

The methods of treatment are acupuncture (fine needles are placed into different points of the body to increase the circulation and balance the energy), moxibustion or burning herbs on certain points of the body used in conjunction with acupuncture, food therapy, and herbal medicines that are individually combined. Other treatments are cupping, creating a vacuum with a cup on the patient's back, meditation and breathing (T'ai Chi and Qui Gong), and acupressure massage (Tui na).

Much of what alternative medicine has to offer sounds promising. There are many studies being conducted to learn more about it because it's becoming more and more popular. However, researchers don't yet know the exact effects of holistic practices—especially in children.

There are more and more integrative medicine programs being established in different medical centers in the United States. CAM doctors work together with practitioners of traditional medicine in some hospitals. If you wish to explore this route in treating your child, research the CAM practitioner's training just as you would for any traditional specialist; inquire whether they're licensed (not all states require licensing for CAM), how long they've been in practice, and most importantly whether they're experienced in treating children.

If you decide to use CAM, don't delay any of the traditional treatments prescribed. Use treatments together only after understanding every procedure and how it will work in the best interest of your child.

For more information about CAM and its use in children, visit nccam.nih.gov/health/children.

Essential Takeaways

- A well-baby appointment occurs at 12 months, where the baby receives new vaccines including MMR and chickenpox and is tested for anemia and lead.
- Know what medications are not safe to give your baby, such as aspirin, chewables, and medication for adults.
- Be familiar with which medical conditions you can treat at home, such as low-grade fevers and colds, and what requires a trip to the doctor or emergency room, such as bleeding and severe allergic reactions.
- Have emergency numbers, including your doctor's number, Poison Control, and 911, readily on hand as well as insurance and immunization records.
- Alternative medicine for children is an additional option to consider in combination with traditional medicine.

Part 6

Twelve Months Later

The first year is an intense, exhilarating, exhausting, sometimes frustrating, and thoroughly satisfying year. So here, we offer a recap of the essentials of your baby's first year—what's most important to accomplish before going into the toddler years. There are children who have special needs, and we cover the different types and avenues of help and support.

Developmental issues and developmental lagging concern every parent. We'll help you understand some of these issues and guide you toward getting the proper evaluation and treatment for your child as soon as possible.

Finally, we'll give you an overview about what to expect in the second exciting year of your baby's life.

chapter 23

Medical Conditions Needing Special Attention

| Hearing and vision deficit or loss |
| Genetic diseases: those that are inherited |
| Birth defects and their causes |
| Cancer in children |

Sometimes things may not go according to plan. Each child who is born is special and unique, regardless of the problems or deficits with which they enter the world. These problems will need attention and may for a long time—and sometimes even for a lifetime.

Some diseases and medical conditions appear from birth (and sometimes before birth) through the first year of life. There are several categories of disease and conditions: genetic, congenital malformations, and conditions resulting from infections or accidents.

With early detection and treatment, many of these medical problems can be resolved. Some may be cured, and many are helped immeasurably. As a result, your child's health and quality of life will be enhanced. Many children who have medical issues go on to live completely healthy and productive lives.

Hearing Loss

Hearing develops as early as 16 weeks in utero, and babies generally hear well at birth. Many states require a hearing test before the baby leaves the hospital. If the test isn't performed, the baby needs to be referred to an audiologist or pediatric ENT (ear, nose, and throat specialist). If the baby didn't pass the hearing test in the hospital, the hearing test will be repeated in one month. It doesn't necessarily mean that he or she has hearing loss, however. There are many causes that lead to hearing loss. The baby can be born with the deficit, or it can develop later. Hearing loss impairs speech, so it's very important for it to be diagnosed as soon as possible.

Before birth (in utero), the baby may have been exposed to infections such as herpes, rubella, toxoplasmosis, or syphilis. Prematurity, congenital malformations, or genetic disease can also account for hearing loss.

After birth, very high bilirubin levels that required transfusions, certain medications, infections, or trauma to the head, face, or ears could also cause hearing loss. Family history of hearing loss is an important factor, and yet another factor implicated is the exposure to very loud sounds.

Ear infections, especially when they're chronic, can result in hearing loss. If this is the problem, your doctor will refer you to an ENT specialist. If there is hearing loss and fluid in the ear, the ENT doctor may recommend placing special tubes in the ear that will drain the fluid.

Many times, there is no family history—and the reason for the loss of hearing is unknown. Very careful observation and follow-up is essential in starting early treatment.

When to Be Concerned

There are signs in the first year that can indicate hearing difficulty. Have your child tested if you observe any of the following:

- A newborn who doesn't startle

- A three-month-old who doesn't turn toward sounds

- A six-month-old who isn't babbling

- An eight-month-old who doesn't turn his or her head toward a sound

- A 12-month-old who isn't talking in jargon (baby talk) or who doesn't react to you unless he or she sees you

Kinds of Hearing Loss

Hearing loss is caused by different conditions. Diagnosing the type of hearing loss a child is suffering from is important in determining correct treatment. Different types of hearing loss include:

Conductive—When something interferes with the sound.

Sensoneural—When there's a problem with the inner ear, the acoustic nerve, or both.

Central—When the brain can't process information that's necessary for hearing.

Mixed—Two or more of these types combined.

Treatment

The treatment for moderate to severe hearing loss is a hearing aid. The ENT specialist will give you the information you need. If there is profound hearing loss not helped by hearing aids at two years of age, the child may be a candidate for a cochlear implant (surgically inserted in the ear to aid severe hearing loss).

In any case, many hearing-impaired children can learn to speak, even if not clearly. The child and the family can learn sign language; many children mix signing and speech. With early diagnosis and treatment, the child will be able to function well and thrive.

Visual Deficit

The fetus's eyes are closed until 26 weeks. It's difficult to say how much they see, but at birth the baby has 20/200 vision (normal vision is 20/20), which improves over time.

MISC.

20/20 Vision

What does 20/20 vision mean? Eye charts have been used since the nineteenth century. The classic eye chart (Snellen chart) consists of 11 lines of letters of different sizes. 20/20, or clear vision, means that a person being tested can see a line of letters at 20 feet—the distance that's considered the norm. People whose vision is 20/200 or less with corrective lenses (glasses or contact lenses) are considered legally blind.

Vision deficit or vision loss can occur in utero if the fetus has been exposed to infections. Genetic disease, congenital malformation, or even a type of eye cancer (retinoblastoma) is implicated in visual loss.

Early premature babies; severe eye infections; trauma to the brain, eyes, or face; or burns can cause visual deficit or blindness. The baby's eyes will be checked at birth, while in the hospital, and at every well-baby visit.

When to Be Concerned

It isn't always easy recognizing visual problems in infants, but there are a few signs:

- If your baby doesn't follow past the midline or has no eye contact by three months

- If your baby doesn't reach for toys

- If your baby doesn't react when you show objects

- If your baby doesn't fixate or try to grab an object placed in front of him or her

- If there's no eye/hand coordination

Other worrisome signs include:

- The baby's eyes constantly tearing, which could mean there's an obstructed tear duct or increased pressure in the eye (called glaucoma)

- Redness or pus that doesn't clear after three days (could indicate an infection)

- "Crossed" eyes after four months, which means the baby has strabismus, or weak eye muscles

- The pupil, or the middle of the eye, is white in color, which could indicate a type of cancer (sometimes noticed in pictures taken by parents)

- Cloudy-looking eyes, which can be cataracts due to infection (rubella) or a lack of vitamin A

Premature babies could have a disease called *retinopathy of prematurity,* an abnormal growth of blood vessels in the eyes. If untreated, this could lead to blindness.

In rare cases, eyesight doesn't develop at all.

If there's a problem, the pediatrician will refer the baby to an ophthalmologist for further evaluation. With early diagnosis and treatment, support, and encouragement, the visually impaired child will be able to enjoy life.

Genetic Diseases

Genetic diseases are the result of hereditary diseases that have been passed on to the baby from the parents.

baby steps

Every cell in the body has about 30,000 genes that determine the characteristics of every individual (eye color, features, and height as well as the diseases an individual may have or may be prone to getting). Genes carry the instruction for making proteins (which form the basis for all the body's functions) and chromosomes.

Every cell has 46 chromosomes. Each parent gives the child 1 X chromosome: 23 from each parent. Girls will inherit 1 X chromosome from each parent, so they'll have 46 XX chromosomes; boys inherit 1 X and one Y chromosome, so they'll have 46 XY chromosomes in every cell.

A genetically transmitted disease results when there are too few or too many chromosomes or when one chromosome is broken or develops in an abnormal way.

One of the most common genetic diseases is Down syndrome. The name comes from Dr. John L. Down, who described the disease in 1887. What accounts for this syndrome is an extra chromosome; instead of 46, the baby will have 47. One in 800 babies is born with Down syndrome.

There are a few distinct characteristics of babies who have this disease. They have upward-slanted eyes, a flat profile, a large tongue, small and low-set ears, and low-tone muscles.

Children who have Down syndrome can also have heart disease, low thyroid function, problems with bones, and intellectual disability. They could also be at a higher risk for developing diabetes and leukemia.

The pediatrician will work with a cardiologist (heart specialist); orthopedist (bone specialist); endocrinologist (specializing in diseases of the glands); and physical, speech, and occupational therapists. Depending on the extent of the disease, many children who have Down syndrome will be able to live a fulfilling life.

Congenital Heart Defects

A congenital defect means that an organ or part of the body developed in an abnormal way or not at all. The most frequent birth defect is seen in the heart. While in utero, even with a heart defect, a fetus can function because the placenta and the mother's blood are working to help the baby breathe and get oxygen to the blood vessels. Once the baby is born, however, the placenta stops functioning and the baby's heart takes over.

Usually, blood that's low in oxygen goes back to the heart. From the heart, the blood flows to the lungs. In the lungs, the blood becomes rich in oxygen, which goes back to the heart and then back through the body.

If there is any disturbance or obstruction in this normal pathway, or if essential organs or parts of the system haven't developed properly or don't function efficiently, the heart won't be able to perform its normal functioning.

In certain cases, heart disease is diagnosed at birth. In others, it could take a while because there may be no immediate signs. The doctors may hear a heart murmur (an extra sound of the heart) that could just mean that they hear the blood circulating in the heart, or it could indicate a more serious problem. The amount of oxygen in the baby's body will also be checked.

One congenital defect seen frequently is a hole between two of the heart chambers, called a ventricular septal defect. It may simply close on its own. But if the baby has symptoms, including rapid breathing, a bluish color, and failure to thrive, surgery is needed.

A congenital heart defect can occur in different parts of the heart for different reasons. Most heart defects obstruct the flow of blood in the heart (and in surrounding vessels) or can cause the blood to flow in an abnormal way. Some defects in this category include aortic stenosis, coarctation of the aorta, ventricular septal defect, or atrio-ventricular canal (a defect of the middle of the heart seen in children who have Down syndrome).

Others are due to more complicated defects, and the babies are very ill. These defects include: **tetralogy of Fallot**, where there is a thickening of the right chamber, a hole in the ventricles, a narrow valve, and the aorta is on the wrong side; **truncus arteriosus**, where there is only one common artery; **hypoplastic left ventricle**, where one of the chambers is not completely formed; and **transposition of the great vessels**, where the major arteries are transposed, or attached to the wrong side of the heart.

Due to great technical advances, heart defects can be seen through fetal ultrasound. There are specialized heart surgeons who can actually do surgery in utero, before the baby is born. The heart doctor or cardiologist will see the baby on a regular basis in addition to his or her primary provider.

Seizures (Convulsions)

A baby can have a seizure when the brain has increased electrical activity and the cells don't communicate with each other. Many times, a seizure happens just once; other times, it's an on-going condition called epilepsy.

Causes of Seizures

At birth—in preemies, very large babies, or if the mother is diabetic—a baby can have a seizure because of low blood glucose (sugar). Seizures can also occur if the mother uses illegal drugs, if there is a low calcium level, or if parts of the metabolic system don't function properly (a condition called galactosemia).

Infections can produce seizures, and so can "shaken-baby syndrome," which is considered child abuse. Other reasons for seizures are accidents, such as trauma or falling on the head, or abnormal brain development. Seizures in infants are more difficult to diagnose, and they're different from those seen in adults.

Symptoms of Seizures

The symptoms of a seizure include repetitive movements of the arms and/or legs that don't stop when you touch the baby, the baby staring into space (even if an object is moved in front of the eyes), head bobbing, and prolonged tongue thrusting.

If you observe any of these strange movements, try to take a video of these movements. The baby may very well not have the symptoms when you see the doctor, and they may be hard to describe, so the video can very helpful. In most cases, the pediatrician will refer the baby to a pediatric neurologist. Many babies outgrow seizures, but there are cases when it becomes a life-long disease.

Endocrine Gland-Related Diseases

Hypothyroidism describes an underactive thyroid gland. Left untreated, it can cause serious physical and mental illness in children. This important gland is situated in the neck, under the

"Adam's apple," and secretes hormones. It determines the body's energy and regulates metabolism.

Because all states in the United States screen newborns, untreated hypothyroidism is very rare—but it can happen if the gland didn't develop, if it isn't in the right place, or if it doesn't produce hormones. The latter condition may indicate that the mother had hyperthyroidism (an overactive thyroid), took medication, and/or was exposed to radiation.

These babies can have very loose muscles, a hoarse cry, and don't develop well. The pediatrician will refer the baby to a pediatric endocrinologist. If congenital hypothyroidism is diagnosed and treated early on, children will have a 100-percent rate of healing—although they'll have to take medication for life.

Bone Diseases in Infants

Several bone diseases can afflict babies. Some are fully treatable, and some are not.

Osteogenesis Imperfecta

Osteogenesis imperfecta is known as "brittle bone disease," and in most cases, it's hereditary. Babies can be born with fractures because the bones are so fragile. In other cases, the fractures begin when the baby starts moving. Aside from fractures, the disease causes short stature, problems with the teeth, and a gray or bluish tinge to the whites of the eyes.

In most cases, children have normal intellect. One famous patient who had this condition was Henri de Toulouse-Lautrec, the great impressionistic painter.

Rickets

This condition causes soft bones because of a lack of vitamin D, which helps calcium and phosphorus be deposited in the bones. This can be seen in babies who are exclusively breastfed and don't receive vitamin D supplements. There are many countries where rickets is endemic due to malnutrition. Rickets is treatable with vitamin D supplements.

Spina Bifida

Spina bifida, Latin for "open spine," is the incomplete development of the spine. The disease can be diagnosed in utero or in some cases may go undetected even after birth. Some children will develop bladder problems, leg paralysis, and hydrocephalus (water on the brain) as symptoms.

The intellect is normal. The causes of spina bifida are not known, although folic acid deficiency has been implicated.

There is no cure, but treatment is available to be able to manage the disease and to prevent complications. Depending on the severity, surgery, medications, catheters to help urination, and physical and behavioral therapy are used. Children with mild spina bifida do not need treatment, just good follow-up.

If children with spina bifida develop hydrocephalus, a condition caused by a problem in the flow of the cerebrospinal fluid, this can be treated by draining the extra fluid through a surgically placed tube (shunt). The shunt runs under the skin to the abdomen. The fluid will eventually leave the body.

Some affected children may have different degrees of paralysis. They'll need braces, crutches, and wheelchairs.

Bleeding Disorders

A bleeding disorder can occur in infants soon after birth. The platelets (part of the blood that helps it coagulate) may be low or not functioning well. There are inherited diseases, such as hemophilia, and those acquired after severe infections, trauma, or impaired functioning of the liver.

Babies who didn't receive vitamin K after birth are at high risk for bleeding. These diseases are treated by a pediatric hematologist.

Cancers in Infants

A very good and thorough physical exam can save lives by diagnosing a malignancy, or cancerous tumor, early on. The most common type found in children is called *neuroblastoma* and forms in the adrenal glands, abdomen, neck, or spinal cord. It affects 1 in 100,000 children younger than five.

Leukemia is cancer of the bone marrow. Any baby who is constantly lethargic, doesn't want to eat, has swelling of parts of the body, or bleeds abnormally needs to be seen as soon as possible. The pediatrician will refer the baby to a pediatric hematologist-oncologist. Early diagnosis, referral to the right specialist, early treatment, and the right support system will ensure a higher rate of cure.

Sickle Cell Anemia

When two parents have the sickle cell trait, their baby has a 25-percent chance of having sickle cell anemia.

baby steps

Normal red blood cells are very flexible; they're round, look like a doughnut, and can easily flow through blood vessels. The cells in sickle cell disease are rigid and not flexible. They look like a sickle and can cause occlusion (blockage) in the blood vessels.

Usually, the baby won't have symptoms of the disease until around two years of age. Symptoms include severe pain in the hands and feet, a spleen that's increased in size and is painful, and a decreased red blood cell count. These children can have respiratory problems, lower immunity, and be more susceptible to infections.

It's important for a baby diagnosed with sickle cell disease to get all vaccines when scheduled. The child will also need to take an antibiotic from six months on, every day. Fever and dehydration have to be treated immediately. The doctor should be notified if a child with sickle cell disease was exposed to the Parvovirus, which causes "fifth disease" in children. This condition causes a decrease in all blood cells in children who have sickle cell disease.

MISC.

Fifth Disease

It's called "fifth disease" because it's the fifth disease with a rash that was recognized and reported as a separate entity. All these diseases have the similar symptoms of fever and a rash. The other diseases in this group are measles, scarlet fever (given by strep), rubella, and Coxsackie and Echo viruses. The sixth disease is roseola, which is a virus of the herpes family.

The primary care doctor will work closely with the hematologist and the parents to prevent infections and give immediate care to all children who have sickle cell disease.

Cystic Fibrosis

Cystic fibrosis is a genetic disease that affects the lungs, digestive, and immune system. If both parents are carriers of cystic fibrosis, their baby has a one in four chance of inheriting the disease. Testing can be done in parents as well as babies in utero and after birth. When testing is not done, it's more difficult to diagnose this disease early on. Many people who have CF are diagnosed later in life.

At birth, the baby may not be able to pass meconium (the sticky, first black stool) for 48 hours. Signs of the disease are failure to grow well despite good nutrition and constant respiratory problems.

The skin may have a salty taste, usually noticed by parents when they kiss their baby. Bowel movements may look greasy and discolored.

MISC.

Understanding Cystic Fibrosis

The disease affects cells that are important in the production of sweat and mucus, called epithelial cells. Because these cells are everywhere in the body, the disease will affect many organs. Due to protein changes in the genes, mucus that is usually thin and can pass through all cells is instead very thick. The balance between water and salt (comprised of sodium and chloride) is damaged. The lungs can't fight germs, thereby causing lung infections. The pancreas isn't able to carry enzymes that are necessary for proper digestion.

The *sweat test* is done after birth. An electrical current that carries a special substance, pilocarpine, is directed to the skin (usually in the forearm). This will make the sweat glands produce increased amounts of sweat. After 30–60 minutes, the sweat is checked for the amount of chloride. A result higher than 60 means that the baby has CF. This test needs to be done twice to confirm the diagnosis.

The pediatrician will work together with the pulmonary specialist (lungs), gastroenterologist (digestive system), and nutritionist. These children will need to take antibiotics and have a nutritious diet high in calories, vitamins, and special enzymes.

A new therapy, gene therapy, under investigation since 1993, is showing great promise for a cure. The most recent research is in protein repair therapy. Early diagnosis and teamwork will give these children an opportunity to have a long and fulfilling life.

Celiac Disease

Also known as nontropical sprue, celiac disease tends to run in families and is an autoimmune disease. It happens because the body doesn't tolerate gluten, the protein that is found in wheat, rye, and barley. It damages the surface of the small bowel to the extent that nutrition will not be absorbed.

Other grains that derive from gluten are farina, spelt, bulgur, semolina, udon, and couscous.

The symptoms begin after the baby has started solid food, especially cereal. Symptoms include vomiting, diarrhea, rashes, poor growth, tiredness, and later anemia. There are many people who consume gluten for years and develop the disease later on in life.

There's a blood test for this disease. If the result of the blood test shows antibodies to gluten, then the gastroenterologist will do a procedure called small bowel biopsy. The only treatment for this disease is to avoid all foods that contain gluten. Researchers are working on medication that could eliminate the toxic effects of gluten.

Famous People Who Have Medical Conditions

It's interesting to know about those in history who endured severe health problems and made great contributions to society during their lives.

Learning Disability

Albert Einstein—brilliant scientist

Hans Christian Andersen—famous author of children's stories

Louis Pasteur—major medical discoveries

Visual Impairment

Homer—Greek poet who wrote *The Iliad* and *The Odyssey*

Helen Keller—author and lecturer who was visually and hearing impaired and had no speech; despite all these conditions, she was the first person with such disabilities to receive a Bachelor's degree

Ray Charles—famous musician and composer

Stevie Wonder—famous musician and composer

Louis Braille—invented the Braille alphabet

Hearing Impairment

Ludwig van Beethoven—one of the greatest composers of all time

Francisco Goya—famous painter

Thomas Edison—inventor of the electric bulb; he held the most patents in the United States

Seizure Disorder

Michelangelo—great painter

Leonardo da Vinci—famous painter and inventor

Aristotle—Greek philosopher and playwright

Physical Disabilities

Franklin Delano Roosevelt—32nd president of the United States; had polio and was wheelchair-bound

Itzhak Perlman—famous violinist who contracted polio as a child and performs in braces or a wheelchair

Stephen Hawking—professor of mathematics and physics at Cambridge University; author of many books; has the incapacitating neurological disease called ALS, Amyotrophic Lateral Sclerosis, which severely impairs speech and movement

Essential Takeaways

- Sometimes things don't go according to plan, and your child may have a medical condition that requires special attention. Seek the necessary medical attention.

- Your doctor will evaluate special problems and refer you to the appropriate specialist(s), who will manage your child's care.

- With early detection and treatment, many diseases and conditions can be cured or helped dramatically. It's possible for a child who has medical challenges to live a happy and productive life—and in many cases, a completely normal life.

chapter 24

Developmental Issues

Detecting developmental delays and what to do about them

Special attention to developmental delays in premature babies

What to do for children with special needs

Autism: what it is, its causes and treatment

Parents or caretakers are usually the first to observe a specific developmental problem. The earlier the problem is diagnosed, the faster one can intervene. Although all children are different and will develop at different times, you have to be on the alert if your baby is not meeting certain milestones at a given time period.

The milestones we're most concerned with are gross and fine motor development and cognitive, language, and social development. By now, you're familiar with all of these. Chapter 4 gave an overview of what developmental milestones and skills to expect for your baby's first year. We also outlined what to be concerned about if these milestones and skills are not achieved. Of course, your baby's doctor will be monitoring these as well.

It's very important to note whether your baby reached a milestone and accomplished the appropriate skills but then stayed with the same set of skills, not moving forward to the next milestones, or slipping backward, regressing to an earlier stage.

Remember that what is developmentally expected and what the doctor will be looking for is *steady growth*. Your child may be lagging behind by several weeks from the expected norm, but as long as the milestone is reached within that reasonable time frame, then that's fine.

Developmental delays may exist in only one specific area, but there are children who have delays in every area—called *global delay.* The delays can also range from a minor speech or motor delay to profound intellectual and motor delays. The delays could be *static,* meaning that they don't change, or *progressive,* meaning that they get worse.

Causes and Signs of Delay

What causes developmental delays? There are many factors and diseases that contribute to or account for delays, including:

Prematurity

Congenital malformations (abnormalities present at birth)

Genetic diseases (cystic fibrosis, fragile X syndrome, and Down syndrome, for example)

Endocrine disorders (congenital hypothyroidism, for example)

Infectious diseases (rubella and cytomegalovirus, for example)

Metabolic disorders (such as galactosemia)

Neurological disorders (such as hydrocephalus, neurofibromatosis, and brain atrophy)

Fetal Alcohol Syndrome (FAS) due to the mother's consumption of alcohol during pregnancy

Deprivation of oxygen

Untreated high levels of bilirubin

In many cases, the reason for developmental delays is not known.

Gross Motor Delays

When a baby has a gross motor delay, it involves the larger muscle groups. If a baby isn't holding the head up by three months, isn't putting the hands together by four months, isn't rolling by six months, has no head control by five to six months, isn't sitting by eight months, isn't crawling or cruising by 12 months (please remember that many babies won't crawl at all but will stand up and walk), and isn't walking by 15 months, there are likely gross motor delays.

Fine Motor Delays

A baby who isn't grasping, is still holding his or her hand in a fist at 3 months, isn't reaching or holding objects by 5 months, has no palmar grasp by 7 months, isn't transferring by 8–9 months, and has no pincer grasp by 10–12 months is showing fine motor delays.

Cognitive Delays

Cognitive delays are demonstrated when a baby doesn't recognize the parents by 3 months, isn't turning toward sound by 3 months, isn't following objects by 6 months, isn't able to follow a command with a gesture by 7 months, isn't following commands by 12 months, and is unable to play with toys or objects.

Social Delays

Social delays are present when a baby isn't smiling or cooing by 3 months, makes no sounds by 5 months, makes no monosyllabic babble by 7–8 months, makes no polysyllabic babble by 9 months, and emits no babble, words, or jargon by 15 months. If the baby makes no eye contact or doesn't show pleasure in hugging or playing at any time after age two months, that's a cause for concern.

If you think your baby is not meeting the milestones, talk to your baby's doctor. Further evaluation will include blood tests, imaging tests (X-ray, CAT scans, or MRIs), and referral to specialists and an Early Intervention (EI) program.

MISC.

IDEA

In the United States, every child up to age five is entitled to services that include free developmental screenings according to The Individuals with Disabilities Education Act (IDEA). If it's determined through testing that the child has a disability, therapy is provided either at no cost or at a reduced rate. Services may include speech, physical, and occupational therapy. The services are provided in the home.

Developmental Delays in Premature Babies

Prematurity means that babies are born before 37 weeks. The earlier the baby is born, the higher the risk for having developmental delays. Because all the organs didn't have enough time to develop, they can be affected.

Premature babies can have bleeding in the brain, disease of the eyes (retinopathy), hearing loss, respiratory problems, heart problems, intestinal disease, anemia, and delays in some or all the developmental areas. Babies hospitalized for a longer period of time and who had more complications are at a higher risk for delays.

Premature babies need to be screened for development more often. There are special follow-up clinics for premature babies in many hospitals, but a pediatrician can screen as well. It's important to correct for the baby's age, meaning if a baby was born eight weeks earlier, one should expect a developmental pattern for a baby who is two months (eight weeks) younger. If the baby doesn't meet the milestones even with age correction, it's a reason for concern and investigation.

Vision problems are seen frequently in premature babies, and retinopathy is common. In this disease, abnormal vessels grow in the baby's retina. If not treated early, it can lead to blindness.

Hearing for all babies is checked in the hospital and followed up closely by a pediatric ENT doctor (ear, nose, and throat specialist) if there's a problem. Hearing loss contributes to speech delay.

Frequently seen in premature babies are problems with speech (sounds) and language (meaning). They either can't articulate a sound or the meaning of the words is not understood. The brain isn't able to make the necessary connections.

The most serious delays are neuron motor delays and intellectual disability. Cerebral palsy (static neuropathy) is a complex and common neuro-developmental disability. The muscle tone can be affected (either very stiff or very loose), as can muscle coordination. These children aren't able to walk, have distorted movements, or walk with a very broad-based gait. Cerebral palsy affects other small muscles; for example, those in the lungs and in the bladder. It's called static neuropathy because it's not changing.

Intellectual disability refers to cognitive difficulties and deficits in adaptive behavior. Day-to-day functioning and learning lags in these children, and they need help learning to perform tasks.

The good news is that early screening and diagnosis of premature babies will lead to receiving all the services in time. Even if not curable, many delays can definitely improve. These children will need a team of specialists and therapists working together with the pediatrician and parents. Also, premature babies usually catch up to full-term babies by three years. While parenting a premature baby poses a real challenge, parents and caretakers need to be familiar with their babies and understand that they'll catch up developmentally later—and that milestones will be achieved, but with the age correction.

Premature babies need frequent follow-ups, and of course, parents should bring any concerns to the doctor's attention.

What Are Special-Needs Children?

The term "special needs" refers to a large group of children who need special medical attention and other services. These services provide not only help for children with developmental delays but also for those with intellectual delays and chronic or terminal illnesses.

It's hard enough to take care of a perfectly healthy child, but it's extremely difficult for a parent to take care of a child who has special needs physically, mentally, and emotionally. Usually, there's a team of doctors, nurses, social workers, and different therapists who are involved with the child's care.

Development in special-needs children depends on the type of disease and the level of physical and intellectual disability. These children will meet some milestones but at a different pace

Toys and activities may need to be individualized for a special-needs child. You can try a toy that is appropriate for the age group, but if the child can't relate to it or gets upset or stressed, remove it. Wait and try it some other time. Occupational, play, and other types of therapists can help you with what's appropriate. Always offer favorite objects or toys. With patience and a good understanding of your child's abilities, this process will become easier. Make sure you involve the entire family in activities with your special-needs child, and as with every child, be consistent.

Aside from special programs for these children, there are also camps that specialize in specific illnesses and disorders and respite programs for the parents and caretakers.

The sibling of a child who has special needs will need attention as well. Many times, these children feel neglected and the parent just doesn't have enough energy to respond to their needs. Enlist a family member or friend for help. The prolonged lack of attention for the sibling can result in behavioral problems, alienation, and sometimes even acting out in inappropriate and dangerous ways.

Parents and caretakers of children who have special needs are undertaking an enormous task. Day-to-day care is more complicated, with extra time and attention for the child, numerous appointments, and hours of physical, occupational, speech, and other therapies. This increases stress and exhaustion and can lead to fatigue—and sometimes even depression and loss of hope.

Parents need to take care of themselves, too. When they're stressed, the child will feel it and react. Even a short walk, exercise, or spending time with friends may be enough to gather back strength and energy.

Every state has a respite program that may offer a babysitter who is specialized and experienced with special-needs children. In addition, there are day-care centers, support groups, therapy, and spiritual help. Other families in the same situation can provide valuable information and insight and much-needed understanding, and can become great friends.

A good support system, a reliable medical team, and knowing when to ask for help go a long way toward enabling families to deal with these situations. Visit the following websites for resources in your area:

> www.ed.gov, U.S. Department of Education
>
> www.familyvillage.wisc.edu, disability-related resources
>
> www.education.com, learning resources

Caring for HIV Positive Babies

Although studied in the early 1980s, HIV (human immunodeficiency virus) was around well before then. This virus can cause AIDS, Acquired Immunodeficiency Syndrome. Not all people infected with HIV will have AIDS. It's transmitted through infected blood transfusions, unsafe sex, sharing dirty needles, and from the infected mother to the newborn. It's important for family members and caretakers to know the universal blood and fluid precautions. One cannot get HIV, however, from hugging or holding hands, sneezing, coughing, and sharing a toilet seat.

The rate that babies used to be infected was over 25 percent. This number is down to 1 percent because of testing of the pregnant mother, birth by C-section, and the existing treatment. Almost all new infections diagnosed are the ones transmitted from the mother to the newborn. An HIV positive diagnosis is one of the few contraindications to breastfeeding.

Babies infected are healthy for two to three months, but after that they don't gain weight, have large lymph nodes, and a large liver and spleen. They can get more infections more often and with specific (opportunistic) infections (Pneumocystis pneumonia).

There is no vaccine against HIV, but treatment with medications has improved dramatically over the years. The parents need to see an infectious disease specialist and the pediatrician often. The doctors and caregivers have to provide good nutrition for the baby and watch the weight. Testing needs to be done frequently for the baby and the family. A social worker, therapist, and nutritionist can provide help for the family. The medication is expensive, but there are state and federal programs helping with the cost.

Overview of the Autism Spectrum

Autism is a complex neurological and developmental disability. There is an autism spectrum disorder that includes at least three different entities to more specifically define different characteristics of the disorder:

Autistic disorder (classic autism) has symptoms of speech delay, unusual social behavior (such as no eye contact, playing alone, doing the same things over and over, rocking, and spinning), an inability to handle any transition, and intellectual disability. This disorder was first described by Leo Kanner in 1943. The name comes from the Greek *autos,* meaning "self."

Asperger syndrome (described by Hans Asperger in 1943–1944) is demonstrated by difficulty in social interaction and by patterns of behavior and interest in subjects that are repetitive and restrictive in nature. This syndrome differs from Autism insofar as language and cognitive development are retained. Physical clumsiness and idiosyncratic language are often noted. First course of treatment is behavioral therapy.

Pervasive developmental delay (PDD) describes the rest of the illnesses that don't fit into either category.

Baby watch

Sensory processing disorder, previously called sensory integration disorder, is a relatively new ailment not in the autism category. In this disorder, the brain can't process information from the five sensory systems that are responsible for sight, sound, smell, taste, temperature, pain, and the body's position. These children are too sensitive to touch, to clothing, have difficulty learning new movements, and are "clumsy."

The Cause of Autism

Millions of doctors and parents would like to know the cause of autism, but as yet, it's undetermined. Autism seen in families and studies with twins have led researchers to believe that a cause could be genetic or hereditary. It's possible that the environment plays a role as well.

Autism has been seen in children who have other genetic or neurological problems, such as fragile X syndrome and others. Much research is now focused on finding a possible gene that causes this disease. The theory that vaccines cause autism is no longer accepted.

It's difficult to diagnose the autism spectrum before 18 months of age. At 18 months, the doctor will perform a more detailed developmental exam called the M-CHAT (the Modified Checklist for Autism in Toddlers). The parents will need to answer some specific questions and provide pertinent information about their child. Hopefully, soon there will be tools and better ways for diagnosing autism earlier.

The Treatment for Autism

Treatment is guided to enhance the child's quality of life and to ease the family's distress. The medical treatment is achieved by giving appropriate medication and following the child's progress closely.

The educational treatment is highly individualized to meet the child's own needs. It consists of special education, including behavioral, speech, social skills, and occupational therapy. Early Intervention (EI) programs are the first to help, focusing on children up to age three.

Some parents use alternative medicine. This is still controversial, although widely used by many people (an increasing number of adults see alternative therapists and holistic healers for themselves and in turn use it for their children). Ensure that the alternative medicine provider or practitioner is certified. Unfortunately, there's still not much scientific research being done to investigate the efficacy of these modalities. Changes in diet are definitely not harmful, however.

There are special schools for autistic children as well as camps and structured programs. Recently, yoga has been shown to be helpful. As devastating as the autism diagnosis is, early diagnosis will lead to a much better outcome.

Discussing the Help You May Need

It's very difficult for a parent to hear some stranger say, "Your child needs to be enrolled in an Early Intervention program because we think he or she may have one of the autism spectrum disorders." There are so many emotions and thoughts that arise—perhaps shock, guilt, sadness, panic, disappointment, disbelief, shame (the stigma), and denial.

Even in these difficult times, it's necessary to start the evaluation and treatment modalities as early as possible. Talk to your doctor, ask questions, and do research. If you don't feel comfortable, ask for a second opinion. Once the diagnosis is confirmed, make sure the lines of communication are open for all the specialists, educators, and therapists.

As with everything else, beware of those offering "miracle" cures. Some of these could be dangerous. Beware of unqualified and unlicensed people making unfounded promises, especially if large amounts of money are involved. There's nothing wrong with having faith and finding alternative healers. Complementary medicine means just that—sound, traditional medicine and other healing modalities working together.

There are special programs, but public schools also incorporate education for autistic children. There are respite programs for both parents and children. The Autism Society of America's website, www.autism-society.org, is a great source of information, providing news, activities, and access to local chapters.

Although there's no treatment yet for autism, the different approaches and therapies available can lead to significant improvement and a good outcome. Intensive therapies, good follow-up, and support are the most important factors.

Essential Takeaways

- If you think your child is lagging developmentally, seek advice from your doctor, get follow-up evaluations and necessary testing, and be proactive in your child's treatment and care.
- Parents of a special-needs child need support. Enlist the help of family members and friends to help take care of other children; therapists and groups can also provide emotional support.
- Get in touch with other families who are going through the same situation. Sharing information and getting the understanding and support you need is invaluable.

chapter 25

Baby's First Year Recap: The 10 Essential Things to Remember

Monitoring your baby's milestones

Establishing and keeping a sleep routine

Feeding and introducing solids

Being consistent and establishing limits and boundaries

This book has provided you with detailed advice and guidance to help you navigate the first year of your baby's life, from first breath to first step. To recap the most important things to know and accomplish during the first year, this chapter is dedicated to the 10 essential things every parent should remember. Every day is special and unforgettable, and keeping these key items in mind during the first year will set the foundation for a very happy and healthy child.

Establish a Bedtime Routine Early On

Newborn to three months: It's never too early to establish a sequence of activities that will become routine. Why is this important? It helps to have feeding, napping, playing, and going out at the same time every day. Make sure everybody follows the same routine and that there are at least one to two hours of quiet time before sleeping to wind down the day.

The very moment your precious baby comes home, begin to establish the difference between day and night. Have more light on during the day. Dress the baby in different clothing, even when the baby naps, to signify that it's a daytime nap as opposed to nighttime sleep. Swaddle the baby differently. If you wish, you may even sing a different lullaby.

At night, follow the same sequence: bathing, feeding, rocking, using the crib mobile, and singing (whatever you decide). You may leave a small, dim light on in the baby's room. When the baby wakes up at night, feed and keep a quiet atmosphere. Remember that co-sleeping could be dangerous for the baby.

Four to six months: If you and your baby are ready, you can start sleep training. Choose either the Ferber or noncrying method (or a mixture of the two). You can do what you wish for the bedtime routine as long as it's always the same: bathing, eating, singing, and reading.

After four to five months, very few babies need to be fed during the night. If the baby wakes up, go into the room to make sure everything is okay, but don't pick the baby up if you can help it. Change the baby only if it's absolutely necessary. Make it short and boring. You don't want the baby to learn to get too excited to see you in the middle of the night. You must be consistent in the night so the baby knows he or she must go back to sleep.

Seven to nine months: By now, babies understand the routine. Make sure that quiet time is respected before sleeping. Give the baby a transitional object, such as a toy or a blanket. Shorten the last nap in the afternoon.

Bathing may take more time now because babies are enjoying it and like to play. Figure out how much time you need for this task in your routine. Watch for babies who are able to climb out of the crib, because they could be ready for a bed.

Try not to run in too quickly if your baby cries at night. Make sure he or she is fine and that things are normal. Many times, babies will soothe themselves and go back to sleep on their own, but they must be left alone—consistently—to learn to do it.

10–12 months: At this stage, the baby will have favorite toys and even books. Play quietly together, have dinner, and give a bath. Maybe now you can add more reading and songs so that the bedtime ritual is actually in two phases. The last nap should be earlier and shorter. Make sure the baby isn't able to leave the room if he or she sleeps in a bed.

Watch Milestones Carefully

Every baby is unique. Comparing your child with others can give you a lot of unnecessary anxiety. Every baby develops on his or her own schedule, at a different pace. This book views your baby's world at roughly three- to four-month intervals to convey the idea that there is a broader span of time in which a baby begins, and eventually masters, developmental milestones.

Being alert to developmental milestones is important, because if your baby doesn't reach any one milestone (or more) after a specific period of time, you need to consult with your pediatrician. All milestones are equally important—gross and fine motor, cognitive, language, and social skills.

Watch muscle tone *at any age:* It shouldn't be too stiff or too floppy. Watch for response to light and sound. Observe eye contact. By three months, many of the reflexes (Moro, tonic neck, and so on) are on their way out. Babies enjoy being held, hugged, and kissed, but if a baby consistently doesn't like this, it's a reason to consult a medical professional.

One to three months: By three months of age, the baby's head should not be floppy and the infant should be able to lift the head and part of the chest. Closed fists will open. The baby will respond to light and sounds, smile, coo, and even start babbling.

Four to six months: By five to six months, babies will usually roll over. They'll push themselves up when you hold them. They'll grab and hold an object. At six months, they may sit with support. They'll begin to grab objects with the palm. At this age, everything goes into the mouth.

Babies will react to sounds coming from behind them. They'll watch an object falling. They'll join their hands together in front of their chest. There's monosyllabic babbling, laughing, recognizing family members, and perhaps the beginning of stranger anxiety.

Seven to nine months: During this period, babies start to crawl and can roll from one side to the other. Some of them can even stand up and cruise. They've developed the pincer grasp and can feed themselves. Remember, it's fine if the baby skips crawling but just stands up and starts cruising.

Babies can understand simple commands, and their babbling is polysyllabic and in response to others. Stranger anxiety has increased.

10–12 months: Crawling or cruising has gotten better, faster, and more coordinated. Some babies will walk at 12 months of age. It's worrisome if they don't take steps by 15 months. The baby will look for and find objects even if they're hidden. The fine pincer grasp is mastered.

Babies understand commands and will react to people's moods. They'll throw toys and retrieve them. The baby will talk in jargon and will now have a one- to two-word vocabulary.

If your baby hasn't reached milestones within a specified period of time, talk to your pediatrician. He or she will perform an evaluation and if necessary refer your baby to the appropriate specialists and services.

Find a Good Pediatrician

Finding the right pediatrician, family doctor, or nurse practitioner is a very important task for parents. You need to like and trust your baby's provider and develop a good working relationship with him or her—sometimes even before the baby is born. Your children will be seeing their doctor for up to 18–21 years.

Know the office policies regarding hours, phone calls, schedules for well-baby appointments, vaccines, and visits for illness. Get to know all the providers within a practice. Always have a copy of the baby's vaccine, allergy, and medication records.

Have a plan and procedure in place for emergencies and night calls. Know the hospital(s) your doctor is affiliated with and where the closest emergency rooms are located. Understand admissions procedures and what happens if the baby needs to be admitted to the hospital.

You need to feel comfortable enough with your baby's doctor to be able to air any concerns and to have open and honest discussions. All questions are important, and it's also your right to have a second opinion. Call or make an appointment whenever you're concerned; it's always better to be proactive.

If you need to change providers, make sure all the baby's medical records are forwarded to the new provider.

Know What to Feed and When

For the first six months, it's recommended that all babies either breastfeed or drink formula. Breastfeeding is considered the most complete feeding for the baby, but if it's not possible or you need to supplement, formula will provide good nutrition. Vitamin D supplementation is necessary for exclusively breastfed babies. Give no water or anything else up to six months of age.

Birth to three months: In the first two months, the baby will eat every two to three hours, starting with ½ to 1 ounce up to 4–6 ounces by three months. In the first months, babies need to eat more frequently during the day—and also on demand.

Four to six months: If the baby appears very hungry or is not growing enough, you may introduce solid food by four to five months, but waiting until six months is optimal. You can use commercial baby food (start with stage one) or cook the food yourself. Make mealtime family time by including the baby (and no distractions).

You don't need to start with any specific foods. It could be cereal, fruits, or vegetables. Start once a day and give the same food for three days in a row. After three days, you can start a new food. This is done to make sure that the baby doesn't have any allergies. After introducing two to three new foods, you can give solid food twice a day.

You may give water in small amounts but no juice or anything else. Don't reduce the amount of breastfeeding or formula until the baby is eating three meals a day. At this point, the amount of formula is around 28–32 ounces a day.

Seven to nine months: Decrease the fluid appropriately as you increase food to three times a day. You may start meat (chicken, turkey, or very lean red meat). White, mild fish can be introduced as well as egg yolk. If you cook the food yourself, don't use salt, but you can spice the food with herbs.

Allow the baby to feed himself or herself with finger food. Make sure that the food is cut as small as half of your pinky finger nail and feeding is always done under your watchful eye.

10–12 months: Many babies won't like baby food anymore and may want to try regular food. Every new food needs to be tried for three days. Never give two or more new foods at once. The baby can eat everything *except for* raw honey, nuts, shellfish, and a whole egg.

At 12 months, you can give whole, regular milk, but not more than 24 ounces a day. We don't advise fruit juice and definitely not soft drinks. A whole egg can be given at 12 months, but still don't feed nuts. Beware of any food that can become a choking hazard.

Watch the baby for any signs of allergies: rash, swelling of the face or lips, difficulty breathing, and/or vomiting. Always have an anti-allergy medication at home for the baby. Never force-feed the baby. When the child is full, he or she will let you know. They'll often keep their mouth closed or turn their head away.

Feedings need to be done at the same time and in the same way. It's a good time for you to learn to eat healthfully as well, if you don't already. By following your example, your baby will develop his or her own healthy habits.

Be Consistent

We can't emphasize enough the importance of consistency. We understand that when a parent or caretaker is tired or overwhelmed, it may be hard to follow the rules set up.

Ask for help from family members and friends. If you're able to afford it, hire a caretaker for as many hours as you need. Remember, if the schedules and routines are changed daily or by different people, the baby will get mixed messages and may react by becoming upset just trying to understand what's happening. Because babies react to a parent's or caretaker's moods, it's wise to take unpleasant or difficult discussions elsewhere and never raise your voice in front of your baby.

Parents, partners, and caretakers need to talk to each other in order to find common ground—a common way of handling the many aspects of raising a child. It's not unusual to ask the doctor for guidance in this situation.

We love and respect grandparents. They raised you and have a lot of experience. Sometimes, though, there may be differences of opinion because many aspects of parenting have changed over the years. Remember, you're the parent; do what you feel is in the baby's best interests.

Bedtime and feeding require the most consistency (and later, discipline). Handle it now. All these issues will only get more complicated later.

Set Limits and Boundaries

Discipline starts early on. By the time the baby is crawling, you'll need to set boundaries. There should be places that are off limits, such as areas of the kitchen and the bathroom.

Talk to your baby in a soft but firm voice. You can say "no" if the baby is pushing the limits of safety, but don't use this word all the time; it will lose whatever meaning it has for your child. Some babies may stop, look at you, and continue doing what they did before. Maybe they're testing you and/or don't understand. If the baby cries, give a hug and a kiss for reassurance. Show them the places they're allowed to go and the things they're allowed to touch.

If the baby starts throwing toys, calmly stop the activity and return the toy to its place. If your baby is biting, pulling hair, or hitting, say "no" and remove the baby from the situation.

Don't ever yell or hit your child—it won't teach them anything but violence and fear. *Never* shake a baby. This can cause bleeding in the brain that can be fatal or cause a disability for life. Instead, remove the baby from the situation and give him or her a favorite toy. Distraction will be the way to discipline for a while.

The distraction method of discipline needs to be performed by all caretakers in the same way. Again, consistency is very important. If you and your partner have real differences about child-rearing practices, therapy together may help.

Learn Your Baby's Temperament

You'll see glimpses of your baby's temperament early on. Easy babies quickly get on a regular schedule of eating and sleeping and are able to soothe themselves. They adjust easily to change. You need to remind yourself to spend time and respond to this kind of baby, especially because they're not demanding.

Other babies may be quiet, serious, or shy or may have more difficulty adapting to new situations. More difficult babies may overreact to their surroundings, get overwhelmed easily, and have a hard time calming down. Change is not readily or quickly accepted by these children. These babies will get upset if you try to force anything. They need a lot of patience, time, and gentle guidance.

Let your baby develop his or her own personality, and always be there to help them in the process. Remember to keep things simple, routine, and consistent.

There may be times when you feel inadequate and insecure as a parent, especially if your baby isn't easy and seems to be having difficulty adjusting. You may seriously wonder, "How could this be my child? I was never like that. This child is *so* not like me."

Temperament is the disposition with which your child comes into this world. Genetics plays a large part, but there are certainly other factors that may explain and express a child's constitution or temperament.

Try to stay relaxed, be positive, and have patience, and the rewards will come. There's a saying: "You get what you can handle." Sometimes what we get in our children is very challenging to us personally. But if you can use the challenges your child brings to you in a constructive way, you'll grow immensely from the experience.

Spend Lots of Time Together

From the very beginning, spend as much time as you can with your baby. Carry him or her close to you everywhere you go.

Talking to your baby and explaining things all the time is the best pastime for the first few months. You can play together on the activity mat or look and listen to lights and music.

Reading can start in the first months. Babies won't understand what you're reading, but they'll know by the tone of your voice that it's a pleasant activity. You can sing and listen to music together. Put a CD with lullabies on if you get tired of singing. The baby will drop toys so that you can pick them up. You can play peek-a-boo and pat-a-cake. All of these are forms of play with your baby. After four months, you and your baby can play together with toys that move. Read, sing, and dance. As the baby gets older, play becomes more complex. Playing with safe utensils, putting things in and taking things out of a container, and banging things together will become favorite—if not very loud—activities. Spreading toys in different parts of the room will allow the baby to crawl toward them and find them, thus helping hand-eye coordination. Cause-and-effect toys are excellent.

Babies will now begin to have favorite toys (and later, favorite books). They'll start imitating you and others around them. Some babies will even sing with you. Your baby will appreciate puppets and busy boxes.

Some babies start scribbling close to 12 months of age, so you can draw together. Physical activity is important, so go ahead and roll a ball and let the baby roll it back to you.

In essence, it really doesn't matter what you do as long as you spend time together. Some classes and playgroups are important, but babies can tire easily and become overwhelmed. Know your baby's signs of tiredness, and stop the activity. Don't overschedule the baby at this age. Don't worry if your baby isn't enrolled in lots of classes; he or she won't fall behind educationally.

At this time of life, talking, reading, singing, and dancing with your baby are more important than any other activities. Babies take everything in and master new skills every day. You can help, guide, and set the example, but babies need to learn how to do things on their own. And remember, just like adults, babies need their own quiet time.

Make Your Baby's World Safe

You may think that a newborn doesn't do very much. But they can move and fall off a bed or sofa. Never leave your child unattended—anywhere—and especially never leave your child in a bathtub alone.

You can start baby-proofing your home as soon as you want, but definitely make sure this job is done by five to six months. The crib, car seat, and any other equipment relevant to the baby's needs must meet the required standards for safety. Check these frequently, and make sure these items are in good operating condition.

Don't put toys, pillows, or blankets in the crib. Change from the bassinet to the crib when the baby is turning and from the crib to a bed if the baby tries to climb out of the crib. The mattress in the crib needs to be firm, and the bumpers should be thin and tight. Remove the bumpers when the baby starts crawling.

Remove the mobile when the baby starts sitting. Don't use the changing table or the baby tub when the baby can roll over. Never put the baby in the adult tub without a bath seat.

Furniture needs to be stable for the cruising baby. Make sure that the carpet is firmly in place and doesn't shift around.

Knobs on the stove or oven need safety devices, and faucets and the toilet need to be secured as well. All cabinets should have safety devices, and window blind or curtain cords need to be placed far away. Patios or balconies should have a safety net, and the pool should have a safe fence surrounding it. All firearms need to be locked away.

Make sure all medications, cosmetics, and cleaning products are out of reach.

Electrical outlets need to be covered, and gates should be installed in front of stairs. Sharp furniture corners need safety bumpers. Check that smoke and carbon dioxide detectors are fully operational.

Make sure that there are no toxic plants around and that the pets have been to the vet and received their required vaccines. Have poison control and all emergency numbers on hand. Have an evacuation plan in case of disaster. It's important for everybody to learn CPR.

Take Care of Yourself

Rested, healthy parents are essential for the baby's well-being. Although your baby is the most important little person in your life, you can't forget about yourself. For new mothers, it's important to recognize the signs of postpartum depression (PPD), talk to your doctor, and seek treatment if necessary. Fathers and partners need to give the new mother support, encouragement, and help whenever possible.

Ask family or close friends to shop, take care of the house, or help in any other way that's needed. Eat well, even if you don't feel hungry, and drink enough fluids.

Don't allow anyone to make you feel guilty. Sleep whenever the baby sleeps if that works for you. Try to get back to exercise after about six weeks or whenever your doctor says you can. These days, many gyms offer babysitting. You can also elect to do exercise classes together with your baby, such as yoga.

Try to meet with your friends, with or without the baby, and have date nights with your husband or partner. Even a quick walk outside or an hour of yoga or meditation will change your entire outlook. If you take care of a baby with special needs, find respite babysitters and daycare centers to help.

Having a baby isn't easy. It's a huge amount of work, worry, and exhaustion. To be fully present for the experience, you need to take care of yourself. But it's worth it, because this will become the best and most rewarding experience of your life.

Essential Takeaways

- Consistency with a baby during the first year is paramount. Strive to establish consistency in the daily routine as well as with discipline.
- Be aware of developmental milestones, and seek advice if you sense your child is lagging.
- Choose a pediatrician carefully; this professional will be part of your and your baby's life for a long time.
- Spend as much time as you possibly can with your baby.
- Take care of yourself.

chapter 26

An Overview of the Second Year

> Developmental milestones: what your child will do in the months to come

> Encouraging individual expression and interaction while teaching limits and social skills

> Establishing eating and sleeping routines similar to the rest of the family

> When to be concerned about developmental and medical issues

Looking ahead to the second year is an exciting time. Congratulations, you will have survived the first year! The memory of that teeny-tiny baby you brought home just a year ago will be fading, because now you will have a walking and talking toddler. Look at all those pictures and videos you took from the last year, and you'll be amazed at all that has happened in such a short period of time.

You will have a little one who is all over the place, who can say a few words, who wants to feed himself or herself, who knows what he or she likes and dislikes, and is able to communicate with you. He or she (and you) will have come a long way in one year.

Now, you're wondering, what's next?

Developmental Milestones Ahead

From now on, bigger and better things are coming your way. Your toddler is learning to be more and more independent. There will be new accomplishments every day, so enjoy every minute. To give you a sneak peek of what's to come, we've put together what to watch for in your baby's second year.

From 13–15 Months

Gross motor skills—Your toddler will start walking or will walk better than he or she had before.

Fine motor skills—Your child will hold utensils and will want to feed himself or herself. They won't want you to help them with this anymore. At this point, your little one will start helping with dressing and will also start scribbling.

Cognitive skills—Your child will recognize himself or herself in the mirror and will begin to follow instructions.

Language skills—Language is developing as your child adds new words to his or her vocabulary.

Social skills—Your child learns to give kisses.

From 16–18 months

Gross motor skills—Your baby learns to run and climb and can kick a ball.

Fine motor skills—Your toddler can scribble well, knows how to undress, and can wash his or her face and brush the teeth.

Cognitive skills—Your child understands what you tell him or her but is still frustrated. Watch for the first temper tantrums. The child is also beginning to learn about body parts.

Language skills—Your child now says many words and learns new things every day.

Social skills—Your toddler pretends to read, recognizes favorite stories, and plays with other children (although this can still be parallel play).

From 19–21 months

Gross motor skills—Your toddler runs well (but the movements are still a little stiff) and climbs everywhere. He or she can now throw the ball in all directions.

Fine motor skills—Your child continues to scribble, but now the scribbles sometimes look like a circle.

Cognitive skills—Your child listens to commands, but the temper tantrums are getting longer and more frequent. Stranger anxiety decreases. Your baby now knows body parts.

Language skills—The vocabulary increases rapidly, with new words being added every day.

Social skills—The child can "pretend" play and now has favorite toys and books.

From 22–24 Months

Gross motor skills—At this age, skills include fast running, climbing, and trying to climb up stairs but needing assistance to come down.

Cognitive skills—Children of this age respond to two or more commands. They mimic everything you do and help in the house. Tantrums may be getting worse.

Language skills—Your child can start putting two words together and make simple sentences.

Social skills—At this stage, children can start to sing, can request to hear stories over and over, and can start to enjoy playing with other children.

More Issues to Come

The second year, just like the first, will have its own set of issues and accomplishments. Knowing what's coming will help you navigate the tough spots and rejoice in the fun ones.

Tantrums

You'll be astonished the first time your sweet little baby throws a tantrum. He or she may get down on the floor, scream, cry, throw things, and kick.

Tantrums are a normal, but not necessarily fun, part of development. Children want to be independent but just don't know yet how to be. With patience and distraction, you'll survive this, too.

Discipline

The kind of discipline you give changes in the second year. Aside from distraction, you'll need to start giving "time-outs" when necessary. Boundaries will have to be set firmly and consistently by parents and caretakers.

Eating and Sleeping

Feeding should never be a fight, although your child will express many likes and dislikes. Always remember that your toddler will eat when he or she is hungry and to have family table time.

Most children in the second year will give up daytime naps. They'll resist bedtime even more than before. Your toddler will probably be sleeping in a bed at this point. Get creative with your child's room; make it a fun place. This may help with the bedtime struggle. Remember to be consistent, keeping the bedtime routine the same.

Playing

Your child will continue to enjoy play groups, educational toys, and reading together, as well as cooking together and drawing. New activities and toys will replace the old ones that once delighted. Trips to the zoo, museums, puppet theater, and even shopping will become more of an adventure for them.

Of course, you'll want to continue all of those things you've done together the first year. The difference is that now you'll have a real partner. Your little one will be bringing a lot to the table from now on. So instead of talking to your baby, you'll begin to have some real conversations. Reading, singing, and dancing together will continue to provide hours of meaningful and purposeful interactions.

Here are some toys and activities you and your toddler can look forward to in the coming year.

> 12–15 months: Simple puzzles, push and pull toys, finger puppets, reading books, singing. And around the house, clearing drawers and cabinets (under strict supervision) and sorting containers

> 15–18 months: Larger puzzles (with more pieces), ride-on toys, simple puppet theater, big buttons (opening and closing), coloring and learning colors, learning opposites

> 18–24 months: Stringing objects, unwrapping, magnets, learning the sounds of different instruments. Around the house, doing simple housework such as wiping spills and sorting utensils

Safety

Recheck all the child-proofing you've done, and make sure that your entire home is now child-proofed. Between their amazing energy and ability to run and climb, safety issues are very important at this age. Anything dangerous to a child should be locked up and put away in places that are hard to reach. Furniture may have to be rearranged or removed if not sturdy.

Medical Issues

Accidents, falls, cuts, burns, bites, and broken bones could become more frequent. Thankfully, most of the time these aren't serious or life-threatening, but your constant vigilance is vital. Your toddler may get 10 or more colds a year, but this is considered normal. All other emergency situations apply to this age as well.

Toilet Training

Toilet training may start now if your child shows signs of readiness, but don't force it if he or she isn't interested. It will happen. As far as toilet training goes, every child is different and has various issues and unique needs. You'll know when your child is truly ready to take on the task. Typically girls are ready around two and half years old, and boys around three to three and a half years old, but remember there is no set age for it.

When to Be Concerned

Watching your child grow and change is a great experience. Please remember that all children reach their milestones at different times. The autism spectrum disorders are diagnosed at this age, so be proactive if you see any signs that concern you.

It's worrisome if your child isn't walking or saying words by 15 months old, isn't running by 21 months, isn't playing or shows a pattern of playing that is the same and repetitive, isn't giving or responding to affection, or doesn't make eye contact.

Your Child, Unfolding

So your child ended the first year learning how to walk. Now, he or she is off and running, running fast, climbing even faster, and opening doors. Little ones fill and empty containers, can scribble, and can even draw.

baby steps

"The journey of a thousand miles starts beneath one's feet."
—Zen saying

Your child understands what you say and can respond to simple commands. In fact, now they'll respond to two-part commands (and you have a little helper in the house!).

Language has evolved immensely—so much so that it's hard to keep track. Your child's speech has moved from a few words to many words and simple sentences. At this age, children know their names.

From playing seated on the floor, your child can now throw a ball and solve simple puzzles. After being content to play by themselves, they're starting to show interest in other children.

Every day will bring changes and challenges. Every day you'll get to know your child better, and your bond will become stronger. You may feel a bit of sadness seeing a real child before you instead of a little baby. These little people are amazing beings—wonderful, challenging, frustrating, and loving.

Your toddler was once that sweet little angel that now has tantrums on a daily basis. You may have to resort to time-outs. Discipline is the most difficult issue now. With time and patience, you'll understand how and why your child reacts the way he or she does, and together you'll be able to find a way to soothe the internal turbulence before a full-blown tantrum occurs. Consistency is, and will always be, essential.

As your child approaches two years, you'll see his or her personality unfolding. Even if your big boy or girl wants to be independent, you'll still be very close, and they'll turn to you for help whenever they need it. You'll be amazed at how much they've learned, at their ability to solve problems, and at how fully you interact with each other. You not only have a child; now, you also have a little friend.

You've given your child a great start, setting the tone for their future. You've given your child the fundamentals for a healthy lifestyle. Introducing good eating habits with nutritional and varied foods, you've laid the foundation for a healthy body. This is so essential now to prevent obesity, heart disease, and diabetes later on in life.

Encouraging movement and exercise establishes the need and desire for physical wellness as life moves forward. Forming healthy emotional attachments establishes your child's ability to trust, to relate to others, and to form healthy attachments in the future.

Enjoy and be part of everything—it goes so fast, and new times, issues, and challenges will surely arrive. In the process, you've learned a lot about yourself. Who knew that you could experience sheer joy at hearing a new word or feel satisfied when your child finished his or her food? Would you ever have guessed that you could make up stories and have the patience to repeat them over and over? Could you have imagined that you could worry about somebody so much? Could you have known that you could spend hours just watching your little one sleep?

Well, now you know. You have confidence in your parenting, and you're ready to confront any challenges that come your way. Maybe it's even time for the next baby.

Essential Takeaways

- The second year brings an entirely new set of wonder and changes.
- Tantrums begin, and discipline will be a challenge.
- Safety is essential. Child-proof everything, and be vigilant.
- Watch for developmental problems and address them immediately.
- Enjoy every moment, and grow together with your child.

Glossary

acetaminophen pain- and fever-reducing medication

acid reflux gastroesophageal reflux (GERD); when the acid from the stomach backs up into the esophagus

acute otitis media ear infection

allergy reaction to known or unknown food, medication, or other substances; can be mild with hives and itching or serious with wheezing and trouble breathing

alternative medicine complementary medicine; healing modalities in addition to Western medicine

anaphylaxis severe allergic reaction, including wheezing, swelling, trouble breathing, and collapsing

anemia lower-than-normal red blood cell count

antibiotics medication given to fight different kinds of bacteria

antihistamine medication that alleviates the symptoms of an allergic reaction

Apgar score five criteria—breathing, heart rate, tone, reflex, and cry—used to assess a newborn at one minute and five minutes after birth; two points are the maximum given to each criteria

Asperger's disorder part of the autism spectrum where language and cognitive elements are preserved, but there is a deficit in social interaction, with repetition of behavioral patterns

babbling sounds made by babies before speaking; could be one or more syllables

bacteria microorganism that causes disease, from mild (strep throat) to serious (meningitis)

bilirubin   a yellow breakdown product of red blood cells; most of it is secreted out of the body in the stools. If there's too much bilirubin, it will give the skin a yellow color (jaundice).

botulism   a serious type of food poisoning derived from the bacteria Clostridium botulinum, found in canned foods and raw honey. Babies are particularly susceptible, causing muscle weakness, impaired vision, and difficulty breathing.

bronchiolitis   a mostly viral infection of the very small air passages in the lungs that causes swelling and increased mucus

bronchitis   the infection of the large air passages in the lungs caused by bacteria or viruses; rare in children

caput   swelling of the scalp of newborns, mostly over the sutures, which disappears in a few days

cardiac   having to do with the heart

cardiopulmonary resuscitation (CPR)   an emergency procedure performed when the heart stops (cardiac arrest); it induces blood circulation and helps maintain the oxygen flow that goes to the brain and heart

CAT scan   multiple images of the body created by a computerized system

celiac disease   a disease in patients who are gluten-intolerant; symptoms include abdominal pain, diarrhea, anemia, and no growth

cephalhematoma   an accumulation of blood under the bone plate covering the skull; takes a while to go away and needs to be watched carefully

chicken pox   a viral disease (varicella) that causes blisters, itching, and possible scarring; more seriously, pneumonia and meningitis

circumcision   removal of the foreskin of the penis

colic   abdominal pain in healthy babies that causes crying and fussiness for more than three hours a day, more than three times a week, and more than three weeks

colostrum   nursing mother's first milk; dark yellow in color and very nutritious

congenital   a disease or malformation that happened before birth

congenital hypothyroidism   seen in babies born with a low-functioning thyroid gland

conjunctivitis   the inflammation or infection of the conjunctiva, the membrane that lines the eyelids

cooing   the first sounds a baby makes, after crying

cradle cap (sebhorreic dermatitis)   a yellow, greasy-looking substance seen on the baby's scalp

crawling   movement using all four extremities

cruising   taking steps while holding on to furniture

cystic fibrosis   genetic disease involving the lungs and digestive system; heavy mucus production; may result in early death

dehydration   loss of fluid from the body without replacement

dermatitis   a red, scaly, itchy rash with or without blisters that can appear on different parts of the body

diarrhea   very loose, watery stools that can happen between feedings; can be benign or may be a more serious condition if it continues

diphtheria   a disease caused by bacteria (corynebacterium diphteriae) that produce membranes that can cover the throat, resulting in difficulty breathing and even death

eustachian tube   a small tube that goes from the throat (pharynx) to the middle ear

family history   all the ailments and diseases of a baby's parents, grandparents, and siblings and any other diseases running in the extended family

fetus   the developing baby in the uterus, from conception to birth

fever   an increase of the body's temperature over normal values; an important defense against infections

flu   known as influenza; a viral disease that changes every year

fontanel   a soft spot on top of the head of infants where the bone hasn't yet solidified

galactosemia   symptoms of jaundice, an enlarged liver, cataracts, and developmental delay because of the lack of an enzyme in the liver that breaks down sugars

hemangioma   a raised red or purple lesion on the skin

hernia   weakness of a muscle that allows protrusion of part of the abdominal organs, such as an umbilical hernia, where parts of the abdominal lining protrude around the belly button

hives   raised red and itchy areas on the skin that occur in allergies

hydrocephalus   "water on the brain"; an increased amount of cerebrospinal fluid in the cavities (ventricles) of the brain

immunity   the body's capacity to defend against different types of infection

immunization   vaccines

infant   a baby from one month to one year of age

infection   the body's reaction to an invading organism—viral, bacterial, or fungal

intravenous   receiving liquid medication via a needle into the vein

intussusception   a potentially dangerous condition when part of the bowel folds into itself, creating an obstruction with bleeding and pain

jaundice   the yellow skin and eye color caused by increased bilirubin level

lethargy   a state of sleepiness and low energy

measles   called rubeola, a viral disease; fever, rash, and possible complications of pneumonia and brain disease

medical history   the medical events in chronological order as recalled by the patient (or caregiver)

MRI   magnetic resonance imaging, which uses magnetic waves to create well-defined images of the body

mucus   slippery, protective fluid produced by cells lining different organs (nose, throat, and lungs)

mumps   a viral disease with painful swelling of the salivary glands

newborn   a baby from birth to one month old

NICU   neonatal intensive care unit, where newborn babies are treated for medical problems

pertussis   also whooping cough, is a bacterial infection of the lungs with a spastic cough that ends with a sigh

phenylketonuria (PKU)   a genetic disorder that results in very high amounts of protein

phlegm   thick mucus

pincer grasp   the baby's ability to grasp a small object between the thumb and forefinger

placenta   an organ that exists only during pregnancy and provides the fetus's nourishment, breathing, and blood circulation

polio   viral disease that weakens and paralyzes the muscles

positional plagiocephaly   flattened part of the head due to a baby lying in the same position

preemie   a baby born before 37 weeks gestation

Prevnar   vaccine against pneumococcal bacteria

projectile vomiting   forceful vomiting that is emitted for a distance

pulmonary   related to the lungs

rash   red, flat, or raised area of skin with or without blisters

reflex   an involuntary action

regurgitation   a small amount of the stomach's contents returning to the mouth

Respiratory Syncytial Virus (RSV)   a virus that causes a severe form of bronchiolitis, especially in premature babies

retinopathy of prematurity   abnormal growth of blood vessels in the retina of premature babies

rickets   softening of the bones due to lack of vitamin D

rotavirus   a virus that causes vomiting and severe diarrhea in infants, leading quickly to dehydration

rubella   viral disease with fever and rash; serious congenital defects in a fetus if the mother gets the disease

scaly skin   thickened, dry, and peeling skin

seizures   convulsions; rhythmic movements of the body or parts of the body and staring into space; sometimes unconsciousness

separation anxiety   the baby's fear in the presence of an unfamiliar person

SIDS   Sudden Infant Death Syndrome; unexplained death of an infant, usually in a crib

strabismus   "crossed" eyes

swaddling   secure, tight wrapping of an infant to simulate the womb environment

symptoms   an indication or signs of a disorder or disease

testicles   the male sexual glands

tetanus   a rare, but often fatal bacterial disease that can lead to tightening of the muscles, including the muscles that help in the breathing process

thrush   white lesions in the mouth caused by a fungus, candida albicans

upper respiratory   the throat, nose, sinuses, and ears

urinary tract   the kidneys, ureters (tubes from the kidney to the bladder), bladder, and urethra (the tube from the bladder from which the urine is eliminated)

vaccine   part of a bacteria or virus given in small amounts to induce immunity without making the person sick

varicella   *See* chickenpox

virus   microscopic organisms that multiply quickly and invade the body

vitamins   organic substances not made by the body, given as supplements for nutrition

vomiting   the contents of the stomach returning to and exiting the mouth

wheezing   a whistling sound from the lungs caused by increased mucus and narrowing of the air passages in the lungs

Toys

Here is a helpful, quick reference list of age-appropriate toys for the first year.

Birth to Three Months

Mobile in black and white or bright colors, with music and movement

Fake aquarium with moving "fish"

Music box that attaches to the crib

Play mat with colors, textures, and sound

Soft stuffed dolls or animals

Rattle to hold

Baby mirror

Squeeze toys and balls

Four to Six Months

Busy boxes with different textures

Baby mirror with more activities attached

Baby gym play mat where the baby can practice kicking

Roly-poly toys (they don't roll all the way)

Soft blocks

Teething rings

Small, soft balls

Soft books with images and textures

Simple action/reaction toys

Linking toys

Toys that attach to strollers

Finger puppets moved by adults

Seven to Nine Months

Simple puzzles with different, big shapes

Busy boxes with big buttons, things that open and close, light, and sound

Bigger soft balls

Action/reaction toys

Stackable rings or blocks

Canisters to fill and empty

Soft or board books with flaps, textures, and images

Push and pull toys

Projectors with stars or other images in the baby's room

Ten to Twelve Months

Familiar-looking toys (play tool box, kitchen items, and vacuum cleaner)

Toy musical instruments

Push and pull toys

Dolls and stuffed animals

Musical and activity tables

Boxes with buttons, open-and-close objects, images, and sounds

Board books with flaps, sounds, and textures

Balls

Dexterity toys (wooden beads on tracks, for example)

Outside activities: swing set, sand box, toy pail and shovel, and a small basketball hoop

Baby Essentials

From sleeping to dressing to eating, this appendix provides a quick reference of the essentials you'll need for your baby's first year.

Furniture and Accessories

Bassinet: sturdy; not mobile; firm mattress; no pillows, blankets, or toys inside during sleep time; check for recalls

Crib: well-made; sturdy; may convert to a toddler bed; slats no more than $2\frac{3}{8}$ inches apart; nontoxic paint; no sharp corners; no crib tent; only thin and tight bumpers; no pillows, blankets, or toys inside during sleep time; older/secondhand cribs okay only if they meet current standards; check for recalls

Play/portable cribs: check the mesh sides for holes; keep all sides up and locked to prevent collapsing; and no pillows, blankets, or toys inside during sleep time

Changing table: serves as storage, too; protects your back; drawers need to be baby safe; discontinue use once baby can roll over (you can continue to using it as storage)

Diaper pail: empty and clean often

Baby monitor: audio or video; place out of reach of baby; works on batteries so you can take it when traveling

Toy storage: baby-proof so hands and fingers don't get hurt from the lid and baby doesn't climb inside

Drawers or small closet for clothing: baby-proof so hands and fingers don't get hurt from closing and baby doesn't climb inside

Diapers: disposable, cloth, or a combination of both

Wipes: fragrance-free

Bathtub: safe and sturdy baby tub or a large sink (cover the faucets); use an adult tub only with a bath seat; never leave the baby alone in the bathtub, even in the bath seat

Soap/shampoo: natural and fragrance-free

Towels: cotton hooded towels and washcloths

High chair: sturdy, detachable tray, and easy to wipe down

Clothing

Newborns: onesies, sleep sacks, clothing that you can put on and take off easily (snaps and Velcro), a snowsuit (if applicable), bibs, hats, and socks

Older babies: onesies, T-shirts, pants, pajamas (flame resistant), socks, comfortable clothing to crawl around in, a sweater, jacket, shoes, bathing suit, hats, and bibs

Diaper Bag

The diaper bag should be large with many compartments.

Contents: two clothing changes, diapers, wipes, diaper cream, plastic bags for dirty diapers, changing mat, sunscreen, two to three non-toxic bottles (plastic or glass), different types of nipples, formula (if applicable), breastfeeding cover up (if desired), two to three burp cloths, water in a bottle, a small plate, baby spoons, small containers of baby food or finger food, and favorite toys

Meal Prep

Homemade: blender, small chopper, steamer basket, ice cube trays, and small containers with lids

Mealtime: baby spoons, small plastic bowls, sippy cups, and bibs

Resources

Here, we provide a quick reference list of helpful magazines, books, and websites for parents and caregivers.

Magazines

Parenting

American Baby Magazine

Family Fun

Parent and Child

Working Mother

Twins Magazine

Living Green Magazine

Exceptional Parent—for parents taking care of special-needs children

Books

American Academy of Pediatrics. *Caring for Your Baby and Young Child from Birth to Age 5*. New York, NY: Bantam, 2009.

Meek, Joan Jounger, and Sherill Tippins. *New Mother's Guide to Breastfeeding,* American Academy of Pediatrics. New York, NY: Bantam, 2005.

Ferber, Richard. *Solve Your Child's Sleep Problems*. New York, NY: Simon & Schuster, 2006.

Sears, William, Robert, James, and Martha. *The Baby Sleep Book.* New York, NY: Little Brown, 2005.

Walker, Peter. *Baby Massage: A Practical Guide to Massage and Movement for Babies.* New York, NY: St. Martin's Press, 1996.

McLure, Vimala Schneider. *Infant Massage: A Handbook for Loving Parents.* New York, NY: Bantam, 2000.

Zaichkin, Jeanette. *Newborn Intensive Care Unit; What Every Parent Needs to Know.* Elk Grove Village, IL: American Academy of Pediatrics, 2009.

Bertshaw, Mark. *When Your Child Has a Disability.* Baltimore, MD: Brookes Publishing, 2000.

Dwight, Laura. *Brothers and Sisters.* Long Island City, NY: Star Bright Books 2005.

Gromada, Karen K. *Mothering Multiples: Breastfeeding and Caring for Twins.* Schaumburg, IL: La Leche League International, 2007.

Novotny, Pamela Patrick. *The Joy of Twins and Other Multiple Births.* New York, NY: Three Rivers Press, 1994.

Websites

www.aap.org   American Academy of Pediatrics

www.cdc.gov   Centers for Disease Control

www.cpsc.gov   U.S. Consumer Product Safety Commission (for recalls)

www.immunize.org   Immunization Action Coalition (vaccine information)

www.lalecheleague.com   La Leche League (breastfeeding information)

www.hometips.com/diy   child-proofing how-tos

www.onestepahead.com   children's products

www.consumersearch.com   car seat safety and other products

www.safekids.org   child safety information

www.drugstore.com   pharmacy and drug store

www.diapers.com   children's products

Preemies

www.prematurity.org

www.preemiestore.com

www.perfectlypreemie.com

Twins and Multiples

www.mostonline.org

www.twinsmagazine.com

Special-Needs Children

www.fcsn.org   Federation for Children with Special Needs

www.napcse.org   National Association of Parents with Children in Special Education

www.bravekids.com

Green Living

www.kiwimagonline.com

www.naturemoms.com

Alternative Medicine

www.nccam.nih.gov/health   National Center for Complementary and Alternative Medicine

Immunization Schedule Month by Month

The vaccines your baby receives in the first year are an important part of maintaining individual as well as public health. Here are the vaccines and their timing in the first year.

Vaccines

DTaP: diphtheria, tetanus, and pertussis

IPV: inactivated polio

HIB: haemophylus influenzae B

Pneumococcal

Rotavirus: there are two Rotavirus vaccines; one is given in two doses; the other one in three. Both are given by mouth.

Hep A: hepatitis A

Hep B: hepatitis B

MMR: measles, mumps, and rubella

Varicella: chickenpox

Flu: seasonal influenza and H1N1

Vaccine Timing

Many pediatricians use combination vaccines so there are fewer needle sticks for the baby.

Please note that different pediatricians may have different schedules.

At birth: Hep B is given in many hospitals. Hep B and the immuno-globulin are given if the mother is a carrier of the Hep B antigen.

One month: Hep B second dose, if the first one was given in the hospital

Two months: first doses of DTaP, IPV, Pneumococcal, HIB, Rotavirus, and Hep B if the first one was not given in the hospital

Three months: no vaccines unless the baby needs to catch up.

Four months: second doses of DTaP, IPV, Pneumococcal, HIB, Rotavirus, and Hep B if the first one was given at two months

Five months: no vaccines unless the baby needs to catch up, or the third dose of HepB if the first one was given in the hospital.

Six months: third doses of DTaP, IPV, Pneumococcal, HIB, Rotavirus (if three-dose version is given), and third dose of Hep B if the second one was not given at four months. The first of two flu vaccines can also be given. All children younger than nine receive the flu vaccines one month apart.

Seven months: no vaccines unless the baby needs to catch up; the second dose of flu vaccine if applicable

Eight months: same as seven months

Nine months: same as eight months

10 months: same as nine months

11 months: same as 10 months

12 months: MMR, Varicella, first dose of Hep A

Another vaccine is given to very small or sick premature babies. It's actually not a vaccine but an immunoglobulin against a severe respiratory disease caused by the RSV virus (Respiratory Syncytial Virus). It's given once a month from October until April until two years of age.

If you're traveling out of the country, you and your baby may need other vaccines depending on the area you plan to visit. Check whether your doctor can give you the vaccines or medications or if you have to see a doctor who specializes in travel medicine. Visit www.CDC.gov/travel for more information.

In Case of Emergency

An emergency can happen anywhere at any time. Be prepared by having a first-aid kit on hand and knowing what to do in different emergency circumstances.

First-Aid Kit

Have a first-aid kit at home and in the car, and take one with you when you travel. Each kit should include the following items:

Bandages

Gauze

Adhesive and elastic bandage

Alcohol pads

Wipes

Hydrogen peroxide

Antibiotic cream

Hydrocortisone cream

Calamine lotion or anti-itch spray

Pain and fever medication

Anti-allergy medication

Epi-pen

Cold packs

Thermometer

Tweezers (to remove a sting)

Scissors

List of medications that a child takes on a regular basis

List of emergency contacts

Gloves

Flashlight

Disposable warm-up packs

Blanket

Medical history

Vaccine record

A bottle of water

Oral electrolyte solution

How to Handle Emergencies

Some circumstances are considered emergencies and will require immediate medical attention.

Allergies

Mild: symptoms include rash, itching, or hives, but the baby is comfortable. Remove what is causing the allergy, if known, and give an over-the-counter antihistamine medication (follow the dose for the age and weight). Call your doctor for further guidance.

Serious (anaphylactic reaction): symptoms include swelling, wheezing, or respiratory problems. Give an Epi-pen if possible and/or call 911.

Bleeding

Superficial cut: wash with water, cover with gauze, and change the gauze every day.

Large and deep cut: wash with water, cover with gauze, and apply pressure for about five minutes. Call the doctor if bleeding doesn't stop or the cut is longer than half an inch and is deep.

Bites

Child: wash well, apply antibiotic cream, and find out the child's medical history and vaccines. Call the doctor with this information.

Animal: clean the bite and call the doctor; the child may need antibiotics or other vaccines.

Insect: if you know the child is allergic (bees, for example), give an Epi-pen. If not, remove the stinger with tweezers, wash the area well, and apply calamine lotion or hydrocortisone lotion. Call the doctor if the sting is on the face, eyes, or mouth or if the child is wheezing or swelling.

Burns

First degree: the skin is red but no blisters appear; run under cool water; may give pain medication.

Second degree: the skin is red with blisters. Apply cool water to the burn, remove clothing from around the burn, and call the doctor or 911 immediately.

Third degree: the skin may be dry, white, or black and very painful. Apply cool water to the burn, remove clothing from around the burn, and call the doctor or 911 immediately.

Chemical or electrical burns: remove clothing from around the burn, flush continuously with water for 20–30 minutes, and call the doctor or 911.

Broken Bones

If you suspect a broken bone (the baby doesn't move the limb and it's swollen or blue), apply ice and an elastic bandage to the site. Call the doctor or 911 immediately. Do not apply heat. If the broken bone or trauma is on or near the neck or spine, don't move the baby. Wait for medical assistance.

Choking

If the baby is choking and is alert and coughing, allow the coughing to dislodge the object. For any other circumstances, call 911. Learn the Heimlich maneuver and CPR.

Cough

Call 911 if the baby has difficulty breathing and is gasping for air, if you're able to see the space between the ribs, and/or if the baby doesn't stop breathing but is pale or becomes blue.

Car Accidents

Depending on the accident, you and your baby need to be evaluated in the emergency room. Even if the accident was minor and you feel fine, don't assume your child is fine, too.

Dehydration

If a baby is vomiting or has diarrhea, he or she can become dehydrated. Symptoms of dehydration are a sunken fontanel, dry lips, a lethargic baby, and no urinary output for 6–10 hours. You can give an oral electrolyte solution to rehydrate the baby at home. Start with 5–10cc (ml) every 10–15 minutes.

Continue to breastfeed the baby, but formula needs to be stopped. After eight hours of no vomiting, you can slowly restart the formula and solid foods. Start very slowly. Don't rehydrate with water, juice, or soda. You can give the baby more carbohydrates and then go back to the regular diet.

If the baby continues to be lethargic, there is no urinary output, and vomiting hasn't stopped, it's an emergency—so call the doctor and go the hospital.

Fever

For babies younger than two months, a fever of 100.4° Fahrenheit (38° Celsius) is an emergency. For older babies, a fever up to 102° Fahrenheit can be treated at home if the baby looks well. You can wash the baby with cool water (a sponge bath), but don't use alcohol. Don't immerse the baby in cold water. With any fever, if the baby is lethargic and/or not behaving or eating as usual, see your doctor.

Frostbite

Frostbite is a frozen body part that looks white or blue and has no sensation at all. Bring the child indoors immediately, remove the clothing, and give a warm bath and warm drinks. Don't rub or touch any blisters. This is an emergency that will need medical attention.

Frostnip is the reddening and tingling of the areas that are exposed to cold (face, nose, and hands). You can treat this at home with a warm bath. Frostnip heals within a few hours.

Head Trauma

If the baby falls and has lost consciousness, is vomiting, is having seizures, and/or is lethargic or very irritable, call 911. Place the baby on the side if he or she is vomiting. For babies up to one year of age, you need to call the doctor—even if the baby just fell and cried and now is acting as usual. If a bump is apparent, try to apply ice. This will last for a while but will eventually disappear.

Watch the baby for the following signs for the next 48 hours: look for any circles under the eye (raccoon eyes), a bruise behind the ears, and any fluid coming out of the ears or nose. If the eye is injured, don't touch it or apply pressure to it. Don't move the baby if there is trauma to the neck or spine.

Poisoning

Call 911 if the baby is unconscious, has a seizure, is very red or blue, drank a chemical solution, or swallowed a sharp object or battery. Call Poison Control at 1-800-222-2222. They will advise you in all cases. Do *not* use ipecac syrup.

Seizures

In the first year, call the doctor or 911 for a seizure. Don't put anything in the baby's mouth. Don't try to stop the seizure, and don't give anything to drink.

Febrile seizures are convulsions triggered by a fever, they can sometimes occur with any fever higher than 100.4° Fahrenheit. You should be concerned about rapidly increasing fever. These seizures usually disappear by five years of age, but the baby may have others. Seizure disorder tends to run in families.

Different Kinds of Families

The simple definition of the traditional (nuclear) family has been a mother, a father, and their biological children. In the beginning of the twentieth century until roughly the 1960s, the father went to work and the mother stayed home and took care of the household and the children. (For most of you who are just becoming parents, this will probably seem like the "dark ages." But just for fun, check out the early television sitcoms.)

The origin of the word "family" comes from the Latin *familiare,* meaning a household, or servants of a household, from the word *famulus,* meaning servant. Essentially, a family was defined as people who are related by blood, who have some kind of affinity, or who co-exist or co-reside with one another.

How things have changed. Today, fewer than one third of families are "traditional," and new family units are becoming more recognized than ever before. The "family" appears to be a very different entity in our times. Today, there are foster and adoptive families, same-sex couples, single parents, stay-at-home dads, and families where grandparents raise their grandchildren.

Family means that people have a strong commitment to each other, similar values and goals, and live together under the same roof (at least, most of the time). It's about the love, support, care, stability, and education that a child receives from adults who are committed to them for a lifetime. One type of family is not better than any other—just different.

Foster Care

It's estimated that in 2010, about 500,000 children were placed in foster care. Foster care means that the child has been removed from the biological parent(s) and placed either in the care of a relative (kinship) or with certified foster parents. The court and foster care agencies have jurisdiction over foster children. The Department of Human and Social Services licenses foster homes.

The basis for foster care in the United States stems from the Orphan Train Movement from 1853–1929. Thousands of neglected and orphaned children from cities on the East Coast were placed with families of farmers in the Midwest. Sadly, this situation amounted to little more than servitude for the children. The first foster care agency was The Children's Aid Society, founded in New York in 1853.

Children are in foster care mainly because they suffer physical or mental abuse or neglect. The parents can ask for voluntary foster care if they're not able or don't want to care for a child. The goal of foster care is to eventually reunite children with their biological families, or if that isn't possible, for the children to be adopted.

Adoptive Families

The adoption rate has increased dramatically in the United States. In 2009, there were 70,000 domestic adoptions and 13,000 international ones—more than anywhere else in the world.

Children can be adopted through foster care (59 percent), by relatives (23 percent), or by strangers to the child (17 percent). Adoptions can be domestic, either from the same state or other states, or international. They can be done through adoptive agencies or independently between the birth mother and the adoptive parents. The latter is not legal in all states.

Domestic Adoptions

If the adoption is done between states, it's important for the parents to know the laws of both states. Agencies probably offer the most assurance; they have been licensed and have specific standards. They also provide the adoptive parents with counseling, home visits, and follow-up.

Independent adoption is supervised by attorneys—most of them specializing in adoption. The adoptions can be "closed," when no information is shared between the birth and adoptive parents (except for the birth mother's medical history). All documents are sealed by the court.

In semi-closed adoptions, the birth mother is given some information about a few potential adoptive parents without identifying them, but she can choose which parents she wants to raise her child. After adoption, there is no more contact.

With open adoptions, there are no barriers between the birth mother and the adoptive parents. Sometimes they can be involved in the prenatal stage and may even be present at the birth. After adoption, they have a choice of future contact, ranging from letters to the birth mother or becoming part of the family.

Adopted children need to have a medical exam within two weeks of adoption.

International Adoptions

International adoptions can involve a lengthier and more complicated process. Every country has its own rules and laws. One must consider U.S. citizenship and immigration laws for children. It's a good idea to have a pre-visit to the country from which adoption will take place. While there, the customs and culture of the country must be respected.

In 2007, many adopted children came from China, Guatemala, Russia, Ethiopia, Vietnam, and many other countries. The main difficulty is largely healthcare related. Some children have no medical records, and no information is available about them.

Most of the time, vaccines (if given) may not be the same as those required in the United States. Within two weeks, the internationally adopted children must undergo a medical exam and blood tests.

Depending on the age of the child, they will need tests for HIV, tuberculosis, lead, and others to rule out endocrine or metabolic diseases, parasites, and infections. All missing vaccines need to be given.

You don't need to find a doctor specializing in adoption; a pediatrician can perform all of the above exams. It's also important for the baby to have continuity of care. In both domestic and international adoptions, it's important to get to know the pediatrician beforehand, to have him or her review any medical records, and to establish a relationship with the doctor in case the child becomes ill before the two-week visit.

The Emotional Journey of Adoption

Parenting your own child is an extremely complex journey. Parenting a child that's adopted will almost certainly raise additional issues for the parents and the child. Many adoptive parents with their own children say they feel no difference parenting their adoptive child and their biological ones. This is the optimum situation, when thoughtful planning and realistic expectation have gone into making the decision to adopt.

But what happens when the process doesn't evolve as planned or imagined? Issues and questions around the reason for adoption, the stability of the adoptive parents (or partners) and the status of their relationship may appear. Was the child adopted to meet unrealistic expectations? Is the adoptive child replacing another child? Is the adoption for companionship? Are family members unwilling to accept the adopted child? These are complex issues that need to be sorted through and understood, or the outcome of the adoption may be disappointing for everyone.

Anticipating the arrival of the adoptive child is a big part of the process. Often the trials and tribulations leading up to adoption can create enormous stress, pressure, and potential difficulties. The adoptive parents need time to prepare for the complete, very complex idea of raising somebody else's child.

Bonding or attaching to an adoptive child is more complicated and may take more time than with a biological one. As long as the parents understand that these feelings may take a long time to develop and unfold, that it's nobody's fault that it's taking longer, that their parenting skills are not to blame for the delay, bonding will eventually happen.

It's important to always be present for your child; to show physical affection the child and to be demonstrative emotionally. Never hesitate to respond to the child's needs. Stimulate all of the senses: talk, sing, play, walk, and dance. Make eye contact all of the time.

If you have biological children, talk to them before the adopted child comes home to live with the family about the changes that will happen and about the meaning of the new sibling. Reassure them that nothing will change in your affection for them.

Don't expect too much too soon. The adopted child will need time to adjust, and might be bringing any number of issues along with him or her. Maybe he or she was in an orphanage with little human contact. Maybe he or she lived with abusive foster parents. Maybe he or she is experiencing grief from the loss of parents. Circumstances like these make adoption emotionally more complex for both the child and the new family.

Even if none of the above exists, bonding will still need time. If you feel overwhelmed, emotionally exhausted, or if you feel your adopted child doesn't respond to or answer you, take time off to gain some perspective. Talk to other adoptive parents and ask the involved agencies for help.

International adoption can be difficult if the child speaks another language. Learn a few words or have somebody spend the time with your child who understands and can communicate with them. Because cultural identity is very important, try to offer this to your child. Later on, you may want to visit your child's birth country.

Even more challenging are the adoptions of special needs children or abuse victims. Once again, time is the key to adjustment and for attachment to eventually occur. Social workers and therapists need to be involved to help find the best support system for the child and the family.

Overall, children are very resilient. All a child ultimately needs to know, and to feel, is that he or she is safe and loved. Adopted children will thrive in a patient, nurturing environment and will become part of a stable family.

When Grandparents Take Care of Children

There are 3.4 million grandparents who assumed the role of parents in the last few years. If the parent can't or won't take care of the child, if it's a teenage pregnancy, or if the parents are ill or deceased, grandparents often take over the responsibility of caring for the child. The grandparents, many of whom have retired, are sometimes forced to rejoin the workforce because they may be challenged by new and unexpected financial issues.

In the case of teenage pregnancy, the mother and her child often end up living with the grandparents. Depending on their age and health, grandparents can offer not only love and care but also experience.

Single Parenting

Single parenting means that only one parent takes care of the child or that there is only one parent. This situation may happen due to divorce, death, or having or adopting a child without being married or in a committed relationship. In 2010, it's estimated that there were 13.7 million single parents in the United States.

Single parenting is definitely challenging but also very rewarding. A single parent can raise a well-adjusted and happy child as well as in any other child-care arrangement. Getting help is important, whether it's from a family member, friend, or someone who is hired. If there is no immediate family, local resources can help. Meeting other parents in the same situation can be a great way to form friendships and help each other.

Same-Sex Parents

There are one to six million parents of the same sex in a committed relationship—lesbian, gay, bisexual, or transgender (LGBT). Generally, one of the parents is the legal guardian and the other is a second parent or co-parent. In many instances, however, one parent is the biological parent—and in that case, the partner can adopt the child. In other situations, both nonbiological parents can adopt the child.

In 1998, the results of a first-published study found that children raised by LGBT parents do just as well as children who are raised in traditional families. In 2010, another study showed that children raised by same-sex parents had the same self-esteem, performed the same in school, and had the same social adjustment as children raised in traditional homes.

For same-sex partners, if another gender role model is needed, there's always family and friends. It's not about the number of parents or their gender but rather the quality of parenting that's most important.

Recently, the American Association of Pediatrics (AAP) supported legislative efforts to give both parents the same legal rights. The legislative effort creates the right for the child to be with the parents, have financial security in case of the death of one parent, and have the right for both parents to give consent in case of emergencies.

Eventually, parents will have to deal honestly with their children. Some will have no problems at all while others may need counseling. Local resources in the community can help, as well as meeting other LGBT families and being prepared that not everyone will understand or accept a same-sex parenting situation.

Step and Blended Families

With more than 50 percent of marriages ending in divorce, step families are increasing everywhere. Blending children from different parents is not an easy task (reality is not exactly like "The Brady Bunch").

The new couple needs to understand the difficulty the children will have with a new step-parent. Children can easily act out behaviorally if not given the right avenue to express themselves. When a new baby is born, sibling rivalry may increase, and if not dealt with properly and in a timely fashion, it can cause harm and division within the family.

Patience, sensible discipline, allowing each biological parent to do what they need to with their own children without the interference of the step-parent, consistency in dealing with children's loyalty issues, and family therapy (if and when it's needed) will make for a healthy, blended family.

Resources for Alternative Families

A variety of resources are available for nontraditional families, offering advice and guidance.

Foster Families

Books:

Temple-Plotz, Lana. *Practical Tools for Foster Parents. Boys Town Press, 2002.*

Green-Baldino, Rachel. *Success as a Foster Parent: Everything You Need to Know about Foster Care.* Alpha, 2009.

Websites:

www.fosterparenting.com

www.nfpainc.org (National Voice of Foster Parents)

Adoptive Families

Magazines:

Adoptive Families

Books:

Caughman, Susan, and Isolde Motley. *You Can Adopt.* Ballantine Books, 2009.

Eldridge, Sherrie. *Twenty Things the Adopted Children Wish Their Parents Knew.* Delta, 1999.

Alperson, Myra. *Dim Sum, Bagels, and Grits: A Source Book for Multicultural Families.* Farrar, Straus and Giroux, 2001.

Websites:

www.adoption.state.gov

www.adopting.org

www.afteradoption.org

Single Parents

Books:

Apel, Melanie Ann. *Let's Talk about Living with a Single Dad*. PowerKids Press, 2001.

Keller, Wendy. *Soaring Solo: On the Joys (Yes the Joys) of Being a Single Mom*. Wildcat Canyon Press, 2001.

Nelson, Jane. *Positive Discipline for the Single Parent*. Three Rivers Press, 1999.

Websites:

www.parenthood.com

www.singlemothersbychoice.com

www.parentstoolshop.com

www.mrdad.com

LGBT Families

Magazines:

And Baby Magazine

Alternative Families Magazine

Books:

Gillespie, Peggy (ed). *Live Makes a Family*. University of Massachusetts Press, 1999.

Benjamin, Judith, and Judith Freeman. *And Baby Makes 4*. Motek Press, 2009.

Websites:

www.lgbtfamilies.info

www.familyequality.org/resources

www.proudparenting.com

Step or Blended Families

Books:

Sheinberg, Elaine Cantle. *Blending Families*. Berkley Trade, 1999.

Deal, Ron L. *Smart Step Families: The Seven Steps to a Healthy Family*. Bethany House, 2006.

Websites:

www.winningstepfamilies.com

www.theblendedandstepfamilyresourcecenter.com

Grandparents

Website:

www.grandmagazine.com

More Great Recipes for 9–12 Months

For all of the following recipes, vegan substitutions include:

One egg with ¼ cup unsweetened applesauce

Milk with soy milk or soy formula

Yogurt with soy yogurt

Cheeses with soy cheese

Meat with tofu

Note: Three strands of fresh herbs are equivalent to about one teaspoon of dried herbs.

Breakfast

Easy Pancakes

Ingredients:

1 cup flour	1.5 oz. vegetable oil
¼ tsp. baking soda	¾ cup milk
1 egg	¼ tsp. vanilla
2 tsp. brown sugar	

Mix flour and sugar. Mix milk, egg, and vanilla. Pour the flour mixture into the milk and mix well.

Pour a quarter cup on the hot grill or a nonstick frying pan that has been brushed with the oil. When you see large bubbles, turn the pancake and cook until light brown.

You can serve with any fruit or any yogurt. These pancakes freeze well.

Frittata

Ingredients:

1 tomato chopped

1 onion chopped

1 zucchini chopped (you can use any vegetable)

1 garlic clove

2 eggs

½ tsp. oil

Fresh parsley and dill (or dried)

Heat the oil in a pan, add the onions, lightly brown them, and add the zucchini, tomato, and herbs.

Beat the eggs. When the vegetables are all cooked, pour in the eggs. Make sure the eggs cover the veggies. Cook until the eggs are golden.
Optional: you may grate cheese on top when the eggs are all cooked.

Easy Yogurt Muffin

Ingredients:

2 cups flour

½ cup sugar

½ tsp. baking soda

4 ripe bananas

½ cup olive oil

½ cup yogurt

½ tsp. vanilla

2 eggs

Warm the oven to 350–375° Fahrenheit.

Use a muffin pan and spray with oil or use special baking cups.

Mix the flour, sugar, and baking soda. Beat the eggs and add bananas, yogurt, oil, and vanilla. Pour the dry mixture into the wet one. Mix well. Fill up half of the muffin cups with batter.

Bake 20–25 minutes.

Savory Muffin

Ingredients:

2 cups flour

1 TB. sugar

½ tsp. baking soda

1 cup zucchini, broccoli or spinach, chopped very fine

½ cup olive oil

½ cup yogurt

½ cup cottage cheese (or any cheese)

2 eggs

½ cup red bell peppers

1 TB. dill

1 TB. parsley

Preheat the oven to 375° Fahrenheit. Spray the muffin cups

Mix the flour, sugar, baking soda, and herbs. Mix the milk, eggs, oil, yogurt, cheese, and veggies. Pour the dry ingredients into the wet ones. Mix well. Fill half of the muffin cup with batter.

Bake for 20–25 minutes.

Lunch

Making up vegetable or chicken stock in advance will help you make excellent homemade soup, and it will help you a lot with all meals.

Chicken Stock

Ingredients:

2 lbs. chicken bones and wings

1 onion cut in two

3 carrots

3 parsnips

2 celery stalks

2 cloves of garlic

7–8 thyme strands

10 dill strands

7–8 parsley strands

1 gallon cold water

In a large pot or two smaller ones, add everything to the cold water. Bring to a boil. Skim the top with a fine mesh or spoon. Simmer for 4 hours. Strain and discard solids. Refrigerate overnight and skim the top again. You can use it as a base for soups, stews, etc. You can place the stock in smaller containers and freeze up to 3 months.

Vegetarian Stock

Use it as a base for soups, vegetables, stews, etc.

Ingredients:

2 tsp. oil	4 stalks celery
4 carrots	10 parsley strands
4 parsnips	10 dill strands
1 turnip	7–8 thyme strands
4 onions	1 gallon water
8 cloves of garlic	

Put everything including the oil into the cold water. Simmer for 35–40 minutes till all vegetables are soft. Strain and discard the solids. Keep in the refrigerator overnight. Pour into smaller containers and freeze for up to 3 months.

Cauliflower/Broccoli Soup (suitable for vegans)

Ingredients:

1 head of either vegetable or half of each	3 cups water (or vegetable stock)
1 clove garlic	Sweet paprika
1 onion	5 parsley strands
1 potato	5 dill strands

Place all vegetables in the cold water. Bring them to a boil and cook until all veggies are soft. Put them in a blender and puree. You can control the thickness by adding more water or vegetable stock.

Easy Pea Soup (suitable for vegans)

Ingredients:

2 cups peas	Fresh or dry parsley
½ onion chopped	1 tsp. lemon juice
2 cloves garlic	Sweet paprika
2 carrots chopped	5 cups water or vegetable stock
1 tomato chopped	3 tsp. olive oil

Heat the oil in a pot. Add onions, peas, carrots, tomatoes, and garlic. Cook until lightly brown. Slowly add the 5 cups of water or stock. Cook until the peas and all veggies are soft.

You may also add strips of chicken and cook them with the vegetables in the oil.

Chicken or Tofu Salad

Ingredients:

2 oz. boiled or broiled chicken or tofu	1 cup lettuce chopped
½ cup broccoli chopped	1 TB. lemon juice
1 tomato chopped	¼ tsp. thyme
¼ onion finely chopped	¼ tsp. oregano
½ bell pepper chopped	1 tsp. olive oil

Place all vegetables, chicken, or tofu in a bowl. Drizzle olive oil and lemon juice. Add seasoning and toss well again.

You can add pasta or rice to this dish.

Easy Sloppy Joe

This is always a favorite. You can use it with pasta, potatoes, rice, couscous, or make it a sandwich (cut the crust and cut the bread in very small—half of your pinky nail—pieces.

Ingredients:

1 lbs. chopped turkey or very lean beef (or tofu)	¼ tsp. brown sugar
	½ tsp. thyme
1 onion chopped	Few strands of dill and parsley
2 tomatoes chopped	1 tsp. of olive oil
2 cloves of garlic chopped	½ cup water or chicken or vegetable stock

Heat the oil in a pan. Add onions and peppers and cook until light brown. Add the meat and cook for 5 minutes. Then add the tomatoes. Add seasoning and sugar. Mix well. Add water, chicken, or vegetable stock. Simmer for 40 minutes until the meat is fully cooked.

Couscous

A wonderful and light pasta, couscous is easy to prepare.

Ingredients:

2 cups couscous   2 cups water or stock

Bring the water or stock to a boil. Stir in the couscous and immediately remove from heat. Cover the pot. Let it stand for around 15 minutes until the water is completely absorbed. Fluff it with a fork.

You can add grilled chicken, grilled, steamed, or fresh vegetables and season it, if you wish. It's a filling and healthy meal.

Dinner

Chicken or Tofu with Fruits

Ingredients:

1 apple (or peach, pear, or apricot), finely chopped

¼ finely chopped onion or scallion

½ tsp. lemon juice

½ tsp. sugar

¼ tsp. thyme

½ tsp. oregano or dill

½ tsp. sweet paprika

2 oz. chicken or tofu cut up in thin strips

1 tsp. olive oil

Preheat the oven to 350–375° Fahrenheit.

Put olive oil in an oven-proof dish. Add the chicken or tofu. Put the onion and seasoning on top of the chicken strips. Arrange the fruit around the chicken and sprinkle with lemon and sugar.

Bake for 25–30 minutes.

Tuna Fish Salad

Ingredients:

1 can chopped tuna in water (drain well)	¼ bell pepper, finely chopped
½ celery stalk	½ tsp. onion powder
¼ onion, finely chopped	½ tsp. lemon juice
½ carrot, grated	5–7 strands of dill

Drain the tuna. Add all vegetables and seasoning. Add one teaspoon of yogurt (or soy yogurt). Mix well.

Fish with Rice, Peas, and Carrots

Ingredients:

1 filet of sole or flounder	½ cup rice (brown is preferred)
¼ onion or scallions	½ cup peas
2 strands of parsley and dill	½ carrot, grated
¼ tsp. lemon juice	1 tsp. olive oil

Preheat the oven to 350–375° Fahrenheit.

Put the fish and oil on the bottom of an oven-proof dish. Arrange the onions, peas, and carrots around the fish. Add the lemon juice and the herbs. Bake for 10 minutes.

Boil the rice in water for 15 minutes. Drain the water. Remove the onions, peas, and carrots and mix them with the rice. Serve it as a side dish for the fish.

Snacks

Simple foods make great snacks! Here are some that are easy to make.

Cheese or soy cheese added to cooked vegetables, rice, and potatoes. Babies love this.

Yogurt with fruits.

Cleaned, peeled, and chopped fruits and vegetables

½ pancake with fresh fruits

Smoothies blended milk or yogurt with fruits

Desserts

Rice Pudding

Ingredients:

2½ cups milk, formula, or soy milk

⅓ cup rice

½ tsp. cinnamon

½ tsp. grated lemon peel

1-½ TB. brown sugar

2 bananas, peaches, or apricots

Add the rice, sugar, and cinnamon into the boiling milk. Reduce the heat and simmer for about an hour. Add the grated lemon and the fruits.

Mixed Cereal with Fruits

Ingredients:

1 TB. of 3 different types of cereals

5 slices of peaches and apples

¼ cup milk or soy milk

Pinch of cinnamon

Mix cereals, then add fruit and milk. Sprinkle cinnamon on top.

Fruit and Cream Cheese

Ingredients:

1.5 oz. ricotta or whipped cream cheese (or tofu)

1.5 oz. plain yogurt (or soy yogurt)

3 TB. fruit: berries, peaches, pears (pureed)

¼ tsp. vanilla

Combine all ingredients until it looks like a paste.

Serve it with a graham cracker, on French toast or a pancake, or as a dip for fruits.

Index

D

E